MW01174049

To: _____

Best Wishes

Jeannette Romaniuk

2008

J. R.

Gathering Roses Among the Thorns

By

Evangeline Jeannette Romaniuk (nee Gaumond)

ISBN: 978-1-4251-7680-8

We at Trafford believe that it is the responsibility of us all, as both individuals and corporations, to make choices that are environmentally and socially sound. You, in turn, are supporting this responsible conduct each time you purchase a Trafford book, or make use of our publishing services. To find out how you are helping, please visit www.trafford.com/responsiblepublishing.html

Our mission is to efficiently provide the world's finest, most comprehensive book publishing service, enabling every author to experience success. To find out how to publish your book, your way, and have it available worldwide, visit us online at www.trafford.com/10510

 www.trafford.com

North America & international
toll-free: 1 888 232 4444 (USA & Canada)
phone: 250 383 6864 ♦ fax: 250 383 6804 ♦ email: info@trafford.com

The United Kingdom & Europe
phone: +44 (0)1865 722 113 ♦ local rate: 0845 230 9601
facsimile: +44 (0)1865 722 868 ♦ email: info.uk@trafford.com

10 9 8 7 6 5 4 3 2 1

Dedication

I dedicate this book to my treasures and all of my brothers and sisters who are so dear to my heart.

Acknowledgements:

I am indeed grateful to my daughter Lucille whose contribution was crucial to the achievement of this overwhelming project. Without her expertise in editing, formatting, printing, and binding the manuscript would have been impossible to complete.

I am also grateful to Michael and Cherrie who fished me out of many predicaments when I was hopelessly lost on the computer

Table of Contents

Part I

The Early Years

At this eleventh hour as I traipse leisurely along the path that surrounds and loops around the lake and contemplate the marvels of creation, my thoughts ramble and wander, engrossed in profound meditation. My reflections drift-drift-drift and I ponder about the meaning, the purpose of existence: my existence. Who am I? What was the Lord's intent when He planted me in the grandiose scheme of His magnanimous kingdom?

At sunrise, the entire lake is a flaming sea of dazzling scintillating light, a sea of silver crystals, twinkling, sparkling, [étincelant] glittering, on the undulating waters. It is a sea of fire, reflecting and ignited by the luminous rays of the rising sun. It is a sea crowned with the glory of the trees robed in their most luxurious festive attire; a sea whose splendor and magical enchantment leaves me breathless with ecstasy and wonder.

As I contemplate the mystical grandeur of this scenic beauty, the drama of my life unfolds and stretches out, displaying in its entity the journey that the wiles of destiny has chosen in its chicanery to lure me, and the lake becomes an illusive mirror, a panorama of all the trials, the struggles, and the heartaches along the way. Every ripple, every drop, a page in an open book, revealing every moment of joy; every moment of anguish. Yet, that same mirror reflects, synonymously, emphatically, the times that compensated and transcended all these. The times when the heart knows and remembers but the rapture, the ecstasy loved ones engender.

As I gaze and gaze upon the agitated waters, I become mesmerized by the depth my thoughts have suddenly drifted. It comes to my mind that even as the wind driven waves in their frenzied haste hurl themselves against the rugged bank, likewise my restless, impetuous spirit, compelled by the Herculean might of obsessive delusion, dashes to reach the other shore.

It is then, while gazing at this exquisite natural marvel, that I wonder. It is then, while in the depth of my confusion, that I ask myself, "Why did the Lord, in His infinite wisdom, deem fit to shower one such as me with such immense blessings?" One who never fails to put her left foot forward. [Or perhaps has two left feet.] One who is so naïve, [My Dad used to call it bonasse, which is much more precise,] never confronting harsh reality head on, never ceasing to color hardship deeply under a mantel of roses. One who lives a life of fantasy and dreams life's reality away. I hope and pray that anyone who reads these lines, will find the key to this dilemma, as he journeys with me along the many winding pathways through which I have wandered.

But I have strayed and rambled from my path. Today, unlike the turbulent waters of yesterday, the lake is a transparent mirror. Not a ripple disturbs its glossy surface. Except, perhaps, the occasional duck enjoying its morning bath. Many are strolling along the path. Some at a leisurely pace, some jogging, some chatting, others waving their arms to accompany the rhythm of their stride. Doubtlessly they are walking as a means of exercise and for the benefit of their health. For very few appear to absorb or appreciate the picturesque scenic marvels stretching before their eyes. In their haste, they do not stop to gaze and contemplate the gifts so freely showered upon them. For these that moment will soon be gone. And I ask myself, "Am I the only one who is completely overcome, enthralled, by the magic of nature's exquisite beauty?"

This inconceivable tale begins many, many years ago, when I set out on the turbulent and dramatic quest along life's precarious journey.

I am ushered into this world by a raging blizzard, a veritable November hurricane. This is an inevitable omen. Every momentous event in my life is prophesied and accompanied by earthshaking upheavals. Veritable pandemonium! The heavens join those who are dear to me to create this exaggerated fanfare. Although I am indeed grateful that my comings and goings are so loudly acclaimed, all this alarum clashes dramatically with my personality. For in spite of all this hullabaloo I feel like sneaking in and hiding in the safety of the shadows, unobserved, and there to remain anonymous.

The gift of life is the most magnanimous blessing. It is the ultimate gift! It has allowed me to contemplate and rejoice in awe at the wonders and the splendors of God's magnificent creation. For this bounteous gift I will eternally be recognizant.

Yet, I often wonder, was another child a blessing for my already overburdened parents! In a family with little financial means the seventh child must have been a serious drain on their meager resources. Perhaps it is the vibes in this stressful situation that instill in my heart the feeling that I was the one "de trop." And it is against this feeling, this accursed "bête noire," that I have struggled throughout my entire life. That feeling of inferiority, of inadequacy, is the factor that is to blame and at the root of the many grievous, sometimes irreparable mistakes I have made throughout my entire life. It is the monster that was forever threatening my downfall. Sometimes, even in the declining hours of my existence, the beast is still lurking in the shadows, undefeated, forever menacing, forever threatening.

"De trop," doesn't even begin to tell the truth of the dilemma my parents must have had to deal with by the birth of another child, for there were already three boys and three girls in the family. Yet at the time large families were part of the traditions of the die-hard Catholic and French Canadian culture and every household was blessed with many children. Every new addition to the family was affectionately welcomed in spite of the extra responsibilities and sacrifices they incurred. And so it was that I was followed by three sisters and two brothers: Marie-Anne, Juliette, Cecile, Gerard, and

Raymond. And so it was that eleven of us besides my parents were squashed in a one-room log cabin way up in North West Saskatchewan. That is all of us besides the family my generous mother had adopted and the countless drifters who always managed to find themselves on our doorstep!

Grandpa Savard Family (Left to right)
Back Row: Neil, Emma, Louis, Hélène, Joe /
Front Row: Armand, Francois, Emeralda, Léonide, Ernestine, Florenst
The Savard family members in the back row all settled in United States.

Front row: Marie-Anne, Cecile, and Juliette. Back Row: Evangeline Jeannette

Back Row (left-right) Cecile, Grandma, Jeannette
Front Row: Raymond, Marie Anne, and Juliette

My parents, in cahoots with my grandparents, set the stage for the inconceivable drama of my life. At the baptismal ceremony they decided to bury me under a mantel, nay a formidable array of names. Evangeline, after my great aunt and godmother, Jeannette, fished out of the skies, and Marie. Marie, our Blessed Lady's name, is traditionally given to all female offspring in our culture. Perhaps a litany of names gave distinction and prestige to such an unassuming, tiny being!

Grandparents Francois and Emeralda Savard

But wait, the christening was not over yet! Not if my Dad had anything to say about it. For my Dad all these fancy names were too elaborate to be remembered in an emergency. And in such a large family there are many of those! So my Dad found a practical solution. A solution that suited him to a T. He gave me a nickname that he must have dug out of the woodwork it was so weird! "Little Ring" no less! And even till the very last, Little Ring remained my father's concept of my identity. Of course, it would be unseemly to indulge in self-pity concerning these outrageous nicknames. The good man did this without a grain of prejudice. Every last member of the family was subjected to the same fate. I dare not reveal the absurdity of these nicknames here for fear of grievous consequences. All I know is that every last one of them was bizarre.

My Dad was not the only one having qualms about my first name. On my first day at school, the teacher had difficulty remembering the word Evangeline, so she called me Jeannette. Of course, I wasn't consulted. I would have objected dramatically had I been. Evangeline is a far more romantic name than Jeannette. But the choice was not mine to make, and Jeannette I have been to this day!

My very first conscious recollections are somewhat unusual, almost incredible! It is indeed incomprehensible that I should at that very particular moment become aware, nay, become cognitive of being alive. That mystery is beyond all imagination.

My Dad had been rocking me to sleep [he did this repeatedly while raising his family]. When I finally went to sleep, he went up the stairs to put me down in my crib. "At last" he thought to himself, "I can relax and smoke my pipe in peace." No such luck! When he was almost at the top of the stairs I woke up and gave an ungodly shriek; waking up from my sleep, and for the first time to the miracle of my existence in this great wide world.

My poor Dad heaved a deep sigh. At this particular time there was nothing to do but to carry me back downstairs and repeat the whole procedure. I had won. In spite of being so young [not much over a year old] I still remember the guilt, the remorse in my heart for my selfish behavior. It is indeed uncanny that after all these years that particular incident should have remained ingrained in my memory.

Looking back, it is quite evident that I was spoilt rotten. Yet it is also undeniably certain that these episodes were daily and normal occurrences in our family. For in that home the younger members reigned supreme! They were kings and the adults were their servants. Exigent sacrifices were expected from the grown ups for the comfort of the younger ones. Yet the devotion to the care and well being of the younger members of the family was never a point of contention or coerced in any way. It was given graciously and unselfishly. Any inconveniences incurred in the process was never begrudged or resented. In our family, the comfort and happiness of these precious little ones took precedence over all else. Adults even catered to their slightest caprice or fancy without complaint.

There is a vivid image of an event occurring in my childhood that keeps flashing back in my mind's eye. It is the image of a scene so painful that at the moment I was petrified with terror and anguish. Undoubtedly, I may have exaggerated the gravity of the situation [I always had a tendency to make mountains out of a grain of sand. It has often landed me in deep waters.] Be that as it may, at that particular moment I was in a state of panic and in no way qualified to make a rational analysis of the situation.

I was about three and a half or four when my sister, Marie-Anne, who was two years younger than myself suffered from a most severe and mysterious illness. The symptoms were so strange that no one was able to diagnose the disease or provide medication that could assuage its excruciating ramifications. On that particular occasion Marie-Anne's condition was critical. The whole family was frantic with anxiety. Undoubtedly to relieve some of the torment afflicting her someone had laid her on the kitchen table. The spasms emanating from the pain were so severe that she kept hurtling herself from one end of the table to the other. It was all the family [who had formed a circle around the table] could do to prevent her from dashing herself unto the floor. It is at this point that the memory of the episode flashes back into my psyche. It is the look on my Dad's face that horrifies me. I have the impression that he is convinced that Marie-Anne is having a temper tantrum. Furthermore I am terrified that he might spank her. The look on my mother's face and that on my oldest sister's face seemed to confirm my suspicions! It is a look of horror, of utter disbelief! It is a look that will haunt me the rest of my life. How I hope and pray that we were wrong and that my dad's expression was in fact a manifestation of desperation and helplessness, a feeling that we all shared in this most critical situation. And as I look back I am absolutely positive that we were all wrong for as far as I can remember my Dad never laid a hand on any of us.

The next recollection that flashes back before my eyes is of a most memorable event occurring in my early childhood. It is of a delightful, somewhat amusing incidence. It is an incidence that highlights dramatically my first day of school. Of course, that special day had to be accentuated by something sensational, spectacular, a big splash no less!

I must have been five years old or maybe a little younger. My Godmother Evangeline had sent me from Quebec a most wonderful present. It was a dress! Not a common every day pretty dress. This dress was out of this world! It was yellow and had all the frills, flounces, and trimmings possible to embellish it. I had never seen such a gorgeous dress. Not even in my wildest dreams! [And believe me those can be pretty wild]!

My Godmother Aunt Ma Tante Evangeline

My sisters, admiring me all bedecked in this ravishing attire, decided to take me to school to show me off. Everything went well until recess. The children were playing the game "Drop the Handkerchief". Of course, it is customary in a one room school for all the children, big and small, to participate in the same activity. Unfortunately, one of the big boys accidentally knocked me down while he was chasing the person who was "It". "You big ...", I screamed angrily. The adjective I used cannot be translated into English, but it must not have been very complimentary as both my sisters felt like vanishing into the ground. Needless to say that was the end of my "showing off".

My childhood memories abound with fantasies and wonder! They are memories of illusive dreams, mysterious, ethereal, and so delightful! They are dreams that only the innocence and the purity of a child can savor.

I often envision [in many remote recollections] my Mother leaving in a sleigh in winter or a wagon in summer. She is on her way to do the grocery shopping. For as far back as 1 can remember my Mother had to do the family business and the shopping. Although it is so long ago, when she was gone, it seemed the whole house was empty! We [the children] all watched the road, noses glued to the window, until the horse drawn vehicle appeared. But it was all worthwhile! No matter how little money was in the budget, a treat or a bag of candy always appeared with the rest of the necessary items.

"The children come first" still echoes in my ears, as 1 visualize my mother putting the groceries away.

Indeed every penny available was for the benefit of her loved ones. Their happiness always came first! Holidays, especially Christmas, a time of rejoicing! The magic, the enchantment of these Christmases will be recounted later in my story.

While yet very young the younger members of the family began to assemble to discuss matters of outstanding importance. I can still see us, all huddled together in a semi-circle, whispering, concentrating exclusively on the topic at hand, affairs of crucial importance being deliberated and meditated upon! Laurence, the leader, always officiating seriously on the procedures. [In my recollection, we're all sitting on the floor, Indian style]. And there I am, silently contemplating, pondering, mulling over what is being discussed. Then, suddenly, after a great deal of deliberation, I blurt out with my contribution, a statement so weird that the rest of the members are appalled!

On one particular occasion the subject is about Santa Clause. The general consensus is that the benevolence of this great elf is beyond question! Everyone is certain that he will, unquestionably, bring the gifts that were requested. The whole group is bubbling with anticipation and joy. But I cannot share the joviality, the unmitigated trust the rest have in Good Old St. Nicholas. After considering and weighing the matter carefully back and forth in my mind, to everyone's consternation I slowly and emphatically declare.

"It's very weird, but when it comes to the matter of Christmas and having presents under the tree, I think Mother is our best bet. My trust in her is absolute. She will never let us down. To tell you the truth I have more confidence in Mother."

The whole group sits there staring at me with their mouth open shocked! At last everyone turns away, shrugging their shoulders and apparently thinking, "She's hopeless!"

Later, at another one of those momentous meetings, it seems that the seating arrangement followed the same pattern, huddled closely together, every one sitting Indian style on the floor. On that particular day the topic happened to be "Beauty" or "Looks". It had long been asserted in our family conversations, that is, my aunt's and mine, that my aunt possessed all the beauty and my mother all the brains! That was precisely the subject being discussed at that specific assemblage. And to my astonishment, the unanimous consensus was that my mother did not possess any personal charm. It was at this point that I objected.

"It is very strange that it has never occurred to me that my Mother might be without personal attraction! To me she is just beautiful!" was my somewhat naïve but sincere observation. Of course, that comment was greeted with the same reaction as the previous banal observation I had made about Santa.

Laurence, being of a very daring and adventurous nature, always concocted some new and rather hazardous schemes to satisfy his yen for excitement. He built sleds that would take us careening down the steep hills near the house; he made slingshots for all of us to practice our shooting skills and stilts so that we could experience the thrill of walking high above the ground. His most daring venture however was his attic exploit. In the middle of the second storey level stood a post upon which my dad had built a shelf for the coal-oil lamp which stood three feet below the attic door. Laurence decided that he would pull us up one by one through the trap door leading into the attic after we had stepped unto the shelf. And so he did! I remember sitting on the floor of the attic just looking at each other and Laurence looking like the cat who swallowed the canary. He was thrilled! He had accomplished his audacious feat. Needless to say he never attempted to do these wild stunts when my dad was around.

There is another incident in my memory bank that typifies Laurence's personality. In those days the only means of transportation affordable to most families was a wagon. Some of the more affluent had automobiles and some had democrats but there were, of course, few of those. Later my parents were able to purchase a democrat but in the early days my family had to travel in a wagon. And the roads, well, there were no roads! There were trails leading from one place to another, rough trails that were almost impassable in stormy weather. Even horse drawn vehicles got stuck in the muddy ruts then. On that particular day the family was going somewhere. It had rained and there was mud, mud, mud everywhere, knee-high mud! Everyone was seated in the wagon waiting impatiently for me to get in but I was struggling behind stuck in mud up to my knees. There I was unable to budge one inch and feeling very miserable indeed! But not for long! Down from the wagon jumped Laurence and with no further ado he picked me up, mud, rubber boots and all and plunked me in the wagon. Well, I was so humiliated, so ashamed! To be loaded up like a dead log was too demeaning to be endured. But as far as Laurence was concerned it was all in the day's work.

During those early years, not only did I come out with statements that were totally out-and-out, but at times my behavior also was incredulous, utterly far-out! My next shenanigan, [at least the one that comes to mind] is so weird that I relate it at the risk of becoming an outcast, and of having my whole family disown me. It takes a great deal of audacity to disclose something so outlandish about yourself. Something that could ruin one's reputation forever. Thank goodness it is in the past. I was not yet six years old.

It happened that as a child, it took me an eternity to swallow even a trickle of water. It may have been caused by an obstruction in the throat, but it has remained unexplained throughout the years. No matter how hot or thirsty I was, the water would go down, drop by drop, ever so slowly down my throat a little trickle at a time! It was unbearably frustrating. One day, being extremely thirsty and unable to swallow sufficient water to quench my thirst I became exasperated; furious! I threw the whole glass of water in my face. There was water everywhere, on the counter, on the floor, and I was drenched! My sister Yvonne was astounded!

"What on earth are you doing?" she demanded.

"Well," I retorted. "Enough is enough. I will get a drink one way or another come hell or high water."

Many episodes that occurred in those blissful days of my childhood affirm the fact that I was desperately naïve. In fact my naiveté had sunk to the very abyss of the term. Therefore, the members of the family had long made up their minds that I was an irredeemable "bonasse".

One of these remains clearly imprinted in my memory. Fall had arrived prematurely that year. Most farmers had not anticipated the early snowfall, therefore the harvest was still incomplete. I remember that my whole family had to harvest a whole field of potatoes late at night. Why it had not been done in the daytime is beyond my recollection. It was dark, and it was cold! Everyone was desperately scrambling to pick mountains of potatoes, shivering and soaked in the wet snow. Of course I couldn't pick; I was too little! My job was to hold the lantern. But holding a lantern was not where my world was at that precise moment. My wings had soared into the vast beyond, the land of the unfathomable. The light was not where it should have been. Naturally! My Dad was exasperated.

"Why can't any of these children do anything right," he stormed most justifiably so.

I, however, was the only one who deserved that reprimand. Everyone else was working frantically to finish that insurmountable task and longing to get out of the freezing cold and into the warmth of the cozy house. That is, every one else but me. I was somewhere, sailing among the clouds impervious to everything around me. No wonder everyone had given me up as being beyond all hope!"

The sequence of these childhood events has escaped me, and they may not be in the exact order in which they actually occurred. I am relating them as the recollections flash back and the images reappear in my mind's eye.

All these incidences center around the daily happenings relative to life on the farm. It portrays the endless toil and hardship farming entails. But to a child it has fascinating compensations. The freedom, the wonders, and the mysteries of the wide-open spaces are treasures beyond the limits of the imagination! These treasures compensate for the extra duties and responsibilities imposed upon those who live on a farm in comparison to their urban counterpart. Hence it is not surprising that most of my earliest childhood misdeeds were committed in the performance of some menial task or other. The next misdemeanor to my discredit happened in this manner. My Dad had dug an outdoor root cellar to keep the vegetables fresh until spring. The scene emerges as my mother and I are preparing potato seedlings. We are both sitting on the top of the cellar, working like mad. My mother is extremely frustrated. She is chewing the rag frantically! Apparently the field where the potatoes are to be planted has not been cultivated and is not ready. She blames my Dad's continual procrastination for the situation. And feeling my mother's discontent, I began to whine and grumble with a passion. Eventually, I say something that is so vulgar, so gross, that my mother is completely astounded! By the look in her eye, it is quite evident that I have committed a major transgression. Of course, the meaning of that forbidden blunder is still not quite clear to me, even after all these years!

At certain times, my contributions to the family welfare deserved approval. On one occasion all the grown-ups were buried under mountains of work. No one was available to do any extra tasks. The potatoes in the cellar had to be cleaned in the near future. In spite of my age, my Mother asked me to sort out the good potatoes from those that were decayed. The task was not difficult. Indeed it was quite simple. That was doubtless the reason why it was allotted to the least capable of the lot. The problem was that the basement of the house was a dirt cellar and there was no air circulation. I remember crawling up the ladder and at the top thinking that I was going to faint from lack of air. Yet I was bursting with pride. At last I had been able to contribute to the daily routine and the well being of the family. In spite of my naivety!

During harvest, everyone was expected to pitch in and help. Thrashing was the time when everything was buzzing with activity. The old fashioned threshing machine was installed right by the granaries so that the grain could be piped into the granary through an opening in the wall by means of a conveyer pipe.

Naturally the grain accumulated immediately below the conveyer pipe. It was the delight of the younger members of the family [myself included] to level the grain across the floor.

One spring, during seeding time, the seed drill was not functioning properly. The ducts through which the seeds are distributed in the soil would continually get plugged. My brother could not clear the ducts and drive the horses at the same time. So I was elected to do the job. Standing on the drill platform beside my brother, I'd clear the ducts using a long stick. I felt ten feet tall! But I nearly froze to death!

And during all these years of my childhood I wondered how my sister Hélène and I could be so different in temperament. She being so rational, so practical and trustworthy and I with my head always in the clouds. It bothered me that she was always depended upon to do the most complicated tasks while I was always stuck doing the menial no-account chores. After many years and a great deal of deliberation and speculation, I decided to make an intensive study of the matter. I had already concluded that each one of us had definitely inherited our unique personalities. It is quite obvious that we were both raised by the same parents and under the same circumstances. But I wanted some definite proof. So I went ahead hell bent on a quest searching for an authentic source that would validate my hypothesis.

Despite the countless researches establishing the fact that nurture is more crucial than inheritance in the development of a child, it is evident that these deductions are not invariably conclusive. Close observation of individual personalities sometimes contradict and challenge the validity of these findings. The results of these studies may be indecisive and vacillate.

Even during my intensive research project and on purely speculative grounds, I still maintained that based on personal and perhaps wild assumptions, I dared to contend that a child's main character traits are inherited and emanates into his individual personality as an adult. Sometimes even physical traits persist into adulthood. In fact, based on my limited personal observations it seems that an infant retains both personal and physical characteristics in adulthood. I have little proof of this physical aspect. Nevertheless, family members who experienced health problems as a child had persistent health problems throughout their lives, whereas those born with a strong and robust physic enjoyed the gift of good health. Subsequently, members of the family with striking character traits retained these characteristics when they became adults.

My sister, Hélène, is verily the most glaring example of my contention that marked character traits persist throughout adulthood. She was but an infant during the Spanish Flu. She was very ill with the disease and the family feared for her life. Nevertheless even as an infant, she displayed a strong and determined personality. She had decided that only my mother could rock her cradle. No matter how stealthily my grandmother's hand crept upon the rocker, she sensed it instantly and raised uproar. This determination has been the most outstanding character trait throughout her life. Even as a child when her mind was made up about something everyone backed off. At a very young age she decided she would make something of her life. Struggling through high school without teacher, book, or any guidance, she was admitted into the Holy Family Hospital in Prince Albert to train as a nurse. She was a credit to her profession. Throughout her life, excellence was her target, and she never let any obstacle deter her along the way.

Hélène's Graduation

Strange that one of my granddaughters should have my sister's identical personality! To succeed, overcoming all hurdles is her goal. As a child she never failed to assert her rights. Beware if anyone dared to step into her turf! Even in high school, the rest of the class acquiesce to her decisions. It was easier than to contest the issue. Such fortitude and strength of character merits commendation indeed!

When I contemplate the philosophy involved in nature versus nurture and all the controversies this subject engendered, I am confounded! The issue is dependent on so many variables that a definite, absolute validation is impossible to achieve conclusively. Were I to base my conclusion upon my own observations heredity would transcend nurture, especially in the psychological development of personality. However, physical development obviously emanates from care and proper nourishment.

Perhaps my assumptions are biased and prejudiced by the observation of a restricted field or sample. My observations have been confined to personalities in my immediate surroundings: my family, my colleagues, my students, my own children, and of course myself. It is through a great deal of soul-searching and contemplation that I have reached these [somewhat limited] conclusions. It is also evident that I could debate the pros and cons of this theory indefinitely. But it is not what my intentions were at the beginning of this project, and I have wandered, adrift on a subject that is too complicated, too controversial, to be discussed in such limited space. I have introduced the issue in an effort to highlight the striking and remarkable difference between my sister Hélène's personality and mine, a factor that is of major import because of the phenomenal influence her fortitude and courage had upon the path I pursued as I trudged along the way. For she was practical, determined to achieve her goal and always able to solve problems with wisdom and insight, while I, in contrast, always had my head in the clouds fantasizing and building an illusive mystical world of my own. Only my sister's steadfast example had the ability to bring my skittish fancy anchored onto solid ground. Alas after all this hullabaloo and after spending hours doing research I am still convinced that nature is more powerful than nurture in the development of a child's personality. And that my sister and I must have inherited genes from widely different ancestors that existed way back when.

Looking back throughout my life from the beginning, the characteristics that I inherited from my parents are the culmination of who I am. That is perhaps besides my passion: my mad obsession for reading. That is debatable! Was that passion inherited or was it inculcated by the constant image of my mother, entranced, blissfully devouring the pages of a book?

The most outstanding characteristic of my personality, however, was my ability to dwell in mystical, illusive fantasies. Flights of the imagination into dreamland where radiance and rapture reigned supreme. Those euphoric ramblings in space monopolized most of my waking hours, hours during which my feet were never firmly anchored solidly upon the soil of reality; a reality that demanded severe and rigid standards, standards too cruel to abide. Therefore, a haven, an illusive paradise I fabricated in the cobwebs of my childish fancy.

At the time, and in my childish imagination, this illusive presence wandering among the clouds in space was the real me, and in the flesh, only its shadow, a figment of illusion. For in the boundless realm of mystical magnitude was where my heart and soul forever dwell. Only when necessity coerced, did I descend from this haven of bliss, where sorrow and sadness did not exist. And that dream world was my secret! It was kept hidden in the deepest recesses of my soul. I was absolutely petrified that someone might discover my secret. In fact, it seemed to me that anyone who would efface oneself from reality, and exist in a dream world would have to be weird, utterly bizarre! Yet I could not escape nor abandon the mystical haven surreptitiously woven in the most secretive abyss of my childhood fancy. In fact that secret was never revealed to anyone until I discovered that the author of "Alice in Wonderland" had day dreamed all his life.

Years later my sister Hélène and I created an imaginary community inhabited by semi-real individuals. Of course, these residents were model, irreproachable citizens. We had created a veritable "Garden of Eden", an island in the skies. Several families lived in this imaginary Utopia. The most fascinating and spectacular aspect of this creation was that each family had been given its own identity, its own particular characteristics and its own place of residence. Most of the family names have eluded me. One however has remained, the EE's. The reality of these inhabitants was so genuine that we actually paid daily visits to each household and engaged in lengthy, sophisticated conversations with the residents. That the visitor carried both ends of the conversation did not matter in the least, it still went on and on. To us, these make-believe people were as real as we were, existing with us side by side.

Right in the center of this Utopia we had erected a haven for children. It was a home where every child was welcomed. The home projected such an aura of tranquility, peace, and sanity, where every child was mysteriously drawn within its domain. And once within these magic walls, the child would be free to be a child. Free to express himself, without being taken to task and with no one breathing down his neck. It was where a child could be liberated from the implacable eye of judgment glaringly scrutinizing every gesture, every move.

Peace, tranquility, serenity, were the gifts so lavishly emanating within these magic walls! How I longed then [and even now] for the solace of their healing and comfort. And how these gifts are the fundamental right of every child to enjoy.

This Utopian creation that had been woven out of the cobwebs of our fancy was much more logical than my flights into the land of dreams. Whereas my imaginary world was jealously kept locked away into the most abysmal chambers of my spirit, these creations were realistic. They had each been given substance, identity, and personality. They, like real human beings, played an important role and participated actively in the drama of our lives. It is impossible to ascertain the point in time when we moved away from our magic realm and abandoned our out-of-this-world imaginary friends. It has long been buried deep in the virtually all but forgotten past!

It is not surprising that this tendency to transport myself into the unknown and the mysterious realms enticed me to seek solitude. I looked forward to any task, activity, or situation that gave me the opportunity to be by myself. Then, undisturbed, unconstrained, I, with the wind, could swoop down into these magnificent, mystical kingdoms of my own creation.

Jeannette Romaniuk

On the farm there were many such opportunities. Berry picking was, perhaps, the task that I cherished the most. Not only was it a pleasure to gather the ripe, luscious berries, but I found myself in my own private paradise. Surrounded by the splendor of nature's grandeur, I luxuriated in its magnanimous radiance.

At the time a wide variety of wild berries abounded in Northern Saskatchewan. Saskatoons grew everywhere, by the roads, in the uncultivated fields, on the hillsides, everywhere! The fruit on the bushes was so plentiful that the branches were weighed down almost to the ground. Dark, juicy fruit, bluish-purple in color soon filled a bucket. My mother never ceased to be amazed when I came back from these expeditions with two buckets plump full of luscious, juicy berries. Strawberries were harder to find. They grew in several scattered locations. A great deal of searching was required in order to discover patches where the berries grew. During the last two weeks of August, the blueberries ripened and were ready to be picked. The family had discovered a patch in our pasture, where the berries abounded. At first we reaped the benefit of gathering the berries uncontested. Unfortunately after the lease on the pasture expired, the patch was discovered by a neighbor. Subsequently a lot of competition for the berries ensued.

Sometimes to my dad's great distress, I even ventured way out to pick cranberries. These grew in the swamps bordering the north side of our homestead. The moss-covered soil at the bottom of these swamps was spongy, soft, soggy, and the underlying layer was waterlogged and dangerously unstable, making it almost impossible to get a secure footing. According to my dad, many animals had been stuck in the mire and had perished in an abortive struggle to regain their foothold. In spite of these precarious conditions, and my dad's insistent warnings, the temptation to get these berries lured me into the swamp. I remember stepping, nay, jumping from one soggy moss clump to another, the water oozing up to my ankles, yet persisting in this mad escapade. How much fruit compensated this hazardous adventure is beyond my wildest recollections. Evidently not enough to warrant the risk it involved!

Raspberry picking was an episode in itself. There were a few raspberry bushes at the foot of the hill used as a potato patch in front of the house. These bushes did not yield much fruit however. Gathering these berries brings back a flashing memory of an event that portrays my idiosyncrasies, my utterly out-and-out behavior! Throughout my life I have lived in dread of anything that crawls or creeps, which explains somewhat my foolish behavior. I remember dashing up that hill, petrified, because I had found a worm crawling inside one of the berries. Unbelievable!

Our friends happened to have a luxurious raspberry patch right near their house. When the berries were ripe some of us would go and spend a few days at their house in order to take advantage of the picking season. It was fun! We had the companionship of our friends, who were the same age group, while amassing great quantities of fruit. Unfortunately that family moved away from our neighborhood. It is almost incredible that they found themselves again situated right near a raspberry patch! Regardless of the distance [nearly thirty-five miles] separating us, and in spite of the hardship such a long trip involved, we ventured out. It meant hours of traveling in a horse drawn wagon. It goes without saying that Laurence was our teamster leading the way into this mad extravaganza. With him on board we were convinced that we could weather any storm and therefore we were undaunted! Nothing could stop us. We were on our way to share nature's bountiful gifts with our friends.

There was one more fruit picking episode. It involved pin-cherries. The only place where these delicious berries could be found in abundance was on the crest of a great sand hill that rose about one-quarter mile from the fence at the edge of our land. That hill was crowned with trees of every description: pines, aspens, birch, and of course pin-cherry bushes. The temptation to get those pin-cherries was impossible to resist. There was a problem. A whole flock of hawks had claimed that haven as their domain. The giant trees provided a natural shelter for their nests and safety for their young. The hawks guarded their kingdom with a vengeance. Indeed, anyone daring to invade their privacy did so at his own risk. These courageous hawks would swoop down menacingly low over the intruder's head with a great rush of their wings and utter the most blood-curdling shrieks. These noble creatures were bravely defending their sanctuary from invaders like me. It was their justifiable, instinctive right. How I longed to explain to them my intent. Alas, they, like men, are ignorant of the language of the conciliatory entente. Peaceful negotiations, compromises are impenetrable, unfathomable, beyond all understanding or feasibility to both species. For birds, it is beyond their ability, for men, it is beyond their humanity.

Even in my earliest childhood wandering aimlessly in the woods, along a wagon trail or following a narrow path that led no one knows where fascinated me. It may have been that once in the great outdoors I was liberated from cares inherent in the confinement of a crowded house. It may have been because of my obsessive fascination with nature. Or perhaps it was a feeling that at last my thoughts were set free to ramble whichever way they chose to go. Whatever the reason, no sooner did the door close upon my exit that I spread my wings and floated upon the breath of enchantment. As I strolled leisurely along those magic byways, I was enthralled by the beauty, the depth of nature's mysterious secrets. The joy and the rapture emanating from these wonders is unfathomable!

Undoubtedly many of these hikes were mandatory and part of the daily chores farm life necessitates.

The most important and time consuming of these tasks was searching and fetching the cows home at milking time. Tracking and bringing these cows home was by no means an easy task. These animals were loosed, or set free, in a grazing field that was indeed not an ordinary run of the mill pasture. That pasture was immense! It stretched and included all the far–flung, endless, wide open sections of uninhabited land lying east of our homestead. This vast area included low rugged mountains, [a continuation of the Canadian Shield apparently]. Covered by swamps, sloughs, bushes, and dense prickly shrubbery it was indeed a very inhospitable terrain, unsuitable for cultivation. But as a pasture it was ideal. The sloughs and the fields were covered with rich, luscious grasses. It provided ample space where animals were free to roam at will. A veritable animal paradise. And it was into this paradise that those cows were loosed every morning after they were milked. No wonder they stubbornly refused to come back home in the evening! After enjoying the freedom of the wide open spaces and the luscious verdure of the grasslands, the restrictive enclosures were a dismal prospect indeed. At night they were not allowed beyond the gates leading to the open pastures and were kept in these enclosures, or corrals. In the morning there was no time to fetch them before milking. As soon as they were milked the gates were opened and the cows led to the pastures. They were hopefully expected to follow their instincts and come home to be milked. Which would have been ideal and did occur on many occasions? But those crazy cows had a mind of their own and many times they decided to wander off the well beaten path. And wander they most assuredly did, as far as those interminable, wide open spaces could conceivably permit. Stupid they may have been but amazingly they apparently made sure that the sound of the cow-bell they carried could not alert the searcher. The bell was lying motionless on the ground.

It was Hélène who for the most part went to look for the cows. She always did the most difficult jobs. But occasionally I was able to persuade her and the rest of the family to allow me to have a turn. It was an opportunity to wander by myself for many delicious moments. It meant endless treks through the vast rugged area beyond our homestead. Sometimes it meant searching for hours. Those stupid cows played a mean game of hide-and–go seek! And I, perhaps as dim-witted as they were, was in my seventh-heaven, savoring the glory of my beloved nature!

On one occasion we had been unable to find these scheming beasts for many days. Every member of the family had searched endlessly and everywhere for them. We had almost given up hope of ever finding them. However the girls decided to try one more time, make one more Herculean effort to locate these wily creatures. So, there we were, all five of us, sauntering along the trail, obviously doing more talking than looking. With all the racket we were making, even the cows would have run for their very lives, let alone rabbits.

All at once we froze in our tracks, petrified. From a thick clump of tall poplars came a thundering, ear-splitting crash and clatter, veritable pandemonium! It sounded like all hell had come loose. There was the deafening sound of pounding, stumping, crashing, and trees falling. It sounded as if a whole regiment was storming a barricade. We just stood there, trying to determine what could possibly be the source of such an horrible hullabaloo, and also trying to figure out what to do next. After we had calmed down a bit, we concluded that our herd had come in contact with another strange herd and that a horrible battle was in process. As usual Hélène knew what was to be done.

"Stay here and watch that our herd doesn't stray further up the trail," she cautioned, "and I will go and chase them towards the trail." Although she was quite apprehensive she slowly, stealthily approached the site and disappeared behind the trees. As scared as we were, our fright was not to be compared with the sheer terror we felt for Hélène's safety. We stood there waiting, hardly daring to breathe. We waited and we waited! We held our breath, not daring to make a sound. No Hélène. No cows! Our alarm increasing until we were in a state of panic. "What could have happened to her?" we wondered. There was no sign of her or the cows. Besides, the noise had turned into a dead, eerie silence. Not a sound. Not even the snapping of a twig! Oh, we were silent alright, indeed we were! Even the sound of our breathing was fantasized as the rumbling of thunder. Time stood still indefinitely. At long last Hélène appeared on the far end of the bush. We breathed a sigh of relief. She was as white as a ghost! We all began in unison to ask the same question. "What happened? Where are the cows?" "Sh, sh" she whispered, walking or actually running away from the bush where the racket had emerged. "But, but," we persisted. "Be quiet!" she reiterated. From the horrified look on her face we began to think, "She must have seen a ghost, or maybe worse, Lucifer himself! Only Satan could make that much racket all by himself." Finally when we had reached a safe distance from the ill-fated bush, she told us the whole story.

"Scared, I was slowly and very cautiously getting closer and closer to the source of the commotion. I was sneaking up on what I thought was a herd of cows and making an effort not to step on dead branches so that the herd would not be alerted and stampede. Suddenly I froze, for there right before my eyes and in the middle of that thicket was, not cows, but a man holding an axe, a team of horses tied to a tree. He was chopping frantically, like a maniac, the trees crashing down everywhere beside him. At first he was unaware of my presence, but he must have sensed that someone was there, because he turned suddenly and saw me. It would have been impossible to judge which one of us was the most thunder struck, him or me. He became rooted on the spot, his eyes bulging in disbelief! We both stood there, speechless, staring at each other. How long? I haven't the faintest idea, but it seemed an eternity. What passed through that unfortunate man's mind as he tried to unravel the absurdity of this freakish, outlandish encounter must have been extraordinary! I was the first to recover! In a flash I turned and like a bat out of hell I fled out of that bush as swiftly as my winged legs could fly! I had no way of knowing what this man was thinking, but as far as I was concerned that was the weirdest experience I had ever encountered!"

Needless to say the cows were not milked that day.

It was obvious to my parents when the incident was related to them that the man had been gathering his winter's supply of firewood. Because it was illegal to use any resources in the area without a permit, the poor man must have thought that my sister was spying on him. He was probably afraid that she might report him.

Once, when on a wild-goose-chase searching for those cows in that extended, unlimited pasture, I realized all of a sudden that I was hopelessly lost. I had followed a rabbit trail that led to a small clearing. At the outer edge the trail encircled the clearing. It was a fascinating little glade. One could almost imagine that it was the rabbits' conference circle, with members hunched around the periphery concentrating attentively to the business at hand. I lingered awhile to admire the spot then turned around in order to retrace my steps. Or so I thought. But after having walked for a considerable distance, I found myself in the same spot. I repeated this several times, always with the same results. I became apprehensive, afraid that I might not be able to find my way home! Fortunately my common sense came to the rescue and I asked myself, "What is the sensible thing to do when faced with a desperate situation?" The answer became obvious. "Don't panic. Sit down and think." Well, that's exactly what I did. I sat right in the middle of that circle and evaluated the situation. I had always turned in the same direction when trying to retrace my steps. So now, it became apparent that I must turn, face, and walk in the opposite direction. That is what I did. Soon there were many familiar objects along the path and I knew that it was the way home. It was at the corner of our homestead that I met my sister. She was riding a horse. [How gracefully she rode a horse.] But my troubles were not over. Coming towards us and dangerously close was a mother skunk and her whole brood advancing imperiously in a single file. I never realized how beautiful these animals were. I was evidently too terrified to appreciate their elegance at that particular moment. Only sheer good fortune enabled us to escape unscathed. The memory of the precarious situation we were in still gives me the creeps. When we got home we realized that my mother, fearing the worst, had been pacing up and down, agonizing over my prolonged absence.

Countless unusual incidents occurred while chasing these cantankerous animals all over kingdom come. Some of these incidents were downright hilarious, priceless! Others would have tested the patience of a saint! Needless to say, Hélène and I enjoyed these excursions immensely. Some, the men especially, were not so impressed. They thought their valuable time should be spent on activities that were more worthwhile, not wasted chasing cows.

There were many worthwhile activities besides berry picking and fetching the cows that took us wandering all over the countryside. For instance, we discovered that it was possible to supplement the family income by picking a wild root, Seneca, that grew in our neighborhood. These roots are apparently used in making certain cough medicine. At one time it seems to me that with the exception of my mother, everyone in the family was digging up these roots. My dad had designed a tool that facilitated the tasks considerably. It consisted of a pole like a broomstick, a foot brace, or prop, and a sharp blade riveted to the lower foot end for digging into the soil. The root was dug by pressing the blade into the ground with the pressure of the foot on the brace. When a quantity had been amassed, the roots were dried and sold to the local merchant. A large sack sold for ten dollars.

To some digging roots must have been a backbreaking and tedious task indeed. But not for me. My mad inordinate infatuation with nature's marvels, the spiritual peace and solace it brought me, besides the sanctuary, the refuge from the constant surveillance of the watchful eye probing my inadequacies and my failures more than compensated for the backaches and the drudgery of the task.

All these wanderings in the open air to accomplish specific tasks could never be compared to the joy, the pure rapture I experienced in the ramblings, the aimless drifting into the wide-open spaces. The exhilaration, the delight these pleasurable wanderings brought transcended all other adventures. Just meandering into the woods, admiring the beauty of the trees and the wild flowers, listening to the bird's mixed concerts, and feeling the soft breath of a Zephyr breeze I leisurely put one foot ahead of the other. Time, destination, and chosen site all acquiescent, obeisant to my slightest caprice. In nature's vast wondrous realm [there and there only] I reigned supreme, triumphant!

Strolling to and around the lake was perhaps the most frequent of these adventures. This lake, shaped like the continent of Africa, was situated in the very center of our homestead about half a mile from our house. It was surrounded by a dense growth of every kind of trees: willows, aspens, birch, pine, and a thick undergrowth of shrubbery. From the house the path led down a hill then winding to the right past a dried out well and thence through a thickly wooded area and to the lake. On the opposite side in the densely wooded area Laurence had constructed one of his many miniature log cabins. Above the lake the path continued, surrounding it and leading to a cultivated field. That lake held a special captivating attraction. On many occasions the whole family would gravitate there with friends or visitors. Once, on a warm winter day, the adult members had taken a young priest to the site, most likely because he had brought his skates. The young priest proceeded to do figure skating on the ice, figures of eight, and countless artistic dynamisms. I was amazed, we all were! It was the first time we had seen anyone skate, let alone figure skate!

The path from the house to and surrounding the lake was the path along which I never ceased to drift. It was my haven, my refuge from sadness or sorrow, an escape to my own ivory tower, to the tranquility and peace I so passionately yearned!

Many times however, my rambling moods led me further afield. When obsessed by loneliness or an urge for solitude I ventured along the trail in front of the house. That trail was the route that led to the nearest town, Shell Lake. It was also used by the Natives traveling or visiting from one reserve to another. Further on it provided the distant neighbor's access to the town. Sadly the trail has vanished. It has been obliterated completely by weeds and shrubs covering the ruts, the beaten path of yester years. But then it was the entrance to a world of freedom I so desperately sought. The freedom to be me, alone with my beloved nature! Indeed I was a veritable coward, [a wimp, spineless]! I could not bear conflict, quarreling, or discord. I could not bear the horror of butchering an animal. I'd run away, far away, and linger until all traces of this dreadful deed had been effaced. On other occasions it was my passion for reading that lured me away. I'd sit on a stump or a stone, reading or knitting, admiring the gorgeous feathers of the blue jays while they came pecking at my bare feet.

It was during these solitary excursions that I gave free reign to my wild imagination, rampaged into the unknown, and indulged in my flighty ecstatic reveries. It was then that my fantasy would run wild and journey into the unknown, weaving magic castles in the air. Magnificent, lofty, elegant and luxuriously extravagant castles built upon a terraced hillside and surrounded by a mythical, legendary moat, overlooking sparkling crystal clear waters. The prohibitive, exorbitant extravagant expenditure was of no consequence ever, for these castles were woven of the ethereal web spun and emanating from an over active rambling chimera.

There are endless incidents from my childhood that keep flashing back on my memory screen. Many of these events are so deeply buried in the past that it is questionable whether or not they occurred before I was old enough to go to school.

One of these flashes brings back a most delightful experience. My cousins, who lived in a town nearby, had come to visit the family. These cousins were very close to us. We always looked forward to their visit as we always had loads of fun when they came. We played games, chatted, and sometimes, unfortunately, got into serious mischief! On that particular occasion they had come all dressed-up. The girls wore dainty dresses and brand new shoes. But what appealed to me the most, [I must confess that I was a little bit jealous] was their exquisite capes. They were out of this world! How I wished that I could have possessed such a beautiful garment. That wish, although it never materialized, remained with me for years afterwards. The desire was so strong that years later I purchased the treasured item for a grand daughter. She, however, did not share my taste, and she never wore the treasured item. Needless to say the capes were soon forgotten, and the joy of being together the only thing that mattered and we sashayed to the little sand hillock on the trail that led to our house. The sand was deliciously soft and deep. Barefooted, [what the cousins did with their fancy shoes is beyond me] we squished the sand between our toes as we raced down the hill. Then we'd fill our skirts to the brim with sand and let it dribble as we skipped and danced our way down. As the sand squirted out we shrieked with laughter. We then proceeded to roll down to the very foot of the hill. Was it the freedom of doing something so utterly ridiculous that was so hilarious? At any rate, we were deliriously happy. Needless to say my aunt must have been appalled. The beautiful dress, the new shoes, must have been in a disreputable state, if not completely ruined. But we did have a terrific time! I regret that it is too late to make amends, at least to apologize to my aunt. Alas, it is too late!

On other occasions when these town cousins came to visit we'd play various indoor games, games we had invented such as "Button, button, who has the button?" or "Charade." Whatever we did we always managed to have loads of fun.

The great enormous cliff the hawks had claimed as their own extended far beyond our land. It extended through the road allowance, continuing to rise further and across the neighbors' fields. It was a curse to the traveler, especially to the motorist. In winter, its icy slippery height was impossible to ascend. Loaded vehicles were barely ever able to reach its crest. As children it appeared that the climb was endless especially after having walked all the way from school. It did possess unique charms of its own however. Especially in the eyes of a child! It was a rock collector's paradise. Rocks of all sizes and of every description, whose exquisite beauty was beyond compare. Multi-colored their brilliance gleamed and glittered in the dazzling sunshine. Often we gathered those whose beauty we could not resist, thinking that they might contain diamonds or even gold. Yet always our treasures were rated worthless. Be that as it may, modern artists shape and form these colorful rocks into magnificent designs. These artistic creations are sold as unique ornaments in art and novelty shops. It is unfortunate that these creative artists never had access to this abundant source, the bounteous source teeming in my childhood playground.

While yet at a very tender age, I was subjected to an operation for appendicitis. Although it was a most traumatic experience, I should have been ashamed of feeling so sorry for myself as seven members of the family were subjected to the same fate and none of them indulged in self pity. However, because of my young age [I was as yet unable to read], my mother was quite worried about leaving me alone at the hospital. Consequently John, my oldest brother, was mercifully left with me in the city. He came to visit me every day, sometimes twice. Every time he came I was sobbing hysterically.

"I want to go home. I want to go home." I kept repeating.

My poor brother was at his wits end. No matter what he said or did he could not dispel my anxiety. He'd buy items dear to any child. Books, stories like, "Little Red Riding Hood", the cover of which was in the shape and had the picture of the main character. They were items I cherished for years afterwards. Despite all his efforts he was unable to calm my fear. Looking back, the image of an elderly lady flashes before my eyes. She may have been mentally disturbed and kept under observation. Be that as it may, she was determined to terrorize me to death. Indeed it was not a difficult thing to do, as I already felt insecure, lonely, and disoriented in these unfamiliar surroundings.

"You'll never be allowed to go home again", she constantly repeated. "They'll keep you here forever if your parents can't pay the hospital bill. You'll never see your mother again." She never stopped. She'd go on and on. Even though John did his utmost to reassure me during his visits, her words kept resurging in my mind. I was frantic.

It is inconceivable that a timid child with an impressionable mind would have been lodged in the same ward as a mentally disturbed patient. Was it the lack of space, staff, or facilities that could have necessitated such a monumental measure? That is indeed another inscrutable mystery that keeps resurging in my mind and haunting me every step of the way.

This medical problem had almost reached an epidemic status in our family. My brother Laurence barely survived the life–threatening operation. Before both he and Hélène could be taken to the hospital the appendicitis had ruptured, complicating the procedures and the recovery period. Others, because of complications derived from the operation, suffered an extended convalescent period. Yet, doctors were unable to trace the origin of the disease. It was the cause of great emotional and financial distress in the household.

Intertwined among all these many joyous and troubled times were events that were sometimes hilarious and at other times somewhat exasperating. Depending on which side you were on. For instance, as far back as my memory can travel, I had been elected [nay coerced] to act as the family chaperon. And I despised it, oh Lord, how I despised it! I felt like a spy, listening on people's secrets, snooping on the young couples' privacy. How they must have resented my presence! And how I longed to disappear or at least to become invisible. The fact that I always had nice clothes and that I had the opportunity to go wherever these lovers went was no consolation.

On one of these excursions, a most dramatic incident occurred. Although the consequences were rather serious. My sister, her friend and I were coming from church in an old model T Ford. We were on the trail that led across the reserve. It was a very rough road, with rocks, holes, and bumps. The old model T hit a rock and overturned, the boiling water from the radiator spilling all over my legs. Needless to say I was badly burned.

"I will never, never, ride in a car again," I vowed. Evidently that promise has been broken.

The unfortunate friend had to walk several miles in order to repair the wheel of his dilapidated yet prized vehicle. Years later my cousin informed me that the friend had secured a wheel to replace the damaged one from my Grandfather.

My sister Germaine was full of energy and enterprising ideas. One day in early April, she decided to take the younger members of the family for a swim in a slough. She was unable to convince Hélène to participate however as Hélène had more common sense than the rest of us. It was soon after the spring thaw and the water was still ice cold. Undeterred, shivering and teeth chattering we all jumped in. We were having a frigid hilarious good time until my dad spotted us. He was livid. In a split second the culprits were home in dry clothes their heads hanging, waiting for the storm to erupt. And the storm did break! An absolute hurricane!

But that wasn't the worst retribution emanating as a consequence of that wild escapade. As a result of the exposure to the frigid temperature of the water, the whole crew caught a chill and came down with a severe case of whooping cough. I still remember the excruciating cough that racked my body for days on end. Truly and for once the punishment was too ruthless and did not justifiably fit the crime.

It is most amazing indeed; it is beyond all comprehension, that my first years at school have completely been effaced from my memory. Besides crowning this perplexing enigma is the fact that "learning to read" has also vanished without a trace to the confines of the past. Although a few rare insignificant incidents flash in my mind's eye, those years remain totally buried in the crypt of time. Years that are but a haze, a blur, a dim shadow, in the distant past. It is so frustrating! As if time had stood still and my life had temporarily taken a leave of absence as a curtain call between the scenes in the drama depicting the role I enacted on this earthly stage!

Yet this revelation, this lapse, is indeed incredible. The adaptation to the school routine in our community was fraught with numerous pitfalls, obstacles, and complications. These difficulties should have fixated in my recollections the trials they engendered. Perhaps the most challenging of these obstacles was that the instructions and the textbooks were almost exclusively in the English language. This was a major impediment indeed. With the exception of one family all the students in the school were of French Canadian descent. Therefore most of the students were unable to communicate and perform effectively in the English language. Our family was no exception. My father insisted that French be the sole language spoken in the home. As a consequence, we were unable to comprehend the instructions and skills that were exigent to our academic education. Besides, the teacher was responsible for the academic growth of students of all ages and at all levels of learning from grade one to grade eight. Sometimes the supervision of correspondence students in grade nine and ten was an added responsibility imposed upon the overburdened teacher.

The school was the typical little red schoolhouse that usually existed in rural areas. It wasn't red however, nor did it reflect signs of impoverishment one might expect pertaining to a country school. It had one main classroom, one cloakroom for the boys, one cloakroom for the girls with an entrance-corridor separating them. This corridor was equipped with a shelf upon which a huge crock containing the daily supply of water stood. The water had to be carried nearly half a mile from a farmer's well. A massive wood-burning furnace towering over the student's desks supplied the heat during the severe winter temperatures. It was, however, the extraordinary collection of books that made this small country school unique. There were books, books, and more books. Under the classroom windows on one wall and projecting onto the back of the classroom were three shelves jam packed with books. Books in both languages, English and French, story books, text books,

books of all kinds and description! It is indeed astonishing that such a small school could accumulate this unbelievable quantity of books. It is most likely that my mother's obsessive compulsion for reading may have been instrumental in the acquisition of such a valuable collection.

The only vivid images of these early years at school that flash back clearly before my eyes are those of one teacher, my dear friend, a major incidence and one minor event. The image of that teacher will remain embedded in my memory because of his unique if not eccentric personality. The affection and empathy my friend and I shared endured throughout our years at school and is a treasure that will remain forever in my heart. This girl, Marguerite, and I, being at the silly age when every thing is funny, had a tendency to laugh at all things. Nobody knew what we were laughing about. In fact we didn't know what we were laughing about ourselves! That was irrelevant. We just kept right on giggling! For some weird reason the teacher thought we were making fun of him. That, of course was the furthest thing from our silly immature minds. Be that as it may, one day we were severely punished. We both felt that the punishment was unwarranted. Being extremely distressed, we vented our anger by barricading ourselves in the outhouse. Unfortunately the teacher was standing at the door and heard all the outlandish blabber. There were severe consequences. The teacher sent a letter to our parents and we were reprimanded. Whenever someone in the family got in trouble my mother always stood by them, always coming to their defense. Why then when I felt that the punishment had been so unjust did she so irrevocably condemn me. Many times in later years, that same question haunted me. For whenever problems or any disagreements arose among the siblings, I was always the culprit. My mother never stood up for me. Except once, but that is another story. And the thought kept becoming recurrent, "Maybe I am just irretrievably, hopelessly bad."

The other incidence that still keeps coming back vividly, again involves Marguerite and I. We were in the process of dramatizing "The Three Little Kittens". The performance must have been quite spectacular because it attracted the attention of the whole classroom. All of a sudden my friend and I found ourselves in the midst a large enthusiastic audience. We were overwhelmed! Needless to say that was the final act of the performance.

I often meditate and wonder about the needless entanglements, the embroilments of these years. The perplexities, the unfathomable compulsions that prompted the inexplicable, irrational behavior of many adults in our milieu. For instance, the obsession of a most capable, competent teacher who was determined to stop two silly girls from whispering secrets in each other's ears and giggling. Little did he realize that this was an impossibility; as futile as trying to stop the raging fury of the hurricane, or the roaring torrent of the cascading waters from the fall. Whispering, giggling, that's what little girls do. And my spirit utters a piercing cry pleading their cause. May this cry be heard throughout the ages by adults who have allowed conformity to become an obsession. To adults who cling tenaciously to the age-old misinterpreted theory of "spare the rod and spoil the child" and are determined to whip children into shape.

Do not envy the laughter of the child, or tear the rapture that gushes forth from his heart. Let that laughter ring out. It is a rhapsody of delight gushing out from the soul, a song of joy, the enchantment of just being alive. It is the wonder, the magic of being a child! Therefore, I entreat thee, be appreciative and generous to the child's laughter. That time will soon be gone. Too soon the cares and toils of adulthood will enslave and dampen the brightness of the spirit.

As I reminiscent about these years other images come to mind. There is a picture of my sister, Hélène, a veritable genius.

Consequently, she has the admiration of the whole class, including that of the teacher. No task appears too difficult for her. She always is ahead of the class. The teacher is amazed at Hélène's ability to retain information and ability to memorize poetry. Besides her phenomenal intellectual ability her shrewd responses displayed such a keen wit that the teacher was often left speechless and stunned. For instance that wise gentleman was always complaining that we were reluctant to join the class in any choral activities.

"That is very strange, "he reproached," for your mother is famous for the quality and beauty of her singing voice."
"That is very true," retorted Hélène, "But you should hear my Dad."
Another time the teacher was lamenting the quality of our spoken language.
"It is inexcusable," he chided, "after all your mother is a teacher."
"That is very true. "responded Hélène, "My mother's spoken language is beyond reproach. But my father's speech is a language of his own making and I," she added proudly, "speak like my Dad."
Needless to say Hélène was the teacher's favourite. It is also quite evident that I wasn't. That was to be expected. I wasn't a genius.

There is also a very clear and joyous memory of a Christmas concert during Mr. L...'s first year at the school. We obviously had to get to the school in a horse drawn sled as motor vehicles were then out of the question. It was bitterly cold. Although we were all bundled up, I remember being so cold that I thought I certainly would freeze to death. It was worth the discomfort however. Once inside the school the festivities began. The concert itself is vague. In a child's mind it was the arrival of Santa Claus that was spectacular! He descended upon the stage with a great flourish, and a roaring "Ho! Ho!" Of course all the children's eyes were bulging with anticipation! Santa's bag soon followed, upside down, and from its entrails came the cry, "Mama, Mama". The delighted children knew the contents of the bag instantly, naturally! They also knew who would be the recipient; my friend and I, of course. Our joy was beyond belief! Hélène, being the star student was rewarded with a unique sewing machine. After all these years that machine is still treasured by her daughter. Every one of the students was delighted with the awesome gift that came out of that enormous bag. Besides, not only was there a generous portion of goodies for the students but there was one for the little ones at home as well. Something tells me that my mother had something to do with that.

A Miss Crow came to the school after Mr. L...left. The storybook tale claiming that "love at first sight" is a possibility must be true. The moment I laid eyes on that teacher, I thought that she must have descended straight from the skies. In my childish delusions I must have thought she was superhuman because it seemed strange to me when she visited the outhouse. She had black hair and brown eyes, and was, to my eyes, absolutely beautiful! Although she was reputed to be a fantastic teacher, the scholastic knowledge I gained during those years has been erased from my memory. There is only one meaningless incident that has remained and that seems so ridiculous that it is a wonder that it has not become obliterated entirely. Miss Crow was determined to teach my friend and I how to sound out words. So she summoned us to the board where she had the letters c-a-t printed neatly and proceeded to say k-a-t cat. Both my friend and I repeated this procedure several times after which we were sent to our desks. On my way back to my seat, I was utterly confounded and my confusion kept mounting. "Why did she not say cat in the first place and not k-a-t. It would have been so much simpler." The poor teacher seemed to think that she had accomplished a great feat. Looking back, I realize that she was probably following the dictates of some ostentatious authorities on educational theories. Other incidents that occurred in the classroom during the year are vague.

The years that Miss Crow taught in our school were happy ones indeed. The students loved her. She had also won the approbation and the esteem of the parents. She was bilingual, therefore she was capable of teaching the required number of hours in either language. She was very popular with the young people in the community. She often came to the house to join in the musical extravaganza. I am fascinated still when I recall the beauty of her voice as to the accompaniment of the organ she sang "Jeanne D'Arc".

During those years there were many memorable incidents that transpired on the playground during recess. The students in a country school all play together, the younger and the older all joining together in the same games. These games in our school were very simple indeed but a lot of fun. Steal Sticks, Drop the Handkerchief, Hide and Seek, London Bridge, and India Over were often the games we played. Soft Ball was also very popular.

On one occasion, the students were playing the game India Over. The children were divided in two equal teams, each team on opposite sides of the school. The ball was thrown over the school, and if someone on the opposite side caught the ball, he ran to the other side and tried to tag someone with it. If he succeeded, the player that was tagged had to play on his team. No one had had the foresight to rule that each team run on opposite sides of the school in order to avoid accidents. Without that precaution accidents were bound to happen. As fate would have it I was the first to be involved in a most unfortunate misfortune. I was running away from one side of the school in one direction and my cousin Paul was coming from the other side in the opposite direction. There was a most horrible collision as our heads crashed into one another! I escaped with a minor bump on the head. But my cousin wasn't as lucky. There was blood everywhere. The impact was so severe that it loosened two of his upper front teeth. I was positive that those teeth were irretrievably gone. I was so convinced that he had lost his teeth and that the damage was permanent that I was haunted for years with guilt, blaming myself entirely for the accident. It wasn't until many, many years afterwards, in the twilight of my life, that I learned that the dentist had been able to save my cousin's teeth. It is almost unthinkable that this knowledge was not revealed to me sooner. It would have saved me many hours of anguish.

There are countless incidents too numerous to relate. Some of these, due to a lapse of memory, are buried forever in the past. It is most likely that the events that are the most impressionable are the events that will be remembered. For instance, incidences that are painful or that tend to repeat themselves linger. Some of these cannot be erased in spite of a relentless effort to make a clean sweep and wipe the slate clean. They are the memories that clog days with anguish and dreams with nightmares. How wonderful it would be if those painful memories could be buried forever in the deepest abyss of eternity.

As I meditate about the school days of long ago there is a recurring vision in my mind's eye. It is a picture of an unfortunate girl. The fact that she was native was not the problem, as there were many different nationalities in the district and her two brothers formed part of the student body. She was, however, slightly mentally handicapped. Most of the students accepted her and treated her kindly. Unfortunately there were some bullies in our midst. As is most frequently the case, bullies tend to tyrannize those who are weak. And so it was that those boys constantly tormented that pathetic girl. They never let up, on the school grounds, in the classroom, walking to and from school, they never gave her a moment's peace! The other children, appalled by this despicable behavior, tried in vain to stop the abuse. All the parents, except the parents of the students involved, were given a daily account of these proceedings. It is beyond all comprehension that the girl's brothers did not alert their parents, urging them to demand that the situation be rectified. Obviously the culprits did not advertise their contemptible behavior! It happened that one day at recess as I was coming in the cloakroom for a drink, I found that poor girl kneeling behind the cloakroom door, sobbing as if her heart would break. The image of that unfortunate girl kneeling and weeping behind the door will remain embedded in my heart forever.

"What on earth are you doing there?" I asked.

"I am praying to God asking Him to stop them from tormenting me." was her most extraordinary reply.

Even as a child, I wondered why no one appeared to be doing something to help that unhappy child. Later, an unprecedented event contributed and coerced the school board to investigate and solve this problem. It happened on the way home from school. The girl, unable to endure the harassment any longer, struck one of the boys with her lunch kit, causing an ugly gash on his forehead. Then all hell broke loose! Out-and-out pandemonium. The father's ferocious rage was frightful to behold. A meeting was summoned and all the parents urgently requested to attend. On the night of the meeting, the father, Mr. F...stormed in. "I want that girl to be expelled from our school!" he declared haughtily in his high-and-mighty overbearing demeanor. "She is a threat to the safety of our children." he continued. Most of the residents in the district were sort of intimidated by this man's imperious nature but not my mother. Like an avenging angel, she stood up and confronted this perturbed father with the truth. She told the father that his sons had repeatedly abused and treated this unfortunate child in a most despicable manner and that in a moment of despair she had tried to defend herself. As is often the case, when one person has the courage to speak out others dare to follow. So the other parents stood up and confirmed my mother's story. "So, my dear Sir," continued my mother, "from all the evidence presented here today, it is quite evident that it is that poor girl who is the victim and not your son." As the evidence was irrefutable, the matter was dropped. Did the boys' reprehensible behavior improve? The answer to that question has been lost with the passing of the years. Unfortunately these malfeasants did not always suffer the consequences for their despicable behavior. Often their victims were punished for the crimes they had committed. One of these incidences was a direct assault on a member of our family, an incidence that caused a great deal of distress and left a painful memory in our hearts.

It happened that the two older boys from that family met my sister Germaine as she was walking home one day and violently attacked her verbally. They used language that was despicably foul, vulgar, abusive and defamatory. Traumatized and utterly devastated, my sister sought the support of her family. Overwhelmed with shock the family made a concerted effort to comprehend what motive had instigated such a vicious attack. At last the matter was brought to court.

The youths' family retained the services of the most reputable and prominent lawyer in the state, John Diefenbaker. He was reputed as being able to acquit his clients of their crimes irrespective of the gravity. Thus the culprits were, of course acquitted. The eloquent lawyer insisted that the defendants were as innocent as newborn lambs and that the victim was the culprit. It is little wonder that many victims of violent crimes remain silent. It is also incredible that this lawyer later became a prominent political leader, the Honorable Prime Minister of Canada no less! With this kind of imbalance in power what chance did our family have. There will always be a question of lawyer integrity when defending their clients. Is it only a matter of winning? Where does justice fit into the picture?

The fact that this capable lawyer was instrumental in the youths' acquittal was to be expected and was probably accepted by the victim's family. It has always been a well-known assumption that money talks and that it has always been the supreme power.

But what was utterly unbelievable, utterly abominable was the fact that the victim's mother with a house full of children was incarcerated to defray the cost of the whole affair. Thus the victims were punished and paid the price for the culprits' transgression because they lacked the almighty dollar.

Philosophers claim that history has a tendency to repeat itself. And so in this story there was almost an identical repetition of the first incident. Indeed it is little wonder that the members of that family were certain that they had carte blanche to crush anyone in their wake for they had the support of a tyrant and backing of an infallible lawyer.

Be that as it may the next time these scoundrels decided to strike, the circumstances were significantly different. For instance the offenders were the younger members of that most belligerent family and the victims were very young and extremely timid. It was years later and to all outward appearances the feud between the two families had somewhat subsided. A truce of some sort had been called and the families were on speaking terms. It seemed perfectly logical to assume that a mutual trust had been reestablished. This was crucial as the children from both families attended the same school. Subsequently, unaware of the peril, my sister and I accepted a ride from these contentious youths. It goes without saying that we were completely unprepared for the ensuing incidence as these boys were our classmates.

No sooner were we on our way that the violent, verbal abuse erupted. Heinous, obscene language spurted out of these boys' foul mouths. The attack was so unexpected, so violent and unwarranted that it was beyond all justification.

There are certain deep emotional crisis that harbor in the abyss of the soul and which are so painful, so hideous, that they are buried profoundly hidden in the deepest chasm of our being. They are the secrets that are unspeakable, too horrid to be disclosed, secrets that shatter the heart with anguish. It was many years after that I was finally able to relate the incidence to my sister Juliette. "I could not understand why these boys were speaking to us that way" I blurted out, "they spoke words that were so vile, so heinous, so obscene that it was as if the venom from Medusa serpents was gushing out of their filthy mouths. I should have jumped out, butt I froze, paralyzed with disgust and repugnance. I was so scandalized by language that I had never heard before, feeling so humiliated, violated, dirty, that to hide in a dark closet forever was my sole reaction.

It is almost incredible that these boys should have chosen two young innocent girls who had barely emerged from their parents' protective custody as the target of their malicious wrath. It is also incomprehensible that I should have assumed the guilt and the shame for their despicable behavior.

Did my sister and I tell my parent about the incidence? Never! Not in a thousand years or under threat of torture. I for one was too obsessed with shame and mortification. Looking back I hope and pray that the incidence did not have the same devastating effect on my sister that it had on me.

There is only one logical conclusion that could possibly explain the boys' infamous behavior. They must have remembered that under similar circumstances the law had acquitted their brothers' criminal behavior. Therefore, they were convinced that for them nothing was beyond limits. The power that their father's wealth had given them was limitless.

Justice! A word that is so awe-inspiring and righteous; a word that descended straight from the skies, a word that has been bandied about and given lip service since the beginning of time and throughout the world. Yet without the vaguest understanding of its true meaning and of its astronomical significance. It is a word that is often used with a double meaning and to serve the speaker's selfish motives. Upon the philosophy and principle of that word the world should revolve.

But the world is held captive by a power that is more lucrative, the almighty dollar! That dual sided coin: one side the mercenary value and the opposite the power that it wields. Yet on this insignificant piece of metal lies the dictatorship of the world and justice a commodity that can be sold to the highest bidder.

Every one missed Miss Crow when she left. A young teacher replaced her. It was her first year and consequently she was somewhat overwhelmed when confronted with the colossal responsibilities expected of a rural school teacher. She had doubtlessly been chosen because her superior qualifications and her ability to speak and teach in both languages, French and English. She was brilliant! That should indeed have been an asset. It was, on the contrary, a disadvantage. She could not bring her thinking to the same level as that of the children. It was entirely beyond her understanding that the students were unable to comprehend or grasp simple, minute concepts. Subsequently, her instructions and explanations were way past the students' level of comprehension. She left before the end of the year.

The next teacher to come to our school was a Mr. L... He was an experienced, competent, and most capable teacher. The year started out great. I was in grade eight and my academic progress was excellent. I thought very highly of and admired the teacher. I was very happy and expected this to be the happiest year of my life. But it was not to be! As fate would have it, when things are too perfect, disaster strikes. And for me that disaster was a catastrophe! I was so humiliated, so ashamed! Of course, it was one of the same imperious family's shenanigans, a secret plot to demean someone. As an adult, I am fully aware that the sensible and practical thing was to rectify the situation. But not as a child! I was so devastated. I could not face my teacher or the other students. It was beyond the bounds of possibility. So I decided to quit school. I never went back. From that day on my education depended on correspondence courses and my mother's instructions. Looking back it is almost inconceivable that I was allowed to have my way regarding such a significant matter. Perhaps my mother felt that it was in some way justified. To an adult the incident was not tremendous in magnitude but to me as a child it was earth shattering even though it could be easily remedied. To me, it felt as if the world had suddenly collapsed, leaving nothing but an ugly bottomless chasm beneath. Yet in lieu of having the courage to confront the problem and solving it, I was allowed to quit school.

Numerous touching events are intertwined and enmeshed with these early years at school. Because of the many years that have elapsed, it is impossible to fixate with precision the exact moment on which these events occurred. The most emotional and dramatic events are, naturally, those that will remain in my heart forever. From my earliest childhood, I remember being responsible for the care of the little ones in the family. My sister Hélène, being much more capable and responsible, was always entrusted with the more difficult demanding tasks. I loved taking care of my two younger brothers! Especially Gerard. He was absolutely, totally adorable! His blond hair and big blue eyes conspired to capture everyone's heart. Especially mine. My love for that child was impeccable, unmitigated, undivided. From the moment of his birth he seemed to have been clutching a hammer in his grasp and he was forever driving nails in the cover of our wooden breadbox. From morning till night he was content just pounding holes in that lid. That is, he was content until he had the opportunity to escape, unobserved, out of the house. For he was fascinated by the great outdoors! He loved the animals, the birds, the flowers, but most of all he loved the freedom to run and play as he pleased in the spacious farmyard. This indeed would have been most acceptable had the adults been aware of his whereabouts and not been searching for him constantly when he sneaked out unnoticed. Besides, many times he would run outdoors without being properly dressed. On numerous occasions he managed to run out in his bare feet and a nightshirt. By the time someone caught up with him in cold weather he was frozen. I can still feel the excruciating anguish, the guilt that pierced my soul when I found him on numerous occasions outside shivering from the cold. Besides, my Dad could not understand how anyone could be negligent to the extent of allowing a child out of the house without being properly dressed, especially in cooler weather. Oftentimes he raked us all over the coals. Yet, in spite of the guilt and my poor Dad's anxiety, the child constantly sneaked out without being seen. I still am unable to forgive myself for the irresponsible behavior that initiated the improper supervision of someone entrusted in my care.

This continual exposure to chilling temperatures had devastating consequences. Gerard caught a severe cold that eventually developed into pneumonia. The nearest hospital was a hundred miles away and the nearest doctor fifteen. When all home remedies failed and the child's condition kept getting worse, we were overcome with anxiety. At last, in desperation, my Mother decided to go and look for the doctor. Evidently she knew that he was on another call but had decided to find him wherever he might be. Unfortunately she was unable to find him. Meanwhile Gerard's fever had reached alarmingly high temperatures. His condition was deteriorating rapidly. Poor little tyke. He insisted that I be the only one that could hold and rock him. That, of course, was what I wanted to do, with all my heart. My father feared that I would get too tired and wanted to relieve me. But I resented that. I wanted to be near him, never leave him with anyone else. That evening, not long after my Mother's arrival Gerard passed away. I did not want to let him go. I loved him so!

Raymond was another story. From the very first he made sure that his presence was felt and appreciated by everyone in the household. It is of little wonder for he was beset by one misfortune after another. At birth he had a serious case of jaundice. When she came from the hospital Mother told us that the first time she saw him he was yellow from head to foot. Then he came down with a disease that my Dad called the seven-year itch. Whatever it was, it was horrible! Without any access to a doctor or modern medication there was little that could be done to alleviate the tormenting itch that plagued Raymond constantly. Bathing in a tub full of soda or Epson Salt treated water relieved the torment temporarily. Consequently, Hélène and I were forever dipping the poor child in that water, taking him out, wiping him, and when the nagging affliction started again, resuming the whole procedure. There was little time for anything else. But it was never enough to relieve the torment Raymond had to endure. Mercifully, the disease ran its course and Raymond's health improved. Meanwhile toilet training became a major hazard. The unfortunate child had somehow become afflicted with hemorrhoids. Sitting on the toilet too long aggravated the condition and caused the hemorrhoids to bleed. True to form, I was elected toilet training supervisor. Dreading the worse, I'd stand there, watching like a hawk, and every few minutes pick him off the toilet. In a frenzy I would twirl him around to examine him and make sure he was alright. Mercifully my older sister, seeing my panic, assumed the responsibility and replaced me as toilet training supervisor. Thank goodness!

It follows that commiserating with Raymond's woes the whole household bend over backwards in order to make him as comfortable as humanly possible. Everyone at his beck and call catering to his slightest whim had rather disastrous consequences for Raymond and the rest of the family. He became incredibly spoiled. However his superior intelligence prevailed. He became a most worthy individual, compassionate, thoughtful, and selfless. He was gifted in music, literature, and science. His extraordinary musical talent endeared him to young and old. His beautiful singing voice complemented by his uncanny ability to memorize the words enabled him to sing most of the songs included in my Mother's enormous repertoire. Although he was able to play other instruments, Raymond's favorite was the accordion. Children constantly exhorted him to play for them non-stop. Raymond inherited his mother's passion for reading. Mother read anything and everything she could lay her hands on while Raymond's literary taste was exclusively science fiction and comics. He had horded a colossal volume of this material. Raymond's passion for scientific research and knowledge was phenomenal. Before the discovery involving nuclear energy he had figured out the theory involving splitting the atom. He had also predicted that one day man would go to the moon. That prediction was not accepted among the elders. Raymond was stigmatized as one living in a fantasy or in a veritable chimera!

The last time I saw Raymond he asked "Why did you have to spoil me beyond all redemption?" Oh, but there I go racing ahead again. What can you do when you're incorrigible?

Hélène passed her grade eight with honors. She was awarded a prestigious gold medal and some historical books as a distinction for having scored the highest marks in the Saskatchewan provincial French exams. There was no high school in the vicinity. So even though she was an honor student she had no alternatives other than finishing her education by correspondence. Fortunately the Saskatchewan Department of Education provided courses in most subjects from grade nine to eleven. Undeterred, Hélène embarked upon the momentous tasks ahead. And I, following unobtrusively in her footsteps, trailed meekly behind her. Day and night, night and day, every available minute, every available second, we sat pouring over the pages of these open books. Not one minute was wasted when the innumerable farm chores were done. After each meal when the dishes had been cleared away, Hélène and I would sit at the table and work for hours until we were required to perform other crucial tasks. In the evening after the daily chores had finally been completed, we studied until late in the night. In winter we studied by the dim light of an old-fashioned kerosene lamp. It is a wonder that we didn't go blind. Sometimes Hélène would still be studying at three o'clock in the morning! It was amazing! Of course by this time, even though I had been pacing to stay awake, my book was on the floor and I was sleeping on my feet. It is incredible that she could concentrate that long after working all day.

Indeed, there was very little time left for studying after the essential farm tasks had been completed. During the winter months the men were working in the bush deep in the northern part of the province. Hélène had to assume the arduous task of doing the outdoor chores. Although the men's winter contracts were indispensable to the family's income, the outdoor chores were, on the other hand, a tremendous responsibility to impose on such a young girl. Feeding the animals, the cows, the horses, the chicken, was feasible enough, although cutting and getting the hay from a towering haystack was a challenge. To water the stock she had to walk half a mile to the lake situated in the middle of our farm in severe winter weather and cut or saw a hole in the ice for the animals to drink. Sawing and splitting the logs into firewood was the most difficult of all. In fact, it was brutal! In spite of my exuberant desire to be helpful my efforts were inadequate, and Hélène struggled most of the day to accomplish all these time consuming rigorous tasks.

Summer did not bring much reprieve. As my Mother's health was very poor she was unable to assume many of the heavy tasks involved in farming. Therefore these tasks became the responsibility of the older girls in the family. There was that interminable garden to weed, the cows to milk, the housekeeping, the wild fruit picking etc. Although Hélène did most of the complicated tasks, my share was also very demanding and time consuming. I was expected to help and sometimes to prepare, unassisted, the meals for the family. It was my responsibility to care for the infants. It was also my responsibility to do my share of the work in the garden, help keep the house clean, and pick wild fruit. I fully enjoyed doing most of these tasks, tasks that for me were not work, but pure enjoyment. Especially taking care of my brothers, and picking fruit. Be that as it may, there was never very much time to study, hence the burning of the midnight oil. In spite of insurmountable obstacles, Hélène succeeded in finishing her grade eleven. Then she trained at the Holy Family Hospital in Prince Albert and became a graduate nurse. Everyone in the immediate and the extended family acclaimed her success and praised her extraordinary courage and determination. Undaunted, even when confronted by incredible odds, she refused to accept defeat.

When Hélène left I was sort of lost. At the time the Saskatchewan Department of Education did not provide correspondence courses past grade eleven. High school was out of the question. My parents certainly could not afford to send me to a boarding school. It seemed impossible to go on with my education. I felt completely lost. It is true that my Mother had enrolled me in the nurses' training program after grade eleven, but nursing was way out of my league. Mother was disappointed indeed that after all the efforts she had made to get me accepted in the program, I felt unable to take advantage of the opportunity. But she understood and did not press the issue when I told her that I would be the most horrible and incompetent nurse that ever walked the floor in a hospital ward. Unable to bear the sight of blood, and unable to endure the trauma of others' suffering and pain, I knew that working with the sick was not my destiny.

At first, the chores on the farm occupied my full attention. During the winter months when the men were up north the stock had to be fed and watered. The logs had to be sawed into firewood, split, and brought into the wood box. The barn had to be cleaned. In the severe Saskatchewan winter temperature providing water for the animals was most grueling. It involved running, axe in hand, to a lake half a mile away, with cows and horses at your heels. Then a hole in the frozen lake had to be dug or sawed to provide access to the water. Sometimes the ice was three feet thick. On one occasion, no amount of digging prevailed. So I ran back to the house in desperation. The animals had to have water! My mother knew what to do. There was a tool in the blacksmith shop called a crowbar. With that tool I made a hole big enough to insert a saw blade. Then it was easy to saw a rectangular opening in the ice and keep that hole open in the future. Thereafter it was relatively simple to head down to the lake followed by all the animals, reopen the thin ice in the rectangular hole, and wait for the thirsty stock to quench their thirst before herding them back to the barn. Coping with the severe winter temperature was however the toughest hardship of all. Indeed, Saskatchewan winters are brutal.

The summer months were less excruciating. It included fetching and milking the cows, weeding the enormous garden, cooking, and the normal house keeping routine involved in any household.

The chronological sequence of this narrative is not, to say the least, in strict consecutive order. Many events were intertwined and occurring simultaneously with other incidences. For instance, while Hélène and I were struggling frantically to achieve our high school education, many episodes and situations were significant in shedding some light upon the development of some personality characteristics pertaining to some members of the household.

One of these episodes stands out glaringly. My Aunt Emma, my mother's sister, [bless her soul] came to visit my grandparents and those in the family that had emigrated west with them. It was a memorable event. Aunt Emma was completely astounded by the conditions and standards of living in the west. The lack of facilities in the homes and especially the lack of educational facilities overwhelmed her. I still remember the presents she had brought, particularly two gorgeous dresses for my mother. Unfortunately because of her inability to adapt to the severity of the climate and the rigors pioneer life entails, she came down with a severe case of influenza. During her illness, she and my grandmother stayed at our house. My aunt's visit brought great happiness to our home.

To my Aunt Emma the most fascinating and incredible aspect that characterized our family's daily way of life was Hélène's unwavering dedication to her studies and her unfaltering commitment to her goal. My aunt admired Hélène's relentless courage and her devotion in the pursuit of her dream. It is in this guise that my aunt offered to take Hélène with her to New York, where she would have access to the most creditable and modern educational facilities available. Fear of the unknown or of being away from her family may have been behind Hélène's inability to accept my aunt's generous offer. Although my aunt was disappointed, she understood the difficult emotional deliberations that had emanated in such a momentous decision. As a result Hélène continued to struggle unassisted in order to achieve her objective. And I, following meekly behind her, kept plodding along.

It was during Aunt Emma's visit that a memorable incidence predicting a certain character trait in my personality manifested itself and in later years became blown out of proportion. The ladies, that is, my grandmother, my aunt, my mother, and the older girls in the family were having a mighty exciting conversation. At least it appeared extraordinary to us, the younger members of the family, and we insisted on being included. But being a kid-sister is being in a precarious position. It is often taken for granted as a miniature servant or Joe-Boy. The orders fly in all directions. "Do this. Do that. Get me this. Get me that. Make it snappy." It goes on and on. That is precisely what happened on that occasion. Being the kid sister I was ordered to do an errand. But I had other plans. I wanted to listen to the conversation.

So I said "I don't have time to do that."

My grandmother, with the Wisdom of Solomon, looked at me calmly, nodded her head several times and said, " I see, I see that you are very busy!"

What could I say? For there I was doing nothing, nothing at all. Zero. That is, nothing at all physically. But subconsciously I was in the process of remodeling the whole world. Sitting there, my subliminal self was frantically engrossed in performing legions of activities in one fell swoop. That surely must be the moment that my innermost self decided that it is not acceptable to do just one task at the same time, but a multitude of them. Otherwise remorse and guilt would forever be your companions. Insane, utterly idiotic. That's what I've been telling myself for years. It is hopeless! So I frantically attempted to do the impossible, dashing through the task at hand while madly contemplating the rapidity at which I could attack myriad others in one shot. Thus, the path I have journeyed along these many years has been, it seems, but a frenetic dash, a blitz throughout, with indeed no time to live its dramatic magnitude.

But it is not so. This deceptive obsession that compelled this frantic rush was an illusion, a fabrication that existed in my mind. For there were many moments of reprieve, moments when the whole world seems to stand still, and breathe a soft, soothing sigh, a hush that heralded peace and tranquility! These were moments of bliss, of pure ecstasy!

Moments of bliss! Moments when our humble home was inundated with music, for in that domain music was the ultimate treasure. The precious moments of rapture its melodious enchantment brought transcended all. It was these moments of pure euphoria that rallied the family together. Delightful moments that attracted friends and neighbors to our home! There in the most prestigious corner of the house stood the organ piled high with musical instruments and sheets. The truth is there were musical instruments strewn everywhere: an organ, three or four violins, a guitar, an accordion, a ukulele, a xylophone, and several harmonicas. That's not counting the makeshift instruments such as spoons, combs, etc. And that was besides the instruments musicians brought when they came to join our jovial concerts. In such an environment, it is not surprising that everyone in the family could play one or perhaps several instruments. Of course, we had a most gifted teacher, my mother! She taught us the rudiments of musical theory and guided us while we struggled to learn different melodies. Looking back, I played the organ quite well, and was able to play several melodies on the accordion and guitar. This, compared to some others in the family, was negligible. Marie-Anne, my sister, had mastered all the instruments. She played the violin like a real virtuoso and even played for dances. Besides, she sang like a nightingale. Raymond had also inherited my mother's melodious voice.

These musical extravaganzas were the ultimate in delight! Everyone present at these shin-dings joined the merry-making: family, friends, neighbors, and even the dogs; musically inclined or not. In fact one of the dogs, Ti-Moose, who apparently did not share the jubilation, just howled. That crazy dog did not need an excuse, however, at times he sat looking at the moon and howled as if he had lost his last friend. Those who couldn't play an instrument either sang along or danced. It was fun!

Marie Anne and Laurence Gaumond

These were the moments in my childhood that were impregnated with delight. Moments filled with music, singing, dancing, story telling, gossiping, and card playing. Perhaps the most fascinating of all was the music, music that emanated from my mother's amazing talent. Although she played the piano with great skill, her most extraordinary gift was in the quality and beauty of her singing voice. She fascinated her audiences, especially her family with endless refrains as they sprang forth full of rapturous joy from her soul. She initiated and nurtured in her realm a passion for the exquisite beauty of melodious harmony. This passion will dwell forever in the hearts of all who were dear to her.

There were these delicious evenings when the family and some close friends gathered around my parents with great anticipation.

Sometimes my parents were joined by my father's very best friend who was a master narrator of tall tales. These evenings were filled with extraordinary recitals. There were sagas of every description: legends, adventures, folktales, fairytales, contes, comedies, and weird stories of every description! My father was a master narrator of folktales, comedies, myths, and especially weird, bizarre tales, tales that made goose pimples go up and down your spine. Mother's recitals were usually stories she had read. They were stories filled with suspense, intrigue, romance, and breath taking adventures. My father's friend, however, was amazing; He was simply dynamite at telling yarns! Indeed these yarns were so out and out that I cannot even begin to tell you how preposterous they were. You would have had to judge for yourself. These yarns were beyond the bizarre; they were outrageous! These evening bring back some of the happiest memories of my childhood days. How I regret not having had the wisdom to write these amazing tales in my memoirs, for although I remember some of them, many have been lost in the past. These stories, these tales, and even the weird yarns are a reflection on the culture and the traditions that our parents had inherited. They are part of our heritage.

The occasions when all the families gathered together at my grandparent's home were treasured moments. These moments will forever be cherished in my heart. Usually these occasions occurred at Christmas, New Year or other important holidays that transpire during the year. The aunts, uncles, cousins, parents, were all there to celebrate those joyous festivities. The adults talked, sang, and just enjoyed each other's company, while the children played games and had fun. Everyone feasted on the delicious food. My cousin, Antoinette and I would always spend these precious moments together.

Antoinette Tremblay as an adult.

Then there were the moments when I would get hopelessly engrossed in the pages of a book. Those moments were [and are still] pure ecstasy! I would enter, get myself deeply inaugurated into the schema of the plot, become one with the characters of the narrative and participate in the drama of their lives. I would share their laughter, their tears, and their pain. I struggled with them through hurdles and difficulties and rejoiced with them over their blessings. And when it was time to go, parting with my book friends was filled with emptiness and longing.

Memories, images of those who have journeyed with me throughout the erratic route destiny has chosen to lead me continually flash before my eyes. Images of so many loved ones that still linger in my heart, cherished forever! They are the treasures upon which my whole life has been fabricated and sustained. My thoughts are constantly inundated and overflowing with visions of those who were my whole life and have enriched my path along its chaotic yet euphoric journey.

Often, in my dreams, I find myself meandering along the woods at the edge of the Indian Reserve. In my nocturnal fantasies it is the route that will lead me to my favorite aunt and cousin's place. It is by no means the shortest way and is rather a round about course that will lead nowhere. But dreams, true to their illusive nature have been known to misguide and point to a winding, confusing, and disoriented nothingness. Be that as it may, I plod along endlessly throughout the night never reaching my destination. Perhaps this recurring illusion is the manifestation of the longing for those loved ones so precious in days of yore.

For my Aunt Leonide and my cousins were so dear to me. Many times I imagined that I belonged in my aunt's family more than in my own. In that home that nagging feeling of being "de trop" never haunted me. My aunt seemed to understand my Utopian world, the imaginary impeccable world in which my mind dwelled. No matter how upset and frustrated, I could always talk to my aunt. She always seemed to be able to soothe the tribulations that tormented me. Her deep religious faith manifested in all her spoken words was a source of solace and comfort. Although there were many small children in the family, harmony and order reigned. No confusion, disputes or commotion of any kind! That indeed was most astonishing, considering the number of siblings that were so close in ages. That mystery was soon enlightened.

"Paul" my aunt explained, "has complete control of the situation. He has everyone of these children in toe. They listen to him indubitably. For them Paul's word is indisputable. Such is their faith in him that they look upon him as their shepherd."

And so it was that peace reigned in that household. It was also a peace that I felt in my soul, a different kind of peace. For in that milieu, the "bête noire" disappeared. Vanished without a trace! The feeling of being inadequate bolted out the door. I felt unconditionally accepted. Indeed the whole family loved me. It was with my cousin, Antoinette, however that I spent most of the time while visiting at my cousins' home, or whenever the two families gathered together. The two of us always found a corner where we could chat uninterrupted for hours on end. What we talked about mustn't have been tremendously consequential [girl talk obviously] because it has been completely forgotten. Yet Antoinette was my favorite cousin.

My aunt had been married twice. She was still very young and had four children when she lost her husband. The oldest, an absolute genius, was continually trying to get an audience to share the vast self-taught scientific knowledge he had accumulated. It was far too advanced; no one knew what he was talking about. I, of course, did not have a clue. He was way ahead of his time. Roland was my idol. She was absolutely beautiful. I do not have a clear recollection of Aline, the oldest, nor of the younger members of the family at this point, except Paul, Irene, Grace, and Antoinette, of course.

My aunt's house stood on a rise at the foot of which there was a lake. My cousins just treasured this lake! It was great for fishing, boating, swimming, and wading. It provided hours of fun for the whole family. My mother was extremely worried for the safety of the smaller children. She wondered how the adults managed to supervise so many at all times while they played constantly in the water. We, on the other hand, were a little envious. We did not have access to such a paradise.

On one occasion, all of us were visiting at my cousins' house. Naturally every one wanted a boat ride. So, in spite of repeated warnings against overloading, my brother Laurence piled all of us in the boat. About half way across the lake the boat began to sink slowly. I will never forget the panic, the terror on Laurence's face as he, white as a ghost, paddled frantically towards the shore. Fortunately we made it safe and sound.

Eventually the families went their separate ways and almost lost contact with one another. Irene, a younger member of the family, remained the only source of communication between the two families. Indeed, our paths often crossed as we both had similar aspirations, and had chosen the same careers. But even at that very young age, I knew that Irene was an exceptional person, that she belonged to the beautiful people, no less! Her calm gentle and serene demeanor radiated with tranquility and wisdom. Like all those who are God's chosen ones her eyes reflected the radiance of her soul. She will always be with me as I journey along this turbulent yet euphoric path, the path along which insidious destiny has chosen to lead me. Many years had gone by before our families were at last reunited.

I was sixteen when my grandmother became seriously ill. At the time my grandparents lived alone in a neat little cabin near my uncle's house. My grandfather being quite old was unable to care for his spouse by himself. So I became my grandfather's helper. I was indeed delighted and felt most gratified to be the one worthy of such trust for I loved my grandmother dearly. Even though my grandmother was ill and bedridden, the time that I spent with my grandparents is one of the most cherished memories of my childhood. For in that tiny little cabin dwell a spirit of peace, love, and faith. God's will reigned supreme. Complaints, reproaches, unpleasantness never occurred. My grandmother accepted her fate patiently, never lamenting or bemoaning her condition. And grandpa, well, he was the greatest! He always seemed satisfied with the way the work was done. His sense of humor, however, was what made him so special. He found the stories that I related to him from my wide readings hilarious. Especially from Charles Dickens's tale of how the waiter had bamboozled David out of his dinner in his book 'David Copperfield'. We'd spend hours discussing books and newspaper articles. Although self-taught, my grandfather was an avid reader. He read every newspaper within his grasp.

Many times the local priest would come and visit. Alas! It was then that the [bête noire] beast would launch its most deadly attack! It was beyond my realm of conception that one such as me should be in the same room as such a distinguished individual. I was literally sick. It was also beyond me how both my grandparents didn't seem at all embarrassed and acted as if the priest was one of them. They were talking and joking without having second thoughts. They also invited the priest to stay for dinner on some occasions. Well, that was the straw that broke the camel's back, especially as I always had to prepare the meal. Nothing would be good enough. The episodes passed however without any disasters or major catastrophes and everyone survived. Much to my surprise!

The next time the beast struck was perhaps less devastating, yet much more embarrassing. Some of my aunt's young female relatives had come to visit. Naturally, as they were close to my age, they came over to visit me. There we were seated around the table, chatting. Alas, the girls began to tell some rather juicy stories. It appears that this was their costume and formed part of their entertainment. As far as the girls were concerned the stories were hilarious, and they roared with laughter. But for me, who had been brought up in an extremely conservative family, the stories were vulgar and gross. Indeed it was my first encounter with this crude language. So, of course I couldn't laugh. I was completely scandalized! I just sat there looking stupid. Anyone with a smattering of 'savoir faire' or cool would have at least pretended to laugh. But not me, I was too stunned. What an absolute idiot I was. Of course the other girls were shocked. They must have thought that I was a prude, or worst, weird! It was a blessing that I couldn't read their thoughts. These would not have been complimentary, to say the least! It is fortunate that these embarrassing moments can, at least, be partly buried in the past forever. They are most detrimental to one's ego.

The reason why I didn't continue to stay with my grandparents is still vague in my mind. I have regretted it ever since. It seems so illogical, because both my grandparents were so dear to me. I loved them so! Trying to explain it to myself is ambiguous. Yet that burden of guilt will never leave me. It was most likely the problem that had plagued me ever since puberty. From the very first, I suffered from the normal problem of an adult woman. It didn't help that it occurred at the early age of ten, and being uninformed, thought that death was at my door. Mercifully, Yvonne, my oldest sister, explained that it was a purely natural physical phenomenon and the whole paraphernalia involved the change from childhood to adulthood. Meanwhile my mother conveniently put on her jacket and went to feed the chickens. It appears that I suffered from an abnormal condition for every single month, for days on end the misery returned. The pain was so severe that my mother kept me out of school for a long period of time hoping that it was a temporary condition. Looking back, it may well be that it was impossible to be amiable and function efficiently while being plagued by this problem. Besides, in the confines of that one-roomed tiny domain there was no privacy. Absolutely none! As a result it was impossible to tend to personal hygienic sanitation in private. This was almost unbearable for a reserved, bashful person like me. There was no place to hide. Indeed, that was probably the excuse that I gave my parents. Subsequently my cousin, Irene took over, then my Aunt Leonide. I still feel that there should have been a way for me to carry on. I still can't forgive myself.

While reminiscing about my grandparents, other memorable dramatic incidences flash distinctly before my eyes. They, my cousins, the priest, my friends, indeed my whole childhood acquaintances were players in this ancient but significant scenic drama that unfolds before me. It happened ages in the past. In view of the fact that religious instructions were legally prohibited in the province at the time, the parish priest gave the children the essential religious instructions before they received the sacraments. Well, both my cousins and my family lived miles from the church where the instructions were taught. So the children of that age group in both families stayed at my grandparents' place during that time. What an ordeal it must have been for these poor old people! Be that as it may, it was too far to walk from our homes, and it enabled us to receive the necessary preparations. The event that remains so engraved in my recollections however [probably because it was so painful] occurred when we were supposedly ready to receive our first communion. All the others were lined up to go to confession the day before the big event. That is all, but not me! No one had taught me what to say, or how to tell my sins to the priest. So I stood on the steps of the church bawling my eyes out, sobbing as if my whole world had suddenly collapsed. All the children stood there, staring at me. To make matters worst, when someone asked, "Why is she crying?" my petty friend answered. "She doesn't know how to confess her sins!" What an atrocious crime! Indeed I felt like the most maleficent criminal, beyond any hope of redemption. With events such as these, it is not surprising that the [bête noire] almost succeeded in shattering my deflated ego.

I did it again! I have gone way back again in my story. So I may as well magnify the transgression, in other words add insult to injury. The incidence happened in the parish church and was associated with the reception of the sacrament of confirmation. As this is a very solemn event, the bishop always performs the ceremony himself. Well, there we were, the girls all dressed in white complete with veils and the boys in suits. The bishop began the ceremony by asking questions. He wanted to make sure that the children knew the significance of this sacrament. All was well until he asked someone to name the seven sacraments. The first two girls knew and answered without any problems. But until then the sacraments had been completely oblivious to me. I listened intently while the other two recited them. Lo and behold, when the bishop asked me, I recited them without the slightest error! My mother, in the choir breathed a sigh of relief. She had been well aware of my ignorance. These events transpired long before my aunt's family moved away from the farm, but as the church, my grandparents, my cousins, and my family were enmeshed, it seemed a logical point to relate these most dramatic episodes.

After the oldest members of the family left, many significant developments transpired. For instance, my mother's concern regarding the family's financial problems became an obsession. Yet, as usual, every winter, my dad went north, in an effort to wreak a living from the forest. Usually his labor yielded substantial monetary gains. It is probable that the lumber industry was no longer as lucrative and that it failed to provide sufficiently for the family's needs. Be that as it may, my mother was ransacking her mind in a frantic effort to devise a project that would augment the family income. Many projects were examined and deemed impractical. With our minimal resources, only one of these seemed feasible. This enterprise imitated the wool textile cottage industry. It was known in England as the "Cottage Industry" before the Industrial Revolution. The raw wool was washed, dried, teased, carded and spun into yarn. Then it was knitted into usable woolen garments such as mittens, socks, scarves, etc. These items brought rock bottom prices. But it was a means of keeping the family together and the wolf away from the door. It was also a project in which everyone could participate and contribute, as every family member was responsible for one of the procedures involved. Hélène, my sister, and I usually initiated the process by washing the wool, wool that was not only filthy dirty, but it reeked! The teasing, which involved pulling the matted fibers apart after the wool was dry, was shared by all. Hélène then carded or combed the wool. This process prepares the fibers for the spinning, disentangling, straightening and facing the strands in the same direction. Spinning the wool was my mother's department. She also was responsible for dyeing some of the skeins.

The final stage? The knitting of course! That was my department. I never did live down the reputation of being a knitting machine! What's more every one avoided me like the plague because my steel needles made so much noise as they whizzed from one end of the item to the other. Sometimes it doesn't pay to be too good at what you do.

The project was reasonably successful economically. However its real success cannot be measured in dollars and cents. It is a success that surpasses material gains, a success that is intangible, ethereal. For, while seated in the performance of these tasks, something unforeseen, something deeper and spiritual was occurring. It was more than the response to a pressing need. It was a time when each in his or her own way shared the inner thoughts, feelings and essence of his\her soul. It was a time for discussions, story telling, study, and reflections. Sometimes the whole lot of artisans burst into a rollicking familiar song, a song that gave momentum and animation to the enterprise in process. A new burst of energy ensued from the euphoric, exhilarating rhythm, stimulating and invigorating it with renewed energy. Precious moments. Moments that will be with me always!

After the eldest members left, my mother's frantic attempts to rectify our financial predicament was not the only radical transformation that occurred in the family's habitual way of life. Soon after they were gone our home ceased to be a haven where the young people of the community gathered for entertainment. Its wall no longer resonated with the echo of laughter and song. Naturally, those who had been left behind longed for the joyous shin-digs of old, when music and song had reigned in their humble dwelling. It is not surprising that they would yearn to find a way to resume or reenact these happy times. Lo and behold an opportunity soon presented itself! There was a little old and dilapidated schoolhouse called Camp Lake School about five miles from our place where a group of local people regularly held old time dances. Whether or not my older siblings attended these dances is beyond my recollections for as far as I can recall they associated with the young people further north in the vicinity of the Shell River district. Soon however the word spread about these shin-dings and my younger sisters and I joined these people and attended the country dances almost every week. Sometimes these dances lasted all night! The master of ceremonies was such a jovial, fun loving man. He organized and supervised all the activities, making sure that everything was in control. He called the quadrilles, or square dances and joined in all the merry-making. Many of the local people played old time country music so they took turns playing for the dancers. It was so much fun. There is a picture in my mind's eye of an old couple, so old that in that picture they appear to be all white, like ghosts. They never missed a dance, and danced all night, never missing a number. One evening, the poor man had a seizure. He was carried out as stiff as a board. I was scared out of my wits! Everyone else seemed unperturbed. "It happens every now and then," they claimed, "nothing to worry about."

My sister Marie-Anne was of course the bell of the ball. And well she might be for not only was she a ravishing beauty with the charm of an angel, but her artistic talents were remarkable. She played the violin or any other instrument that were within her grasp. She was therefore able to relieve the musicians for part of the evening. Her grace on the dance floor was sensational! Indeed, in a dance competition, she won an award for her performance of the French menuet.

And it was at those dances that the black beast descended on me with a vengeance, in all its ferocity and malice. I was very unpopular. Very little wonder, as I didn't even have enough confidence to look anyone in the eye. At the time I couldn't figure it all out, for there was nothing wrong with my looks, but as I look back the whole scene is illuminated before my eyes. The monster with its venomous tentacles was destroying my scant opportunity to enjoy myself. It is a wonder that I didn't lock myself in a dark dungeon. Mercifully my flights of fancy and my obsessive passion for the written word rescued me. Later, when confronted with insurmountable obstacles, I had the courage to look that monster in the eye and say, "Who are you?" and thenceforth be on my way.

Well, every good thing has to come to an end so they say. My dad did not believe in this kind of entertainment. He believed that dancing was evil. To us it was a mistaken assumption. We just thought it was a whole lot of fun. Mother could not understand why my dad was so against this form of entertainment, and did, in fact encourage us to participate. Sometimes our enthusiasm and desire for amusement induced us to make unreasonable demands. On one occasion we had made up our minds to go to a dance miles away right in the middle of winter. That, of course was absolutely preposterous, absolutely insane! It's still a mystery to me that my dad allowed us to go, with his horses and sleigh, no less, without going on a violent rampage. Be that as it may, that episode must have been the last straw. From then on, he raised such ruckus every time we dared to go, and it caused so much trouble that at last we decided that it wasn't worth the torment.

It was some time during those years that a granary was installed next to the house and used as a kitchen, evidently to keep the main part of the building cool. So late on a summer night, I had been elected to bake the loaves remaining unbaked. The kitchen was beastly hot. To make matters worse, John, my brother, who had come for a visit, was sleeping on the floor of that tiny kitchen. [Why he slept there is beyond me!] Be that as it may, every now and then, he would wake up in a panic, sweat pouring down his face and scream," I'm suffocating. Open the door." Well, there was little else to do but open the door. But as soon as the door was open the mosquitoes came swarming in. What with the heat and those pesky mosquitoes, it was a bit much. So I'd close the door with the same results. Until that blasted bread was all baked, this went on and on. John waking up in a panic, the door being opened, the mosquitoes coming in, the door being closed. Time after time! After all these years, I still haven't figured out what was worst, the heat or the mosquitoes. Ten to one John hasn't either!

There is something else about this bread that keeps resurging back in my thoughts. After it was baked, it was stashed away in a huge wooden box, covered by a thick wooden lid. Our neighbor, Sam Legros, had laid a lien on that box claiming it to be his reserved seating privileges when he stopped over for a chat. I still see him, standing there, tugging frantically on his trousers, as if he feared they would drop, staring straight ahead at the clock, with everyone in the room waiting, spellbound, trying to comprehend the significance of such erratic behavior. When he did finally sit on that box, he had, indeed, captured everyone's undivided attention! The suspense always paid off. His conversation was as exaggerated, as pompous as his dramatic entrance, pretentious, ostentatious, bombastic! On one occasion after he had executed his most sensational entrance and while still frantically tugging at his trousers, in a state of extreme agitation he blurted out, "For goodness sake, throw that thing out. Throw that thing out at once!" When everyone realized that he was referring to the clock everyone burst out laughing. The clock was five minutes slow!

It was during this period of time that I went to help Yvonne, my oldest sister. She was cooking in a lumber camp in the densely forested area north of Big River. My cousin, Maurice, had a humongous contract in the lumber industry that winter. It was an extensive enterprise indeed, with all the modern equipment engaged in the process. It included a sawmill with the millwright to operate it, huge trucks, skidders, the whole works. It involved the whole process from felling the trees to the finished product:

lumber. Obviously to operate a project of such a magnitude a large crew of experienced workers was essential. Consequently Maurice employed several men, fellers, skidders, and those who worked at the mill, besides many others such as truckers. Naturally these men had to be lodged, fed, and have some means of washing their clothes. It is incredulous that Yvonne was expected not only to cook for all these men, but she was also responsible for doing their laundry and balancing the food budget. Unbelievable! She was desperately frustrated as she was unable to fulfill all these unrealistic and exorbitant expectations. Subsequently, I was chosen to go and assist in whatever way possible. There wasn't much that an inexperienced person could do and it was most unquestionably insufficient. In a short period of time I was relieved of my duties and replaced by my cousin, Marie. It is still debatable in my mind whether this replacement was because of my incompetence or because Marie was Maurice's sister and she needed a job.

It was during my sojourn in the far north that I had another strange, astonishing dream. Indeed, it was a most unusual, mystifying dream! I am still not absolutely certain that it was a dream. To the best of my knowledge, I was fully awake. But that seems beyond the realm of reality. If, on the other hand, I was awake, and it was not a dream, then it was a vision! That question has tormented me ever since. Besides, it wasn't the first time that these mysterious dreams or visions had troubled and confused me, always followed by the same uncertainty. My nephews and I slept in an annex adjoining the main cookhouse where Yvonne and her husband had their bedroom. The boys' bed was along the back wall to the left, mine was along the right wall. In the front left corner there was an old fashioned tin heater, with pipes rising straight up to the ceiling. That ancient method of heating the homes was a fire hazard, thus, as a precaution, it was necessary that someone older be with the boys in case of emergency as both of them were too young to be left alone at the time. Therefore while I was there, that cot on the right side of the annex was where I slept. And it was then that it happened! I woke up from a deep sleep, [at least I thought I was awake] and [you won't believe this!] to my utter amazement I beheld a vision that, although unmistakably distinct, my eyes stared [it seemed for an eternity] in disbelief, unable to accept the presence that was, beyond doubt, plainly visible, right before them. I continued to rub my eyes, thinking that perhaps they were playing tricks on me and that the whole thing was an hallucination. For there, beyond any doubt, standing life size behind the stovepipes was the Blessed Virgin Mary! She was staring at me kindly saying "Pray. Pray. Pray the Rosary constantly." And as I gazed upon this mystical vision, paralyzed with fear, She kept reciting the "Hail Mary" over and over again. I do not remember when or how She disappeared. I was too terrified and confused. And forever afterwards, I was plagued and bewildered. "Why me? Surely I am not worthy of such a blessing. Was it a dream or was it a vision?" Or was it a warning? Did that blessed Lady intend to warn me against the insurmountable obstacles, the struggles, the thorns and tears that lay ahead in my path, to urge me to pray that I would have the fortitude not to stumble as I trudged along the way. The next day, when I told Yvonne, she was amazed and wondered!

It wasn't long after the episode at the lumber camp that I was again sent on a mission. The rationale accountable for the fact that I always was the one chosen for these missions is still way beyond my comprehension. But it never failed, whenever anyone in the family was in a bind, or some sort of predicament, no one else was dispatched hither and thither, all over the countryside on a rescue mission. It may be that my mother realized my dilemma and was trying to help me find my way. Or perhaps I was the only one available and too complaisant to refuse or, God forbid, I was so unbearable that those who were at home, wanted to get rid of me at all cost. On this occasion, it was my oldest brother, John, who was in a bind. He was going up north to work in the bush and needed someone to be with his wife while he was away. He couldn't leave her alone because she would have to do the strenuous chores on the farm, chores that were too heavy for her to do during her pregnancy.

Although I was reluctant and had so many misgivings at my departure, the year that I spent with John and his wife, Victorine, turned out to be one of the happiest years of my entire life. Victorine was an absolute angel. She did the housework while I struggled to feed the animals, keep the wood box filled with firewood, and do all the things that had to be done outdoors. These tasks were not a problem, especially for one who has been brought up on a farm. The compensations far surpassed the menial efforts involved.

Victorine (John's Wife) and Jeannette

My niece, Simone, kept the two of us on our toes and keenly entertained. Inquisitive and extremely intelligent, she came out with the most out-and-out hilarious comments imaginable. She kept us in stitches constantly. One day, as I was trying desperately to have a sponge bath [bathtubs were none existent at the time], she was apparently about to intrude on my privacy. So I must have yelled at her something like," Stay out." Well, this little lady was not to be outdone. So she yelled back at me, "You wash your belly and be quiet". Pretty strong language for a two year old. Although we were both blown away, we didn't dare laugh, so we just stood there, stunned! She also kept teasing me about someone who kept coming to get me [in a big clumsy old wagon, if you please] when there was a dance at the hall or any activity that happened to be going on in town.

The outdoors chores were not too heavy. As a matter of fact I enjoyed doing most of the tasks involved, especially feeding and caring for the animals. There was one little bay mare belonging to my brother that I just loved. Her name was Pearl. Intelligent, alert, and responsive, it was fun to work with her. She was a very nervous horse and did not respond to everyone. She did not trust men in particular and became extremely agitated when they approached her stall. She reacted by pulling or breaking the rope restraining her with her front legs as she reared backwards. Consequently many thought her unruly and difficult to handle. Every time my dad came near her she would panic and rear backwards. It is no wonder that he thought she was wild. Yet, Pearl trusted me implicitly. She even responded to my voice. Once or twice a week, I'd hitch her to a cutter and go to Leoville or Ranger to get groceries or get the mail. It was fun.

Many humorous incidents occurred while I worked with Pearl. I blamed the severe Saskatchewan weather and the family's mischievous puppy for one of these, but it happened because of my downright clumsiness. When the temperature drops to fifty degrees below zero it is imperative to dress up to the hilt, one warm garment on top of the other. Awkward! Whew! With all these clothes on one could barely move let alone be agile and walk with some degree of alacrity. Of coarse animals don't have that problem. They are endowed naturally with a warm fur coat that protects them against any weather. Consequently they are not impeded in their movements by all these superfluous accessories. Cognizant of their advantage, they appear to be laughing in their beards at our clumsiness. Well, on that particular day, I was trudging along beside that loaded stoneboat pulled by my faithful helper Pearl, when that puppy dashed inconspicuously between my legs. Of course, I fell flat on my face and it took awhile before I could get my klutzy self on my feet again. The first thought that came to my head as I lay there, flat on my face, holding on to the reins desperately, was, "She's going to panic and drag me all over kingdom come". But that horse had the Wisdom of Solomon. The moment that I fell she stopped instantly. She turned and looked at me with contempt, and said [in horse language, that is] "What the hell are you doing down there?" Well, there wasn't anything else to be done but to pick my klutzy self up and keep on going. From that moment on it was most reassuring to know that that horse and I had a steadfast understanding, a covenant of trust and dependability. That covenant was never broken.

My thoughts are filled with joy as they stray and meander along the path that destiny led me to dwell with my brother's family. There were so many kind acquaintances, many friends, whose companionship was dear to my heart. Hortense, Victorine's sister, was the dearest of them all. She had such an amazing sense of humor, always managing to turn everything into a joke. I just loved her. We had so much fun together. Then there was her brother with whom I became very close friends. In fact, I thought that I was in love with him. No wonder! He was so thoughtful and considerate and always treated me like a queen. Indeed everyone made such a fuss over me in that small community that while I was there the bête noire disappeared almost completely. I began to feel that maybe, just maybe, there was, in this great universe, a niche where I belonged. It was such a wonderful feeling.

Many incidents transpired during that time that were perhaps insignificant in themselves but delve so deeply into my innermost self that they cast a clear portrayal of my personality then. John's neighbors lived about a quarter of a mile from his place. There were many children in the family and although they were very poor, they always seemed to be in good spirits. They were expecting a new addition to the family at the time. One of the boys came running to the house in a panic one day. His mother had sent him to get help. She was in labor, the father had gone to get help and only the very young children were at home. It is quite evident that in an emergency they wouldn't know what to do. My sister in law was pregnant. She felt it would be unwise for her to go but she knew that it was urgent that someone be there with that unfortunate woman. So she sent me! In spite of my frantic protestation that I did not know what to do! "As long as someone is there," she kept repeating. I was terrified! I didn't have a clue about what to do if the baby came before help arrived. The lady tried to reassure me, but I was beyond reassurance. Fortunately help arrived in time, and I was sent home. I was never so relieved or thankful in my whole life.

Then it happened again! I had another one of those extraordinary experiences. One morning I was startled out of my sleep, my whole body bolted upright as I sat transfixed, staring straight ahead. For there, kneeling at the foot of my bed was a man I had never met, yet I knew who he was. Somehow I even knew his name. He was entirely dressed in white; a white cloak and a white hood covered his head and almost hid his face. As he knelt there he prayed with extreme fervor, beckoning me to join him in his supplications. I don't remember how long it was before he disappeared or how; I was paralyzed with terror. In the kitchen there was the sound of many voices. Someone had come tell the family that a fatal accident had claimed the life of Victorine's uncle. The voices were hushed, filled with anguish. As I entered someone tried to tell me what had transpired, but there was no need. They were all utterly astounded when they witnessed my horror as I said, "You do not have to tell me. I know about that horrendous accident. Mr. Perron, your uncle came to me and as he knelt at the foot of my bed he urged me to join him in prayer."

They were appalled! Incredulous! None of this made any sense, least of all to me. Yet it had transpired. The bizarre, the unknown, the incredulous, the unfathomable! Who can penetrate the abyss of that realm?

The years that followed are sort of blurred, the events full of shadows, awakening but a few significant and memorable incidents. They were years in which I continued to search for a port, a harbor where I would find the essence to sate my restless spirit. They were years in which I worked at various insignificant jobs and was extremely miserable. Although some of the employers were most righteous and decent, some were vulgar with despicably low moral values. These attitudes were dehumanizing and demeaning.

One of these worthy employers was a neighbor of ours, the Good Samaritans, Cayo by name. Good Samaritans they truly were. Wherever there was a need, they came to the rescue. Emergencies, illnesses, and any necessities besieging anyone in the community was always dealt with the same compassion and efficiency by that magnanimous family. Being the owners of one of the few motor vehicle in the vicinity, they were constantly and gracefully transporting patients to the hospital or fetching the doctor for a house call. These were major responsibilities as the nearest hospital was one hundred miles away, and the closest doctor was fifteen. Besides, the family's economical status was more stable than most in the region, consequently they were in a position to assist or lend a hand to those less fortunate than themselves. It seems we were always borrowing something or other from them, especially medicine. How every one of us hated to be the messengers, or the borrowers! It was so demeaning, so humiliating! Or so we thought.

I am still gratefully beholden to the youngest member of that family, Walter. It is because of his generosity that both my sister and I were able to complete our high school education. He, upon his graduation, lent or gave us his correspondence courses and his books, as we could not afford to purchase them.

It was in that home that I was first initiated into the working world. It was a most enjoyable experience. Helping that gracious lady did not seem like work. Unfortunately the bête noire struck full force. My self-consciousness and bashfulness prevented me from having a pleasurable association with the family. To make matters worse the local teacher with whom I had had a previous unpleasant encounter was boarding there. On one occasion, he came down with his saxophone, sat on the stairs, and began to play. His musical performance was indeed delightful. He seemed to be playing for my enjoyment. But I just sat there almost paralyzed with malaise, unable to even look up at him, let alone show appreciation for his splendid melodies. Presently he gave up and went back to his room. It is incredible that personality imperfections, blemishes, can emanate into such irrational weird behavior. That incidence still makes me cringe with embarrassment. In spite of my struggle with this problem, I was reluctant to leave these wonderful people at the end of a very short term and seek my fortune elsewhere.

My next assignment was considerably more demanding. I was to take full charge of the household in addition to being solely responsible for the care of four little girls under the age of six. That in itself would not have been spectacular as the regular household management did not present any particular concerns. There were two significant problems however. The little girls were almost out of control. Indeed that may have been the reason why the mother was completely exhausted and needed some time to recuperate. It is unfathomable, bizarre, that a child, a mere infant, can be malicious! No child is born evil according to all authorities. Yet, it is absolutely astounding to see a child deliberately determined [doggedly] to destroy; to willfully inflict pain on any one in their midst. And what is yet more mind-boggling is the fact that this despicable behavior fosters utter jubilation, and is done as a means of diversion. Surely this behavior is the result of ignorance of child psychology and child rearing principles. The image that flashes back in my mind is disturbing. It is the image of freshly laundered snow-white sheets hanging on the clothes-line and of those little girls, with sticks covered in mud, smearing dirt all over these clean sheets until they were verily covered with black smudges and laughing hilariously all the while. There were other comparable incidents of course. Although these have been forgotten, they rendered life intolerable, and I was greatly relieved when my services were no longer needed.

There was another problem. Children raised on a farm are usually competent, that is able to perform almost any task that is before them. Indeed all the members of our family had been trained to be resourceful and be able to manage whatever was required of them. It goes without saying that the tasks involved in household management were uncomplicated [except, of course, the discipline] for me. Meal preparation, baking, etc…were not problematic. And I could bake the most scrumptious bread. And that's what caused all the problems. Mr. T… kept praising me because I could bake such fantastic bread. He kept on and on. It is obvious that being plagued with a formidable inferiority complex, and having been denied such gratification all my life, I should thrive on such compliments. I simply devoured, soaked up, and regurgitated this appreciation! [Perhaps due to my immaturity.] It is little wonder that the wife, seeing the sparkle in my eyes, thought that I had fallen in love with her husband and decided that the situation was inappropriate. It is indeed unfortunate that this wonderful lady did not know or have any idea that the object of my passion was not her husband, but her husband's approbation and appreciation.

Unfortunately there was another episode in which the care and supervision of exceptional children was my responsibility. Being ill prepared, with no knowledge of child psychology, I may have been partially to blame for these children's behavior. However, both parents were frantically engaged in promoting their business, the father as a mechanic, and the mother as the owner of an elite beauty salon and neither one had any time for their two girls. So the girl's misbehavior was a cry of protest. Neither parents heard that plaintive cry; they were too busy! So they directed their anger at the one most likely to pay attention to their woes, the caregiver. It is indeed regrettable that she was unable to console and sustain them in their need. A pity that many young parents, in their frenzy to gain financial security for themselves and establish a sound future for their children, lose what is the most precious treasure they possess, their loved ones! Too soon they realize that they cannot recapture what for so many years has been neglected. It is too late! And so it was for these unfortunate parents. Many years later their lives ended in tragedy.

My next assignment, had it not been for the interference of an unpleasant episode, could have changed the path along which I had previously journeyed. I was caring for a lady who had a rather severe case of influenza. She lived on a farm with her son. Although she was reputed as being difficult, she was very kind to me. The problem was her son. His charm, his gallant mien distinguished him as the most popular bachelor in the community. Numerous young lasses had lost their hearts trying to attract his attention. Needless to say, being very young and very impressionable, I fell [hopelessly?] in love with him. The mother, thinking that perhaps the situation was inappropriate, tried to warn me. She did so in no uncertain words. She was aware of my inexperience and knew that many girls had been seduced by her charming son. Well, I was devastated! Young and fool-hardy, it was intolerable that my integrity was being questioned. So with no further ado, I quit. Some time later my help was urgently solicited as the poor lady was again very ill. It is most regrettable that I refused to assist someone in dire need. My mother was shocked. It is also most regrettable that my mother failed to persuade me to go. Again destiny interfered. Had I consented, it is almost certain that I would have eventually married this man. It was not to be! I still thank my lucky stars. My dreams would have been shattered. Dreams that somewhere, somehow, there is something, the essence of which is worth more than life itself. Something that gives meaning and purpose to that otherwise futile existence. Had I married at this time, I would have been doomed, wandering aimlessly in a hopeless search for the impossible gratification of an illusive dream.

Sometime during that interval I became fully responsible for managing a household on a farm. Due to the harshness of farm labor the unfortunate lady had suffered a stroke and was incapable of performing work of any kind. It was very disturbing to me that her two daughters, her son and her husband did not seem to be the least bit concerned about that poor woman's predicament. I felt very sorry for her indeed.

There were numerous inconsequential positions following these incidents. During that time, nothing of particular significance or memorable comes to mind, except perhaps that they were years in which I was bored, miserable and felt that my life was being wasted away. I felt that I was drifting here and there aimlessly, like a ship adrift on a boundless, uncharted sea, being tossed and buffeted about by the tempestuous winds, the wiles of capricious destiny. And my rebellious thoughts continuously challenged this fate in an angry cry of protestation. "Oh wild, inexorable destiny, you have spun, whirled, and twirled me around till all is but a blur, and I am weary. You have led me into these dangerous, unknown waters. Yet, I must find my way, and dare not flounder or crash onto perilous shores."

After burrowing into the very depths of my recollections, and clearing away the cobwebs that loiter in that realms I see myself returning home. It seems that I made that decision after having wandered here and there, doing a great deal of soul searching, and being incessantly incapable of finding the essence that would appease my restless spirit. It was a most propitious decision. In order to alleviate the family's economic dilemma my parents had ventured into the dairy business. They had purchased a small herd of cows and were selling the milk to my uncle's cheese factory in Victoire. Although it was a small operation it proved to be rather profitable. There was a huge problem however. Milking cows was the last thing on earth that my dad wanted to do. Everyone else had left the farm; consequently the chore fell upon his shoulders. That is, until I came back home. Then, as expected, that chore became my responsibility. It was not a problem. After the milking the milk cans were loaded into the wagon and taken to the factory which was about seven miles away. Driving the team of horses all by myself, and being responsible for the whole operation was exciting. It was fun.

It did not last. Unfortunately! My sister Yvonne's baby girl came down with a malignant case of whooping cough. Still weak from her pregnancy, it was almost impossible for my sister to care for the child alone. So my mother persuaded me to go and help. As it happens so many times in our journey through life I did not know which path to follow. My dad needed me; he relied on me. It was difficult to leave him in a bind. On the other hand, the child's illness had created a crisis in our whole family. There was no alternative according to my mother; my sister's need was more crucial. Unfortunately, fate doesn't always allow one the privilege of choice, the choices are unalterable, and unquestionable.

When the child [Lorraine was her name] recovered, it was too late to resume my duties as helper at the farm, apparently. My recollections of this period are somewhat vague. It seems that my parents had moved in the small hamlet of Victoire. There is also a vague flashback in my mind's eye of my aunt's family temporarily settled in that vicinity. All these images are but a blur.

It was while we were living in that hamlet that I baked a most delicious cake for Hélène, who at the time was training as a nurse in Prince Albert. It had to be mailed, of course. Inexperienced in the wrapping business I proceeded to wrap the cake in layers of newspaper. My mother was shocked. "Do you mean to tell me that you are going to send your sister this abomination?" she exclaimed. "Your sister will die of embarrassment when she opens it in front of her friends." It goes without saying that my mother must have rewrapped the parcel. Be that as it may, the cake was much appreciated by all who shared it.

Then there was the cheese-making episode. My uncle had a reputation for making the most delicious cheese in the world. No one was able to deny that. He decided to start a cheese factory in the farming community of Shell River. This was indeed a wise business venture. It would provide a market for the milk produced on the nearby farms and a living for my uncle. Besides I became Uncle Charles's apprentice in the cheese making procedure. It was absolutely delightful. There was a lot to learn from the time the milk was poured into a great reservoir to the finished product. Yet when the golden wheels of cheese were stacked in neat rows on the shelves, it gave me such a sense of accomplishment. For some unknown reason Uncle Charles did not continue with this enterprise. The family must have been, during that period of time going through difficult times. In a very short time, the family had moved from the farm to Victoire where Uncle had built his cheese factory then to the village of Debden, then to Manitoba, and finally to Victoria Island. The family was no doubt wandering far and wide in a desperate search for a haven where they could set roots in a milieu that would foster a sense of belonging. It was on this island that their search ended. It was also when our family lost contact with them for many years. It was also the period in my life when I was wandering, hither and thither, desperately seeking of a niche where I belonged, a frantic search for a meaning, a purpose for my seemingly useless existence. Indeed, I deeply empathize with my aunt's dilemma. Both her family and I were hopelessly lost, adrift upon a boundless realm, on a never-ending quest for a sanctuary, where all our yearnings would be realized. She and her family finally fulfilled their dream, while I kept aimlessly wandering along that seemingly futile crusade.

It was sometimes during those years and before my brief sojourn in Vancouver that my sister managed to get me a position in the dining-room at the Prince Albert Sanatorium. That sanatorium was a prestigious establishment reputed for its success in the treatment of consumption during the years when that disease claimed so many lives, especially among the native population. Indeed, their success was so spectacular they managed to eradicate the disease completely. Subsequently, the sanatorium was closed and it is no longer in operation. But during these years it was filled to capacity. To prevent the spread of the disease it was managed with great precision and under very stringent operational rules. Therefore I considered myself most fortunate when I obtained a position in such a reputable establishment.

The dining-room staff worked on a split shift, setting up the tables for the patients before meals. We wore light green uniforms with white aprons and white hats. The work had to be done at lightning speed as each task was timed to the second and an exact schedule had to be maintained. The work was a lot of fun. The staff residence was, to a country girl like me, super. But it was my first encounter with the ways of the world. The world's mysterious, paradoxical ways! I learned that that world was indeed the opposite of the world that I knew. The moral values that had been so firmly nurtured in my childhood seemed strange in this new milieu. For instance, the first time my roommates came in the room and saw me kneeling saying my prayers, they were dumfounded, completely awed. Perhaps they had never seen anyone praying before. They were respectful, however. They all withdrew, leaving me alone to pray in peace.

The girls' buffoonery and horseplay was also contrary to my moral values. The tom-foolery they performed for diversion was not my idea of proper conduct. Needless to say their crude vulgar antics were repulsive to someone who had never been exposed to such rude behavior. Besides, what was most disturbing was that I soon learned that for some, when their well-being is in peril, especially their financial security, integrity and honor does not exist. It was indeed a bitter lesson for me, as these were the principles, the moral values that were inculcated most emphatically in my childhood. It happened one day as we were setting the tables and getting the meal ready for the patients. The supervisor had instructed the girl in charge to serve peaches for dessert. Unfortunately she made a mistake and served pears. The supervisor was furious! It was an honest mistake. In order to excuse herself, and to my utter disbelief, she told the supervisor that I had made the error. It was useless to try and defend myself; this girl had more seniority, and it was taken for granted that she was telling the truth. In that high and mighty establishment error were not permissible. Consequently I was dismissed.

The way home proved to be fraught with pit-falls and hazards. At the very beginning a lady realized, to her utter consternation, that she had boarded the wrong bus. The poor woman was frantic. We had almost reached the terminal. Nonetheless the driver turned around, and drove right back to Prince Albert without a murmur or a word of complaint. Such patience! Although I felt sorry for the unfortunate woman the situation struck me as being hilarious. At the bus terminal in Shell Lake there was of coarse no one to meet me as my arrival was unexpected. I had no alternative but to walk home. It was late on a very dark night and home was ten miles away. Besides there were some dogs on the way that could not always be trusted. Needless to say, I was frightened. As it turned out the dogs had been at my house many times, recognized me, and did not make a fuss when I went by their house. It was indeed a blessing to be home safe at last.

The next phase of my life, although very short in duration, is a time abounding with excitement and significant developments. It is a time filled with dramatic and stirring events, a time of serious soul-searching accompanying deep emotional and passionate incertitude. It all began when Hélène wrote a letter asking me to come and visit her in Ladysmith where she was working as a nurse. The decision was made on the spot. In fact, it may have been a conspiracy between my mother and my sister. Looking back, I have finally realized [at long last] that my poor mother was desperately trying to help me in my frenzied search to find a haven, a niche, where I belonged. Needless to say, there was no hesitation on my part. Where the money for the bus fare came from is another one of these deep dark mysteries that will forever remain buried in the great beyond. Be that as it may, the arrangements were soon made, and I was on my way.

The first part of the journey has been lost through the years in my memory. The bus route led through Medicine Hat. I was overwhelmed, absolutely fascinated, by the scenic beauty of that city. Perhaps my enchantment was contingent on the fact that it was my first encounter with the staggering grandeur of the mountains. There was also all along that journey a woman whose stunning beauty was bewitching. She had decided to befriend me, either because she could sense my insecurity and wanted to be kind, or perhaps she just wanted company. She kept extolling my looks [to my amazement] and I wondered how someone so beautiful could find beauty in one such as me [the bête noire at it again!]. At last we arrived in Vancouver. I had never been in a metropolis before and was completely unprepared for the scope of the spectacular panorama that unfolded before my eyes. Blinded by the brilliance of the dazzling, glittering lights promoting the myriad theaters, shops, etc.; it seemed that I had suddenly entered a world illuminated by a blazing fire. To say that I was scared would be to say it mildly indeed; I was terrified! Providentially my cousins, Claire and Lucille, rescued me at the bus depot, then took me to their apartment. The next morning they escorted me back to the bus terminal en route to continue on my journey. All this had been prearranged by my mother who had the foresight to anticipate the problems an inexperienced traveler would encounter. I still thank my lucky stars to this day that she had the presence of mind to do so. I was never so glad so utterly delighted as the moment that I beheld those familiar faces. I am still most grateful to my cousins though it is too late to tell them so.

I deeply regret that both Claire and Lucille are no more. I have little but shadowy recollections of Lucille. She was a few years younger and did not participate in our games and shenanigans as actively as the rest of us. The only picture that has remained clearly engraved in my memory is the fact that she was so beautiful. But it is unfathomable to imagine that Claire is gone. She was vibrant, enraptured with the sheer joy of living and the thrill of just having fun.

The next part of my journey was fascinating indeed. For many years I thought it must have been a dream, it seemed so incredulous. But it was real! The bus route from Vancouver to Victoria was [and is] under the sea. It still seems too extraordinary, too implausible to be true. Yet it was absolutely breath taking.

Hélène was, of course, waiting at the end of my journey. She was working as a registered nurse in the Ladysmith Hospital. We did not remain in that town long. Soon after my arrival, Hélène decided that her conscience could not allow her to tolerate the hospital's operational policies and we left, Vancouver bound. We might just as well have landed on Mars! The contrast would not have been greater. This monstrous gigantic metropolis dazzled me with apprehension and dread. Hélène however, resourceful and courageous as usual, was right in her element. She had all her papers ready, documents that included all her credentials, resume, cover letter, references, etc. everything she needed to apply for a job. Her accreditation was impeccable and she was directly employed as a registered nurse at the St. Paul Hospital in Vancouver. She found her work most rewarding. There were no controversial moral issues to contend with, and besides, the supervisor and the staff were most complaisant.

My mother had told us that the Sisters of Service, a Catholic charitable organization, provide lodging to young ladies when they are strangers in a large city, sometimes penniless, and desperate to find a place to stay. Needless to say, we soon found ourselves comfortably lodged in that institution. The sisters who managed the home were angels of mercy. Even though several girls had sought asylum in their refuge, these generous sisters treated every one with the same sensitivity and kindness as if a member of their own family.

Hélène found herself in a remarkably favorable situation. She was employed by an eminently prestigious institution, she had a decent place to stay, and she was right in the midst of a center where every imaginable form of entertainment was available. A veritable paradise! And she took advantage of all this auspicious good fortune. She skated on ice and on roller skates; she went swimming; to the theatre; the movies and the museum. In fact, she always found something interesting to do when she had any leisure time. Besides, she had numerous boy friends who took her out for dinner. She must have felt on top of the world.

Amazing indeed that my sister's world had reached such excellence. [She certainly deserved the best.] But as usual, destiny again was up to its old tricks. Everything was too perfect. So, it was decided deviously, to plant a thorn [trouble] in Hélène's Utopia, thus to spoil her unblemished happiness. The thorn? Why me, of coarse! Who else could generate that much turbulence, or such turmoil? True to form, as soon as we landed in Vancouver, I came down with an ungodly case of measles. Ungodly is putting it mild! I was covered with these wicked red spots from head to toe, burning with fever, and as sick as a dog. As luck would have it, there were complications, an excruciatingly painful abscess right in the ear canal. Before that cursed thing broke, or the infection had run its course, the pain was driving me insane. Then it took months for it to drain. To make matters worse, no one was to know about my illness. Measles is a very contagious disease and we shared a dormitory with quite a few girls. It could have become an epidemic, spreading like wild fire. Or if it had been discovered, we would most likely have been evicted. Indeed, Hélène was scared stiff that if anyone found out about my plight we would be evicted. So being a nurse she knew, how to conceal our unfortunate situation. Under no circumstances was I to leave my bed while others were present to go for meals, or not even to go to the bathroom. To this day it still seems improbable, almost miraculous, that no one even suspected the truth. Yet, somehow, my sixth sense tells me that the good sisters knew, but sensitive to my sister's anxiety, her dread of the consequences that would inevitably ensue its disclosure, plus their awareness of the meticulous precautions being taken not to spread the disease, enabled these benevolent souls to remain silent.

At long last, when I finally recuperated from that dreaded illness, another major challenge confronted me, videlicet, the search for suitable employment. That was indeed a challenge. Unskilled laborers were a dime a dozen, thus employers were very discriminating about their employees. Hélène, a registered nurse, was immediately employed. I, however, had no specific training. Therefore it became necessary for me to work as a governess in

Jeannette Romaniuk

some cases, or to take complete charge of a household while the parents worked. My first position was a disaster. The people had all the outward semblance of belonging to the upper class, the elite. They lived in a luxurious home with the most luxurious décor and enjoyed all the luxury wealth can buy. But, to my entire dismay, they had all the attributes of the low, common masses. Although they professed to be religious they certainly did not live according to the dictates of any religion. Their moral behavior was despicable, absolutely vulgar, and so was their speech. They were insensitive to anyone that [they thought] was below their rank. They were almost cruel to those who worked for them, treating them with contempt and as inferiors. Fortunately this hell did not last long. A construction crew who were supposed to do some renovations on the house decided to wreak havoc and lay waste to the plums that grew bountifully in the garden. They threw the plums at each other, hurled them at the house, and wasted most of them. And I, young and timid, was supposed to stop that carnage. That, of course, had never occurred to me. [Would these men have paid any attention to me?] This created a veritable uproar! I was blamed for the whole thing, everything! This incident had occurred because of my inability to understand English, they claimed. Preposterous, as if it could have any bearing on my language proficiency. Subsequently, and to my tremendous delight I was dismissed. Amazing that many of these arrogant hoity-toity scorn and despise those who are less fortunate than themselves. They should turn their contempt inward, because many times the unfortunate's wealth does not abide in riches, but in wisdom and integrity, gifts that they themselves may not possess. [There is a wound festering in the abyss of my memory. Walking home from church some distance behind that family one Sunday, the boys began to hurl stones at me. The stones did not hit their mark, but it was the malicious intent that left a gaping wound in my heart.] I bear those boys no evil, but only hope that the malevolence and hate has vanished from their hearts.

Compared to that first devastating experience, my next position was a breeze! I was employed in the home of a rather prominent physician's family. There were three small children besides the doctor's elderly mother who, because of her declining years, lived with her son and his family. They were beautiful people, considerate, thoughtful, and kind. It would have been an ideal situation, but again fate intervened.

The family spent their summer vacation at the beach some distance from Vancouver. The lady, being most solicitous, thought that it would be difficult for me to be away from my sister all summer. She realized that my sister and I were strangers in town; as a consequence, such a prolonged separation might be problematic. She left the choice to me. After a great deal of deliberation, wavering and debating the pros and cons, I decided [although still very uncertain that it was the right decision] to stay in town. It meant that I had joined the rank of the unemployed. Again!

My next assignment was incredible, just as if it had emerged right out of a storybook of fairy tales, complete with a ravishing princess and a knight in shining armor. A fantasy? Perhaps! But this fantasy was not a figment of my imagination. Not this time. This fantasy happened to be real. For once destiny dealt a good hand, or it might have been a stroke of good luck. Who knows? Be that as it may be, the good sisters recommended me besides the fact that this lady was looking for someone who was bilingual. That was, no doubt, the reason why I was chosen.

Upon arriving at the premises, I was overwhelmed by the grandeur and the luxurious appearance of the home. A lady welcomed me at the door. She had been instructed to introduce the two boys, Michael and Raphael, to me and to teach me the general routine of the household. I was to be in complete charge, the shopping, the cooking, cleaning, besides being the boys' guardian. The monthly budget allowance for groceries was not to exceed ten dollars, and my salary was to be ten dollars a month. Although I made an enormous effort to concentrate on what that brave lady was saying, the magnificence of the décor and all the furnishings distracted me completely. She [the lady] went on and on, trying desperately to give me clear instructions regarding the pattern of my responsibilities. Yet the phenomenal affluence of the ambience so dazzled me that I was too enthralled to fully comprehend her explanations. It felt as if I had been suddenly immerged into an illusion, a chimera.

On the shelves across the table from where we sat was a complete coffee and tea service set wrought of solid silver engraved with a crown insignia. The buffet in the opposite corner of the room held the dinnerware, plates, silver ware, etc. also of solid silver and engraved with a crown insignia. That emblem was engraved on all the expensive silver services but not on the dishes used every day. These were from the beautiful blue pottery made in Holland. From the dinette, I was taken for a grand tour of the whole house. The salon or living room was astonishing, unlike any ordinary family recreation rooms. It was huge! It must have been approximately forty by twenty feet. Upon entering, facing the entry was an immense mirror. It covered the whole wall, the length, the width, and the height. It was amazing! There was practically no furniture in that spacious, elongated salon, except a grand piano. The mirror was not the only extraordinary feature about that room. What was indeed phenomenal, utterly sensational, was the carpet! Pure original Persian carpet covered that extensive floor, thick and luxurious. Walking on that carpet was like wading ankle deep in a dense canopy of soft voluptuous silk. The amazing beauty of these carpets was breath taking! My Uncle Florent, on his first visit, was absolutely overwhelmed by this carpet and couldn't contain his laughter. He entertained us all evening by poking fun at their exorbitant luxury.

"It is hazardous to walk on these," he jeered, "You do so at your own risk. You're apt to sink hopelessly and forever into their depths."

The rest of the residence was not as spectacular. It was just comfortable. As we toured the premises, I kept thinking to myself, "This is a domain fit for a princess."

And indeed it was! A home for a princess! A true, genuine, bona fide, honest-to-goodness princess! That's what my guide had been trying to tell me all along, and what I had been too dazzled by the splendor before me to conceive, or fully comprehend the impact of her discourse. It was indeed too formidable, too incredible to even imagine that here I was, modest, unassuming, plagued by la bête noire all my life, standing in the kingdom of a princess! It was too much to digest all in one fell swoop.

"That is why," that patient lady continued, "I refer to her as madam. She is a real princess, and she must be treated accordingly." Then she proceeded to explain the extraordinary circumstances that had led this most distinguished individual to take refuge in our beloved country. Europe during World War 11, was plunged into the chaos of warfare. Madam's husband, a captain in General deGaulle's underground army in France, feared for his wife and his children's safety. Subsequently, as the fighting did not transpire on Canadian soil, he hoped that the country would be a safe haven for his family. Thus it was that this noble lady escaped the horrors of the German occupation to find shelter in our land. She was forced to reestablish herself and her family in a strange land unaided. She was confronted with the difficult task of purchasing a home in a suitable location plus all the necessary household furniture besides being solely responsible for the care of her two boys. She had managed to accomplish all this all by herself when I came into the picture. Besides she had managed to find a dedicated, reliable governess for her boys.

"She is a Persian princess, daughter of the late Persian King, or Shaw, who recently abdicated the Persian throne because of severe political unrest" continued the lady. "She was a student at the University of Paris when she met her husband, who was also a student at the university. After their marriage, he became the French ambassador to Afghanistan. (I am trying to research under what authority or situation this occurred, but so far my search has been fruitless.) The couple's sojourn in that country brought them great happiness it seems, as Madam always spoke of it with enthusiasm. Soon after they returned, the war broke out and the captain joined the underground movement under general de Gaulle's command."

I was delayed for a whole week as I became obsessed with the exigency to validate the authenticity of what had been related to me and what I had witnessed irrevocably many years ago. After many long hours, having discovered many historical documents that corroborated my story, and being unable to find some other verifications, I realized that to print such information might be inappropriate, even a violation of the person's right to privacy. Subsequently, I had almost abandoned the thought of doing further research and of documenting the information that I had discovered to this point. However, now that my curiosity has been aroused, I will not rest until I have explored the history previous to this episode, information that did not concern me in the least at the time, yet information that was so dramatic, so exhilarating! I am still debating whether or not the authentic documents will be used in this narrative, and will leave this decision to be resolved and perhaps inserted later.

Besides purchasing the weekly groceries on a very tight budget, meal preparation was the most problematic task involved in this position. For an inexperienced shopper to purchase sufficient food to nourish a family of four on a ten dollar weekly budget is unfathomable, utterly impossible! Preparing and serving decent meals is beyond the bounds of all possibility. Not that there was any other alternatives. That noble lady's total monthly living allowance was a meager forty dollars. Perhaps her husband's wages could not get through, that is if he was getting any wages. The boys were absolute angels. It is almost unbelievable that two preschool boys should be so well behaved and never cause a single problem. The other tasks did not seem to worry me. The daily chores that involve housekeeping such as keeping that monumental mirror sparkling clean, besides vacuuming these immense carpets, among other things, did not seem to be problematic. This is rather weird as polishing that mirror alone was a huge and time consuming undertaking.

It was, however, not the grandeur, the opulence of the premises that was so overwhelmingly striking, but the elegance of the princess herself. She over-shadowed and stood out among these treasures as a ravishing crimson rose flaunting its radiant beauty alone in the detriment of the arid desert. In a great crowd irregardless of its magnitude, all eyes seem to converge in her direction and she often became the center of attraction. It wasn't that she was a ravishing beauty although she was attractive in a striking, alluring sort of way. Her dark brown eyes highlighted the luster of her golden hair. Her tan complexion accentuated the attractiveness of her oval face. She was very slim, which is not surprising. She practiced her ballet for hours before dawn, besides she ate very little. But it was not her looks that contributed to her charm. It was a certain uniqueness, a sort of refined grace that radiated the splendor and greatness of her personality. Indubitably she was of royal blood, not because of her royal birth, but because of her amazing nature. Her whole being was a manifestation of nobility. Although I abhor the class system in society, the categorizing of individuals into neat little packages according to their status, I must concede that this "Madam" was distinct and unique with an essence of superiority to the common individual.

She was of the great. Verily, she was the embodiment of the truth that greatness emanates not from material goods, but from the soul, the very essence of one's being. One who possesses that gift, that greatness, never demeans others in order to glorify themselves. It is a gift that cannot be acquired with material gains evidently. Some who have gained enormous fortunes and who profess to belong to the most prestigious class are more vulgar and disreputable than the most deprived homeless people. Although these truths are self evident, it is rather gratifying to find them in the writings of Ann Frank entitled the "Gift". These are her words, words that are so simple, yet so profound and so full of enlightened wisdom. "Human greatness does not lie in wealth or power but in character and goodness." It is amazing that one so young, a victim of human treachery, living in an impossible situation, should possess such insight and wisdom.

Never did this noble lady treat me in a condescending manner or speak to me in a patronizing tone of voice. She treated me as an equal, in spite of our different status in society. In fact, when some tasks were not done to her standards, she did her best to help change and facilitate the situation. On one occasion, she had the whole bathroom repainted so that it would be easier to keep clean. She was always most appreciative and praised me whenever the occasion presented itself. She was astounded one day because I had managed to fix an appliance in disrepair. "Nothing is impossible for a lass who was raised on a farm," she said. "They can do anything. They are never stuck."

On another occasion she complimented me on the style of my clothes, and in my appreciation of the arts. "You know," she said in surprise, "you have excellent taste."

One afternoon, on her way home from her dance class, she became acquainted with a journalist, a Mr. Hall, who was employed by the Vancouver Sun. The two of them happened to be seated next to each other (on the bus) and a conversation ensued. Mr. Hall was utterly amazed, completely overwhelmed. He could not believe that destiny had smiled down upon him and had given him the phenomenal opportunity to meet a real princess, let alone be sitting next to her and conversing with her. Subsequently, the two of them became good friends. Mr. Hall, a very well-educated man, cognizant of the many intrigues of the business world and being fully at ease in the Canadian entourage, became a most valuable counselor and guide in madam's professional pursuits and manageable affairs. He wrote a brilliant column in the Sun proclaiming not only her dynamic personal characteristics and charm, but her outstanding professional skills as a ballet dance teacher. Following his advice, she opened a school of ballet dancing for young girls. This proved to be a tremendous success. In a very short time madam had many students which must have alleviated the strained condition of the budget. To promote the excellence of her school and the quality of her teaching methods she invited the girls to a party at her house. The party was fit for a queen (for a princess?). There were mountains of luscious sandwiches, all sorts of pastries and all the goodies that could possibly be the delight of any girl in that age category. (The delicate sandwiches, indeed all the refreshments were the result of my handiwork.) The party was a great success and must have been a useful modus operandi in the promotion of madam's elite dancing school. In fact, this enterprise proved to be most economically advantageous.

Mr. Hall's expertise was not confined to his illustrious writings or to his business sense however. He seemed to be proficient in many fields, a sort of jack-of-all-trades. He knew what was logical in any situation it seems. The manner in which he could stand apart and analyze a situation was uncanny. He told me about a closeout sale in downtown Vancouver that demonstrates how irrationally people can behave under certain conditions.

"The people were lined up for hours before the doors were opened," he said, "and when the doors finally opened, pandemonium! It was a zoo, no less. These ladies came crashing in. It's a wonder they didn't break the doors down). Pushing, shoving, falling over each other in a mad rush to be the first to take advantage of the bargains. Then these ladies, (can you believe it) would swarm like a pack of wolves over merchandize, grabbing the items out of one another's hands and actually fighting over it. Soon the bickering would gain momentum and explode into fist fights all over the store. It was a regular freak show. It is indeed amazing that normally dignified ladies can behave in such an unseemly manner just to save a few pennies! As for myself, I was having the time of my life. I had been treated to an hilarious comedy. Admission free!"

One day he asked me a rather embarrassing question. "Why do you pretend that you are unaware of complicated and sensitive situations," he asked "when you have figured it all out and have a perfectly logical and humane explanation for its occurrence?" It was most obvious to me that there are certain truths that are best kept in your heart, and that nothing but grief would be the outcome of their revelation.

On another occasion, he noticed that I was very depressed, and trying to cheer me up, he said something that because of its wisdom has given me the courage to go on in desperate situations. "Thank you, Mr. Hall." These are the words that have sustained me when the path seemed insurmountable, beyond all hope of pursuing on the way. "Remember," he said. "All this will pass. All this will pass. Tomorrow you may not remember what caused you so much anguish today." Quite a philosopher wasn't he. Indeed he was, along with all his other pursuits.

In order to gain publicity for madam, this gentleman made arrangements for her to entertain the soldiers by doing a dance performance. At first madam refused. It was against her husband's moral principles. "Women should never perform in public or make a public display of themselves" was his dictum. However as the performance was to entertain the soldiers, he allowed her to do it. It was a grand affair. The dress she wore could not have belonged to anyone but a princess. It was a dream! Gold, adorned with brilliant sequins that sparkled, and fitted with a hood, it had layer upon layer of tiered skirts. When madam put on that gown, she was indeed the fairy princess in the children's books of fairy tales. (It is a minor detail, but I had spent hours and hours pressing all these flounces.)

The ballet performance must have been absolutely fantastic! How I wished that it would have been possible for me to see it. But of course I was too timid to say so. Afterwards, Madam told me that had she known that it would amuse me, she would have made arrangements for me to go. But alas, it was too late. Madam was a professional ballet dancer. She had been taught by a famous Russian ballet teacher, who settled for nothing less than excellence. "He had a whip," Madam recalled, "and if any of his pupils made a mistake, he would hit them on the legs with his whip. No one dared make a mistake." Besides teaching regular classes at the school, she was up in the wee hours of the morning practicing without a break or reprieve. She had a phonograph player and always danced to the music of the same melody (or so it seems after all these years). That regular thump, thump of her foot as it pulsated to the rhythm of the beat is still clearly audible in my consciousness in spite of all the years gone by. To the pulse of the music she was able to make eighteen rotations balanced solely on the point of her big toe. She was indeed a prima donna, a maestro.

Sometime after I had been with the family, the Captain was wounded in the French army and came home to join his wife and children in Vancouver. If righteousness and merit are the criteria on which greatness is based, then Captain Bonneau was of the great. His moral values were beyond reproach. In fact, by today's standards, he would be considered inexorable. Yet he was kind. But the strict army discipline had been assimilated into his nature and became part of who he was. He believed that man should live and behave according to certain ideals consistent with and exigent to his superior intelligence. Thus every detail, every action followed an impeccable pattern, right down to his relationship with his wife and his role as a parent to his sons. Daily routines such as eating, retiring, and personal hygienic habits were performed with meticulous precision, a methodical polish and refinement disregarded in most households. Simple things like answering the door or visiting the bathroom had to be performed with a dignity hitherto unknown to me. His high standards complemented his rank and his distinguished station in life. Indeed it is of little wonder. After all he was married to a princess! It is likely that nobility must obey rigid rules and follow an exemplary pattern of life.

Soon after the captain came home the old restlessness again began to possess me. I claimed that I was ill. Actually it was the old feeling of discontent, the feeling of being displaced, unfulfilled, that tormented me. The princess very graciously gave me a leave of absence with pay with the stipulation that I train someone to replace me.

Soon after that the princess sold the school. Many years afterwards the captain became the French ambassador to Canada. It was while I was in Saskatoon training to be a teacher that these wonderful tidings came to me. How fascinating it felt to have had the opportunity of knowing that amazing couple and their adorable sons.

It wasn't long before another job opportunity was available. Strange as it may seem, although it consisted of the same type of work, I actually enjoyed this new position. The sisters of Charity needed someone to do some extra tasks in the convent and the Mother Superior recommended me. It was pleasant working and chatting with the sisters. They were so kind. It seems, in retrospect that there were more coffee breaks than anything else on the agenda. But again destiny stepped in and I embarked upon another adventure, an adventure that proved to be most exciting and delightful.

George, the second eldest brother, had been in British Columbia for many years before Hélène and I set foot in Vancouver. We couldn't wait to see him. As soon as we were settled, we began to make inquiries in an attempt to locate him. We didn't have his address or any idea where to look for him. It is indeed strange that George didn't write to my parents and let them know where he was and what he was doing. Be that as it may, Hélène and I were at a loss not knowing where to begin our search. It is quite evident that trying to find someone in Vancouver is as useless as trying to find a needle in a haystack. After many futile expeditions we were most gratified to hear that he was likely in the town of Malardville, it being a French community. So it was in that town that we resumed our search. We inquired at almost every hotel, every restaurant, the police station, everywhere! Not a trace. On one occasion, after having walked miles in the burning heat, exhausted we went into an hotel to cool off and rest. No sooner had we sat down when a waiter came and plunked two gigantic glasses of beer before us. We were astounded. Our eyes probably popped out of our heads. (In our family, women did not drink. It was unheard of. An utter sacrilege no less.)

"We didn't order that!" my sister said emphatically.
"Well" retorted the waiter. "What the h... are you doing here?"
It goes without saying that we were out of there in no time flat. Instead of sitting in the lobby we had unknowingly sat in the beer parlor. Within these four walls dwells a world hitherto unknown to us, hence our blundering naiveté. How embarrassing!

After many unsuccessful searches, we did manage to find George, our long lost brother. He apparently had befriended a family who lived not far from the town. He often visited them, sometimes staying at their home for several days. It was through these people that we were finally reunited with our brother. Then we visited with him as often as circumstances permitted. We were delighted that at last we could enjoy just being together. It was from this reunion that my next adventure emanated.

George's favorite in that family was Adrian, who was approximately his age. This confused both Hélène and me as Adrian's temperament was completely opposite from George's. While Adrian was a go-getter and went ahead with his projects regardless of the consequences, George had a gentle unassuming nature. In fact, just in case I have neglected to do justice to that man's most generous nature, I will endeavor to do so now. To say that he was kind would most certainly not do justice to the extent of his generosity. He was magnanimous! Even at a very young age his concern was always for the welfare of others. During our childhood, when he thought the girls would be accused of being irresponsible because they had not been able to do all the many tasks at hand, he would join in and do anything that needed to be done. Anything. He'd knead the bread, wash the dishes, or sweep the floor; anything at all. It is little wonder that the girls loved him. He never failed to be there when they needed him. That is why, even after all these years; my sister and I had not forgotten his kindness and were overjoyed to be with him.

George's friend Adrian

George and Adrian had bought a boat in the hope of using it in a dual business enterprise. Although most boat owners on the coast were fishermen, these two had no intentions of catching fish. They were looking for a more lucrative, more sophisticated means of making their living. Apparently they had discovered that a plant, Huckleberry, used in making floral arrangements, abounded on the island of Van Anda, off the coast of British Columbia. They had also discovered a building that they could use while they worked on the island. How convenient! So they decided to pick these plants, transport them to the mainland and sell them to the flower shops in Vancouver. It was at this point that my new adventure ensued. The boys decided that it would be nice to have help and company while they were picking the plants. (Actually it was the twigs or shoots of the plant that they picked.) So Juliette, Adrian's sister, and I joined the Huckleberry enterprise. We worked in teams, I with George, and Juliette with Adrian. We'd tear off the shoots from the plant, tie them in bundles, and stack the bundles until we had a shipload. Then we'd take it across the channel to Vancouver.

Gathering shoots from the Huckleberry shrub turned out to be one of the happiest adventures of my life. There I was, in an enchanting woodland, mesmerized by the wonders of my beloved nature, as free as those wild creatures that surrounded me. My own personal heaven. For surely this rapture, this magic could only be the manifestations of the celestial kingdom. Besides, I fell madly in love with Adrian. I loved him as only a young inexperienced girl can love, unconditionally. George did not seem to be entirely in favor of this mad infatuation, but as usual he very wisely advised me to be prudent. The age difference, my inexperience, and the fact that Adrian had at one time been in some kind of trouble were the obstacles that concerned my brother. His concerns were unwarranted however. For one thing, la bête noire irrupted with a vengeance. It goes without saying that with that fierce monster on my back, I felt that I was unworthy of his affection. Thus I did everything in my power to hide my feelings. He (Adrian) probably never knew my secret or had the faintest idea that it existed, if he based his opinion on my demeanor. Whether he had any affection for me, I will never know.

Perhaps what fascinated me the most during this adventure was the crossing of the channel between the island and the mainland in a small vessel. I would watch the reflection of the sun upon the waters for hours on end. I fancied myself sitting on a sea of flames, sailing spellbound on a spectral raging inferno. I was mesmerized by its glorious magnificence. Oh, how I loved the sea, the boundless sea in all its majesty

Crossing that channel transported my imagination into another world, a world of magic, a world of illusive rapture. I was overwhelmed, utterly captivated by the enormity, the immensity and wonders of the waters that stretched as far as the eye could see. To my youthful romantic eyes, the sea was all splendor, glamour, and beauty.

Yet, an adventure that occurred on the way from the island to the mainland should have made me realize the hazards of this sea. This sea in all its splendor, grandeur, and its beauty is at times treacherous. When the tempestuous winds sweep over and disturb the serene tranquility of its waters, the ferocity of its wrath is atrocious and frightful to behold. It wasn't, however, the fury of the sea that caused and nearly resulted in a fatal tragedy. It was pure negligence. The skipper had not taken the precaution to make sure that the quantity of gasoline was definitely sufficient and would last until we had reached the mainland. (Adrian, to my brother's utter desperation believed in living dangerously.) He had considerably miscalculated either the distance or the amount of energy that particular engine used. Be that as it may, we ran out of gasoline long before we had reached our destination. There we were, stranded halfway between the island and the mainland. It was late and darkness would soon be all around us. The wind was also beginning to toss the boat helter-skelter in every direction. Well, at this point, even our dauntless skipper became desperate. Juliette and I were unaware of the serious situation we were in and therefore we did not panic. It is the wind, strange to say that came to the rescue. Although it threatened to tip the boat, rocking it dangerously back and forth, it did push us in the right direction towards the mainland. To prevent the boat from capsizing or turning upside down when it tilted or leaned too far on one side, Juliette and I, one on each side would bounce with all our might on the elevated side balancing it and restoring it to a stable position. The wind managed to propel the boat into a small cove along the shore and as it was safely sheltered from the wind, the boys were able to go for gas.

My dream world soon came to an end. It was too perfect. Such perfection is unrealistic and is bound to come crashing down at your feet at any moment. I am not certain why the boys did not carry on with this enterprise. It may be that they could no longer find a market for their product or perhaps the two of them could not see eye to eye. That would not be surprising, as their personalities were unequivocally irreconcilable; one being extremely cautious, and the other daring, throwing caution to the winds, content to live on the edge. Be that as it may, both my friend and I were devastated when the boys told us they couldn't make a go of it and had to dissolve the partnership. We both loved these two, as each of them in his own way was indeed meritorious. We knew that they also cared deeply for each other in spite of their differences. Not only were we devastated at being separated from the boys, but we had become completely enchanted with the boat, (the name of the boat has escaped my memory) and the hours we spent sailing between the island and the mainland. What I missed the most, however, was the boundless, majestic waters of the ocean. The compelling mysticism of these magical waters mesmerized me. As I gazed upon its magnificent grandeur, the oscillating waves, swaying gently, wooing me in an unfathomable rhythmic chant, beckoning me to join their enchanting, perpetual journey. Although I couldn't go, I cherished these magnificent waters with a passion.

Back on the mainland, my friend and I were fortunate to get work in a New Westminster hospital. I worked in the diet kitchen preparing meals for patients who were on a special diet; Juliette's duties were probably in the wards. Three of us girls had an apartment near the hospital. We got along well together. Those were happy times!

During my sojourn in Vancouver I met several friends, both male and female. The memory of these dear friends will forever remain in my heart. My relationship with my girl friends was open and uncomplicated. We'd go dancing, bowling, swimming, or just walking in the park. We had fun, pure unmitigated fun! The dances were out of this world. Not only were the dance halls immense, the floors like mirrors, it seemed that every dancer's skill was amazing. What fascinated and thrilled me the most was the square dances, when all the sets would join in one great assemblage and stepping all the way around the hall, the ladies and gentlemen, dancing in opposite directions, clasped hands with those they met as they skipped merrily along.

My relationship with male friends was, however, entirely different. That is, if I happened to like that person. Casual friends did not seem to bother me. I could be myself without the least bit of inhibition. It goes without saying that, not caring one way or another; casual acquaintances (there were a few of those) were more fun to be with. There were two very decent friends. One was indubitably a special person. His character was beyond reproach. He had an implacable religious affiliation, his faith being inflexible. His spirituality was not restricted to religious matters, however. He was well educated, intelligent and poetry was his obsession. Unfortunately, although I admired his qualities, with my usual will of the wisp attitude, I did nothing to encourage the relationship.

Hélène introduced me to someone she had known for some time. He was supposed to be a millionaire; at least my sister thought he was a millionaire. He had made his fortune in the wholesale business. But as far as I was concerned, the matter went in one ear and out the other. What attributes distinguishes a millionaire from others is knowledge that is way beyond my expertise. Casting the technicality aside, he was a most charming gentleman. He treated me like a queen, taking me to fancy restaurants, to the theater, and other forms of entertainment. I liked him a lot, but as a friend. Perhaps if the relationship had become serious I would have run. It was most incredible to me that such a successful man could be interested me, and I wondered. Was it because I was French (he had asked me to teach him the language) or was it because of my modesty. As for me, the fact that he accepted me just as I am with all my shortcomings, was what pleased me the most about him. He never seemed to mind that I was so unpretentious, always being me; just me. Unfortunately, he was transferred to Winnipeg. He wrote to me from Winnipeg. The reason why I failed to answer his letters is beyond my comprehension. It certainly doesn't make sense in hindsight. Indeed, looking back, there were so many things that didn't make any sense; so many. And that was just one of the many gauche, awkward blunders that kept increasing dangerously and of which I was so blatantly culpable.

Although that episode in my life brings back countless delightful souvenirs, there are other incidents that are most painful and that I yearn to blot out of my mind, and completely erase the past. I was unfortunately fully responsible for these occurrences. That is, of course what makes it so painful! And to add insult to injury, all these misfortunes I managed to create without intent. With the best of intentions, I constantly found myself in preposterous situations that I had initiated. My ignorance, naiveté, ineptitude, plus a lack of (savoir faire) are the only excuses that can be presented in my defense. Or perhaps my make believe world was so perfect that it was inconceivable for me to accept the world as it really exists. Armed with the philosophy that most people are good, it was impossible for me to realize that it is crucial to beware of those who are abnormal. Walking across Burrard Bridge unaccompanied, hitch hiking, going on a blind date are some of the preposterous blunders that left me in very precarious situations and still send shivers up and down my spine just thinking about these foolhardy shenanigans. (Indeed they were downright stupid.) It is a wonder that I always was able to extricate myself unscathed every time. My guardian angel must have been totally dedicated to my cause, and working twenty-four hours a day, desperately trying to keep me out of trouble. Such dedication is surely beyond the call of duty. It is amazing that he didn't quit. It is also amazing that he didn't lay a grievance against the celestial workers' union on the grounds that he was being coerced to perform under impossible and hazardous working conditions without a break or any form of compensation whatsoever.

Sometimes these predicaments were not entirely my fault. On one occasion, as I was walking across that humongous Vancouver bridge in broad daylight, I heard heavy footsteps some distance behind me. There was no cause for alarm however as many prefer to walk rather than ride on the crowded streetcars. The footsteps seem to be getting closer and closer. Becoming a little apprehensive, I took a quick look behind me. There, gaining pace every step of the way, was a giant. He was colossal! He was probably Hindus because he was very dark. His appearance did little to reassure me. So I began to walk faster. But no matter how fast I walked, the closer he got behind me. Soon I began to run; still he was right behind me. I was frantic. At last, the hostel gate was right before me. In retrospect, my fears may have been unfounded as it is questionable what that man's motives may have been. His destination may have led him along the same direction as mine, or being aware of my terror, he may have been enjoying it as a big joke and having a good laugh about the whole thing, or he may have been a stalker. Be that as it may, I was indeed grateful when the gate locked behind me.

One evening as I was returning home after visiting with my sister at the hostel, someone followed me. It was very dark so it was impossible to see who it was. In a panic I began to run. Not fast enough, however, as the intruder was steadily shortening the gap between us. There was no doubt about this man's intentions. I was filled with terror. Lo and behold, all of a sudden, and out of nowhere came this God awful deafening clamor and commotion. There was banging, clanging, and jangling. Alarmed, I held my breath, too frightened to look behind me to find the source of the hullabaloo. I needn't have troubled myself, however, for soon the racket caught up with me, mercifully! The banging came from a bag full of golf sticks that a man coming back from golfing was carrying. In the split of an eye he sized up the situation. Turning back to me he declared, (jokingly) "One of these days," said he," we'll have to beat them off with a club." To me the whole thing was not funny as I shook with fright all the way home. It goes without saying that as soon as the golfer came on the scene the intruder fled. My guardian angel must have been there again, as vigilant as ever. Or maybe that golfer was the incarnation of my angel.

Then there were the times when I'd get lost. (Lost, that's me. I'm always lost somewhere. I even manage to get lost in the backyard.) That nearly drove my sister to desperation. One evening, on the way home from the theater with a friend, I got off the streetcar at the wrong stop. I walked and walked completely confused. After what seemed to be an eternity, the streets and buildings became familiar and I knew which way to go. No wonder my guardian angel was frustrated!

Working at the hospital in New Westminster was enjoyable. Indeed it was almost too perfect to last. The dietician always wrote down the menu for each patient and the instructions were easy to follow. The sisters were pleased with my work. My roommates and I got along well together. We had a lot of fun. Alas, destiny stepped in and our Utopia was left behind.

Part II

Reaching for the Stars

At dawn as I meandered around the lake this morning, I gaze with wonder upon the turbulent wind driven waters towards the other shore. Spellbound I am magically transported to the shores of the mighty Pacific with its towering billows crashing upon the sands. It's a continuous rhythmic and melodious rumble mesmerizing my soul. I hear its bewitching and seducing call pleading, "Come with me." It is an illusive call luring me to the magic and thrill of exploring the unknown and all that lies beyond.

It may have been that same mysterious summons that seduced my mother to throw caution to the winds challenging the unknown and embarking on a most hazardous venture. Perhaps she heard the same alluring whisper that prompted the explorers to venture across an unknown and perilous sea or the pioneers to dare the hazards of the wilderness. Be that as it may the adventure she had formulated and upon which we ventured was froth with uncertainty and hazards. The risks involved added excitement and thrill to the project.

After my parents came west my mother had failed to find an opportunity for the manifestation of her extraordinary musical and dramatic talents. True, she had participated in many activities that involved music and drama, but these activities were mediocre, and did not by far effectuate the mysterious ecstasy her passionate yearning aspired. She had given music lessons to all the members of the family and every one of us played the piano. Some even played two or three instruments, including the violin, the guitar, and the accordion. She also gave music and singing lessons to some of the neighbors' children. Besides, she was the director of the church choir. Almost every year, she prepared an impressive concert to raise money for the church. The preparations for these concerts were a most demanding and exhausting task. Especially as no one in the community had the skills that such an ambitious project demanded. Therefore the entire burden fell on my mother's shoulders. The instructions, coaching, drilling, practice, voice production while singing or speaking, musical accompaniment, the whole kit and caboodle was dumped right in her lap. Some of the rehearsals were held in the church basement, however most of them transpired in our home. Although these rehearsals took place when I was still very young they are still crystal clear in my memory. Repetitions of lines in the plays, words and melodies of the songs over and over are still ringing in my ears. All this going on in a house full of kids. It was unreal, absolute pandemonium! How can one have the courage to go through such an ordeal is beyond me. There were compensations. The concerts were always a huge success and always managed to reap in enough funds to keep the church operational. Hopefully my mother will be rewarded for her grueling efforts where she now resides in the celestial kingdom.

This discourse would not be complete however, if it did not include my mother's fantastic voice, the rapture she experienced when she sang and the incredible collection of songs included in her repertoire. In my mind's eye, I still see her leaning against the wall, or spinning, or doing whatever, and bursting into a song. She had a song for every situation, every activity, every theme, indeed for everything! It was delightful to hear these melodies gushing forth with joy from her enraptured spirit. Her songs have remained deeply inscribed in my memory. Even after all these years they walk with me where ever I go. And whenever I hear anyone giving a rendition of one, my heart is overwhelmed with nostalgia.

It was while Hélène and I were in Vancouver that my mother had a phenomenal inspiration. It is rather strange that this inspiration had not occurred to her before, for all these years her talents had been exploited, always used to the benefit and amusement of others without ever receiving any recognition or even gratitude. All these years she must have been deliberating, wondering how she could unleash these gifts that God had lavished upon her for the welfare of her own family (for a change) and especially to alleviate the desperate economic predicament that had tormented her relentlessly for an eternity. So she entreated Hélène and I to come home as we were part of the plan she had painstakingly conceived and meticulously put together. She didn't dare reveal the whole scheme to us for fear its magnitude would frighten us away. We had barely crossed the threshold of the doorway when we were bombarded from all sides. Everyone in the house bursting to tell us about this extraordinary project.

Mother had a large collection of plays that she had amassed when she was producing concerts for the benefit of the church. Although most were in French, she had managed to acquire a few in the English language. One of the French plays seemed to have been written exclusively for our family. Even the number of characters coincided exactly with the family members that were still at home, besides Hélène and me. That is perhaps what might have inspired my mother's sensational idea. Although the English comedies she had selected were most entertaining, (they were hilarious) the French play was the crux of the project she had conceived.

She had spent days, nay, months and countless sleepless nights deliberating, mulling over the feasibility of a plan she was formulating and putting together in her mind's eye. She had dreamed that we would, as a family, form a traveling show and perform these plays in villages along the way. We would perform the French play in the French speaking communities and the English comedies in English centers. It was a tremendous idea! We had everything required at our fingertips it seemed. From the sisters at the Roberval Convent she had learned the techniques of performing and directing a performance. She could play the piano and many other instruments. Besides, she had the voice of an angel! She had taught every one of us the rudiments of music; consequently, every one in the family played an instrument. Some even played several instruments. She had also trained us in voice production. With all these assets, she was confident that her enterprise would be successful.

So we set to work with great enthusiasm. Under Mother's capable direction we rehearsed, practiced, learned how to project our voices, correct body language, and countless other skills involved in dramatization. Our main feature called *"Les Chaussons de la Duchess Anne"* or *"The Duchess' Slippers"* was evidently a musical. Each one of us was meticulously trained to sing a part of the play that was significant to the development of the plot while another member of the family accompanied him/her on the piano. (It was indeed fortunate that everyone of us had been given some musical training.) After days of constant dedicated practice Mother thought our rendition of the performance was satisfactory and we were ready to launch on our wild hazardous venture. Everything was ready even the costumes. All the time we had been practicing we had worked frantically on these. From the eighteenth century style they were extravagantly elaborate. The hats were especially impressive. They were tall and extensively decorated probably designating the rank of those who wore them.

Indeed the characters in our main feature were aristocrats, the heroine being a duchess no less! The events take place in a small dukedom in France. The story is about a duchess who is trying desperately to hold on to her possessions. As the first scene opens, she is anxiously waiting for news from the captain of her army. Meanwhile, her maids of honor, tempted by the delicious aroma from the kitchen, each steal a slipper-shaped pastry. When they are caught, they apologize and ask for the duchess's forgiveness, to her utter confusion. In the meantime, the page who is the bearer of the crucial message (that is hidden in a knitted slipper to escape detection) puts the slipper on a fence post in order to gather a bouquet of roses for the duchess. Unfortunately, when he returns, the slipper is gone. A peasant woman, seeing the slipper, and thinking it may be important, takes it to the duchess. She beats about the bush, goes on and on, not able to come to the point, until the duchess, exasperated leaves. At this point, the pageboy enters. Weeping convulsively, he admits having lost the message and begs for mercy. But lo and behold when it appears that all is lost, the old peasant woman bursts in upon the scene, recognizes the page, produces the slipper containing the message, and saves the day!

The plot of the play was filled with intrigue, suspense, and humor. We felt confident that it would be a success.

There was one major problem. Transportation! That was indeed a major obstacle. It proved to be the crucial factor that determined the success or failure of this courageous and daring enterprise. My mother, with much difficulty, managed to persuade my dad to transform a hayrack into a prairie schooner, or what looked like one. He did a magnificent job. There was a place for everything that was needed on our journey, including cubicles overhead to store our elaborate costumes. Of course the whole contraption was situated on a horse drawn vehicle. (Alas, a motor home would have been just ideal but at the time they were unavailable, and would have been beyond our means regardless.) My poor dad was exasperated. He was strictly against the whole audacious venture. He was deeply concerned for our safety, and especially for my mother's health as she had not been well for many years. To him, the whole adventure was off the deep end, reckless, and he felt that we were going out on a limb. (He was probably right.) However, due to Mother's insistence, and in spite of his anxiety, his skepticism, he helped us to get ready. (Indeed it occurs to me that this was a déja vue incidence, a repetition of the western exodus episode, that in spite of his misgivings, his great reluctance, he acquiesce to my mother's bidding.)

So, throwing caution to the winds, we set out on our precarious, yet exhilarating adventure. No one, but my mother surely, was concerned about the risks or mishaps that might occur along the way. The enthusiasm, the excitement of it all was too over-powering and transcended care and prudence.

The first performance, or opening night, occurred in the parish church of Shell River or Victoire, as it is now called. The play was in French, of course as that is a French community. It was successful in terms of audience appreciation as most of the parishioners were present, but surely not in terms of monetary gains. Tickets were twenty-five cents each and half the proceeds were given to the church. That didn't deter us. We were undaunted, determined to succeed in that bold and audacious venture. Next we proceeded to perform in Debden, a small French village about fifteen miles away. The next French village was quite a distance away. It must have been a most grueling journey for both the actors and the horses. I cannot recall the exact sequence of the events after our arrival. Our performance was received with great enthusiasm however. Years afterwards, the residents were still saying how impressed they had been with the show. It was in Leoville that we met our first Waterloo. After the performance we set out to visit my brother, John, who lived on a farm about five miles from town. Then disaster struck! It had rained for days and the road, or trail was inundated, completely submerged in mud. It goes without saying that we got stuck, the wheels buried axle deep in that murky stuff. As usual Hélène, without a word, dashed to my brother's house to get help. He, of course came to the rescue with a team of horses (or a tractor?) and pulled us out. This episode made us realize that unless we had a more efficient means of transportation we had to abandon our project. Mission impossible! Although we did the English performance on the way home, we realized that our dream was just that, a wonderful yet impossible dream. It felt as if our gift from the Gods had come crashing down at our feet and been shattered into dust.

We never did live this episode down. The men made sure of that. The teasing, the razzing, and the buffoonery never ceased; in fact it became a family joke. These men could not believe that a group of women on their own would have the audacity to attempt such a precarious adventure. It was the traveling gear, the whole kit and kaboodle, that was the butt of their ridicule. They christened the make shift van" la platform crémeler or crénelé" which translates into the crenellated platform. Of coarse, that was just a scheme to poke fun at us and our fly-by-night adventure. What could we do but laugh with them even though in our hearts we all felt disillusion and regret.

Part III

Drifting

Rambling slowly along on my habitual daily trek around the lake a feeling of intense oppression overwhelmed my spirits. It may have been because the memory of a most difficult period of my life came back to torment me.

It is perhaps John Steinbeck's words that have brought on such a wave of emotions to possess me, for his words have the power to tear my heart to shreds. Amazingly "The Grapes of Wrath" did not wreak such an emotional tempest within my soul. For the tragedy in which the characters of the novel continually found themselves was too horrendous for me to bear leaving me unable to appreciate the author's artistic genius. In his novel "Travels with Charley," however he depicts such a profound insight of human nature that the reader is left spellbound. One observation is especially sensational and I quote. "You can't go home again because home has ceased to exist except in the mothballs of memory." How true! On numerous occasions I have visited the site of our old home, the home of every one of my brothers and sisters, where they were born and nurtured until each reluctantly departed and sought his own way. Alas it is no more! Not a trace or a sign remains as evidence that it ever existed. Indeed the very existence of those whose lives had transpired here seem to have vanished, or perhaps lies buried forever under a mantel of nature's devious chicanery.

As a matter of fact, that novel is bursting with comments illustrating the author's gracious personality and keen understanding of human nature. It seemed incredible to me that there could be someone else like me with the ability to get lost in his own back yard. His comments about governments are so true. When the people elect certain governments they are selling their freedom away unconditionally.

The years that followed that most extraordinary episode are full of shadows. Indeed, the cobwebs blur my vision so that there is only a vague picture before my mind's eye of the events that transpired after our return. Perhaps this letdown feeling was so overpowering that it eclipses the desire to embark on any new project. I was lost again, drifting aimlessly hither and thither, adrift on a boundless, uncharted sea, my destiny! There seems to be a void, a chasm, during these years as if time had stood still, creating a lull during which life ceased to exist. It may be that this period which conjure a complete blank in my memory and leaves me in limbo is painful and is buried deep in my psyche where it will remain forever. Be that as it may, if I am unable to envision in my mind's eye what transpired during that interval, logic and reason have enabled me to determine some of the most important events that occurred within that time frame. For instance my sister Marie-Anne got married and became the proud mother of a girl, Fern, and a boy, Ronald. While the children were infants, Marie-Anne lived with us. The children were the pride and joy of the whole family. Hélène had been long gone; in fact she had left as soon as we got back. As for me, I was in limbo (as I mentioned before) and I cannot recall doing anything significant or worthwhile during that whole interval. Although reconstructing the information, I was able to gather, it was during that time that I spent some time with Yvonne, my sister. Not having recovered from childbirth, she was yet too weak to care for her baby who was dangerously ill. It also is, according to the time frame, during those years that my uncle was trying to teach me the art of making cheese. There might have been many other happenings during that period, but they were insignificant, completely immaterial to me and they have been entirely blotted out of my mind. I was just coasting, aimlessly drifting with the tide, wherever the capricious current of destiny chose to lead me.

At last my parents realized that their struggle to make a bare living on the farm was hopeless. During the depression the debts had accumulated drastically and although they attempted myriads of projects in order to solve their economic problems, the situation was insurmountable, beyond all human feasibility. So they decided to abandon the farm and make their home in the small hamlet off Léoville. It must have been excruciatingly painful to leave the home where they had labored most of their lives trying desperately to make ends meet, relocate, and start all over again. Although they had very little financial resources, they managed to establish a comfortable dwelling for themselves and those in the family who still remained with them. Juliette and I did not stay with them long. Juliette married a boy from the village, and I decided to write my grade eleven examination. That was an ambitious project indeed. For an ordinary student it would have been anticipated as part of the yearly assessment program. For Hélène and I it was overwhelming! We had studied the grades nine ten and eleven from the department of education courses without having had the opportunity to get any of our assignments corrected, or writing one final examination. It was a matter of doing it by hook and by crook and hoping for the best besides having a dogged determination. Somehow we managed to correct our own assignments by using the material in the text. It goes without saying that to be confronted with departmental exams after all these years would be a tremendous undertaking if not downright scary. Besides, I had to review all the grade eleven program to prepare for the tests. Fortunately my brother Laurence was working out of town and was renting a cabin on the work site. He graciously allowed me to stay in the cabin where I would be able to study undisturbed. His only stipulation was that I would prepare his meals. This was not a problem. When he came back to town he gave me the same opportunity while I wrote my exams in town. The only subject that worried me was algebra (which is strange because algebra is relatively easy once it is understood). At last that ordeal was over! The next step was, obviously, where do I go from here. And it was at this point that my life took on a new meaning.

Part IV

Settling Down

On this fine April morning it was an effort to get myself mobile as I didn't have one spark of energy or motivation in my bones. Indeed it was a toss up. "Either I throw myself out and go for a jaunt around the lake or throw myself to the dogs." I argued within myself. Well as option number two was out of the question and all my inspirations seem to materialize as I leisurely and slowly saunter along the path that encircles the lake, it dawned on me that the first option was a better choice. So by hook and by crook I managed to throw some warm clothes on and shove myself out the door. Believe you me it wasn't easy! But the fresh air and the wonders of spring's mystical rhapsody again performed its magic. The wild geese's mating call, the seagulls' plaintive wail, the shrill cackling of the plover joined by the crow's noisy chatter filled the skies with rapture and harmony. The pussy willows still clinging to the willow twigs plus the new leaves just bursting from the buds formed a panorama of greenery and splendor enchanting to behold. Mesmerized by all this exquisite magnificence the threads of my intent began to replace the lethargy by which my imagination had been of late so mercilessly held. And slowly the train of thought began to drift back into my mind and I was able to plan the sequence and the direction that my story was to follow.

Mercifully providence intervened, taking matters into its own hands. During the war there was an acute shortage of teachers. Many of them had enlisted in the army. Many schools remained closed due to this situation. In order to alleviate the problem the department of education decided that after a very brief period of instruction grade eleven graduates would be given a temporary certificate and be allowed to teach in public schools. The heavens must have been smiling down upon me when this announcement appeared in the newspaper, for when my mother asked if I was interested, it was as if a door into the land of promise suddenly (and at long last) stood wide open for me, welcoming me to step in. I knew at once that this was a golden opportunity, and that it was what I had always wanted (unknowingly) to do, what my restless heart had always been searching for, yet had never envisioned it or focused on its realization. My exhilaration was overwhelming; the prospect was too terrific to be true. However, when a general consensus had been reached, it seemed that everything fell into place as if by magic. All the arrangements were made, transportation, lodging, admission documents, the works! I had always wondered where the money for these expenses had come from until John told me that it most likely had come from Laurence as he was the only one employed at the time. It is indeed deplorable that I never had the opportunity to tell him how grateful I was (and still am) for his generosity. Alas, it is too late!

Thus I embarked on a life long career; a career that proved to be my salvation; a career that turned my whole world around. I now envisioned an exhilarating future filled with challenging and exciting adventures. In lieu of drifting along from one monotonous and boring occupation to another, I felt that at last an opportunity to do something worthwhile stood before me.

The students involved in the program were given a six-week course at the University of Saskatoon. It was basically an academic course, comprising basic high school skills such as English, Math, and Social Studies. In fact all the material presented to the students was elementary and relatively unchallenging, with one exception. The professor had decided that the students should have the ability to speak in public so he gave various students assignments to be presented to the rest of the student body. And who was his first target? Why me of course! I was to give a detailed presentation about the ramifications of the Quebec Conference, a hot item in the news at the time. My report was excellent. But it was when I presented it that I met my Waterloo. Fresh from the farm with absolutely no self-confidence the whole thing was bound to be a disaster. And it was! As I walked upon the stage and looked at all these eight hundred students staring at me, I froze. My knees were shaking so badly it felt that they were knocking on both sides of the stage. I haven't a clue as to how much of the speech I got through but mercifully it ended at last. My nightmare wasn't over however. That wily professor made up his mind that he was going to find the solution to my dilemma. So the next week he insisted that I give a preview of a film before that same audience. It was a matter of do or die! After watching the film and being prepared, I walked on that stage, faced the same audience and said to myself," the hell with it." And got through with the presentation with flying colors. That phrase became my lifesaver for whenever things got unbearable and I thought it was impossible to go on I'd say "the hell with it" and go straight ahead without further ado. It could well be that the magic phrase got me through the thorny path destiny had chosen to lead me.

It is most regrettable that the instructions were not entirely based on teaching procedures or methods, such as the preparation of lessons, scheduling, classroom management, discipline, and an innumerable number of instructional techniques so crucial in the teaching profession. Concrete examples of lesson plans and observation of professional teachers at work in the classroom would have been a windfall to these inexperienced students. (Green, in every sense of the word.) All the students were sent out to various rural schools without a clue regarding specific teaching procedures. They (and me included) were thrown to the wolves! In fact, most of us were as vulnerable as if we had been cast into the sea without knowing how to swim. It is indeed incredible that most succeeded. But these unfortunate circumstances turned out to be my salvation! I cannot believe that scheming destiny, after spinning me around for so many years, mockingly using my reeling confusion as divertissement; the butt of its cunning chicanery, was at last going to give me a good turn. It seemed that the tide was turning, that that crafty prankster had finally given me a reprieve and was opening a door to an amazing opportunity. There aren't any words that can adequately express the gratitude that I felt (and still feel) towards the authorities who had the wisdom to put their faith and trust in us believing that we had the courage to confront and tackle the colossal challenge. It would be interesting to know how many of the students succeeded in their teaching career, obtained their grade twelve diploma and their bachelor of education certificate. Being an idealist, I am confidant that most of these students did. But that accomplishment is a story in itself. An achievement that is replete with striving and heroic effort.

I was determined that no obstacles would deter my success. To obtain a bachelor of education certificate a grade twelve diploma is mandatory. Therefore, that was the first hurdle. Mercifully, by this time grade twelve correspondence courses from the department of education were available. So I ordered one course at a time, completed it, wrote the exam and sent for the next one. On and on. English, Social Studies, Biology, Home Economics, Philosophy, Modern Problems, etc. It was a blessing that I loved to study. In fact, I would have been content to spend the rest of my life doing just that. Literature was (and has always been even to this day) music to my soul. The inspirations of the masters allow me to dwell in my world of fantasy, the mystical realm where I can let my wild imagination stray and wander wherever the author's fancy pleases to take me. It is my world, my enchanted kingdom, the realm where my exotic wondrous dreams dwell, my chimera! These great geniuses have the power to invoke wonders and bring down the celestial stars for you to gaze at in wonderment and awe. There are so many of these great men, giants in their field, who have the power to elevate the reader to fantastic heights, and transport them to a world of ecstasy, a world of pure delight. Masters such as Shakespeare, Dickens, Zola, and Camus have brought so much joy to me that without their inspirations my life would be but an empty shell, devoid of all spirituality and meaning. It goes without saying that while many would have found these endless hours of study insurmountable, for me, these hours were pure delight. That is excepting those in which I spent nights struggling with mathematics and algebra. Without assistance these two subjects were a nightmare to me until I began teaching them. All the other subjects were a breeze. It was, however, quite a few years before I succeeded in obtaining my grade twelve diploma. In fact, I was married and had a family. As soon as I accomplished this feat, I began taking University courses by correspondence, one at a time. English was first, of course! That was not surprising indeed. It was my favorite subject.

An incidence that is rather amusing but most regrettable happened when I was writing my grade twelve biology exams. Students who took courses from the department of education correspondence school had to make special arrangements in order to have their exams supervised. On that specific occasion, a teacher had been appointed in Prince Albert to supervise the departmental exams of students from surrounding districts. I was writing three tests, English, History, and Biology. Well, everything was superb until the morning of the Biology test. As soon as I entered the room I was confounded and greatly unnerved to realize that no one else was scheduled for that test. There was the teacher in that immense room, and there I was, greatly distraught, in a state of panic. Although the teacher did his best to ease my agitation, it was to no avail. With the test paper right before me and having the knowledge to answer all questions, I was too nervous to answer even one. In fact, my hand was shaking so violently that I couldn't even hold my pen. In spite of all the years that have gone by that incidence keeps flashing back before my eyes and is the source of a great deal of speculation. It was indeed a source of all kinds of guilt and recriminations. Yet it may well be that many factors contributed to this unfortunate incidence; for instance the fact that the examination center was miles from our home. It is fortunate that the next day I redeemed myself. I managed to obtain a mark of excellence in my French examination.

At the end of the six-week course the students were sent to various rural schools in different areas of Saskatchewan. My first assignment was near the Manitoba border, in the small community of Hazel Dell. The resident farmers were mostly of Ukrainian origin with the exception of one French family and a few that were of English descent. The Ukrainian settlers had retained most of their culture, including their language, their attitudes, and their overall way of living. That was a culture that was completely foreign to me. I felt as if I had been suddenly transported into another world, a world that was unknown to me, and into which I did not belong. It was a world in which the male species was dominant, and in which women were regarded as chattels with no rights whatsoever. It was a world in which men were privileged or licensed to behave in random unconstrained fashion irregardless of their spouses' feelings or protests. (And woe to these unfortunate who dared to protest.) That was the world in which I was, incognizant to the program director's cast. There I was, timid, naïve, inexperienced, green to the hilt, without a speck of expertise as to the ways of the world. They might as well have thrown me to the wolves!

How I managed to survive in that insurmountable situation is beyond the bounds of all conceivable imagination. If my memory is correct, there were about twenty students from grades one to ten in that class. Included in this conglomeration were older boys, sturdy, uncouth farm youth, a little rough around the edges. Teaching in such circumstances would have challenged the ability of an incredibly gifted professional, indeed no teacher would have been audacious or stupid enough to tackle such a task as the chances of success were very unpredictable. It is likely the reason why the assignment was delegated to a first year inexperienced teacher, who being ignorant, had no idea that she/he was walking straight into the lion's den, to be gobbled up in one fell swoop. Well, there I was facing this impossibility; scared, no teaching experience, armed with the philosophy that there is good in everyone, and not the slightest idea about the technique of self-preservation. (A veritable tragic mish-mash.)

Did I teach these children anything that year? That matter remains speculative therefore, can be envisioned only by the philosophers and the chronicles of the past. But even in the face of such impossible odds I remained undaunted. I was determined to succeed and refused to accept defeat. So I struggled and struggled working till all hours of the night, preparing lessons, planning the next day's schedules, agonizing over the deviant behavior of these children, and racking my brains trying to find solutions in relation to the improvement of their strange behavioral patterns. Only the heavens know how I made every effort. I went all out, bending over backwards in an attempt to reach these children. But the odds were too great! My inexperience, the difference and lack of understanding of the culture, besides the wanton manner of these people's ways were obstacles that proved to be invincible. As the year went by, I became more and more disillusioned and extremely discouraged.

The year was not a complete disaster however. There was an event that proved to be an outstanding success. It is customary in rural districts that the teachers prepare a Christmas Concert. The local residents look forward to it and it is the limelight of the year. The parents don't seem to realize how much valuable time is devoted in rehearsing and practicing; time that should be devoted to academic pursuits. Indeed in some cases the teacher's competence is rated according to her/his ability to put on a dynamic concert! Fortunately the plays that we had performed on our concert tour were still very fresh in my mind and I set about tenaciously rehearsing some of the comedies with my class. Using one of my mother's talent as a producer, I succeeded in whipping these students into incredulous actors. The concert was an amazing success. Some of the parents became so rapt up in the action at certain parts of the plays that they'd leave their seats and stand holding their breaths right at the foot of the stage. The reviews were unanimous! "There are reservations concerning her teaching skills," was the unanimous comment, "but she sure can throw a spectacular concert." I was bubbling over with pride.

Although that first year of my teaching experience was so formidably challenging it had many positive and rewarding aspects. These compensated for the tribulations I endured and made it worthwhile. As the odds were so incredibly insurmountable, I learned the most valuable lesson that is crucially indispensable to anyone hoping to join the teaching profession. I learned that it is a career that demands unconditional dedication, perseverance, and devotion. It is a career in which no amount of effort or sacrifice can be spared in order to meet the demands that this profession dictates. It is an all-encompassing life long commitment. It also necessitates a deep affection for children. Indeed a sincere concern for the well being of the child is the most essential requirement, for it is for their welfare that the whole educational system exists. (Hopefully!)

I was also most delighted that my sister, Marie-Anne and her children spent the first part of the year with me. Their company was a blessing. I felt that they had brought a little bit of home with them. Their presence created an atmosphere of warmth that dispelled that strange foreign and displaced feeling that constantly kept haunting me. The children, Fern and Ronald, were most dedicated in their mission. They kept both of us occupied and entertained nonstop with their amusing antics and playful childish attitudes.

Another providential godsend that probably descended straight from the celestial kingdom to rescue me (and my sister perhaps) from total distraction was a single French family who resided in that community. As soon as I landed in that district that benevolent family took me under their wing, veritably adopting me (and later my sister) as their own. We spent many happy moments together and shared many delicious meals, including Christmas dinner. Without the understanding and kindness of these extraordinary people, I would probably not have survived that most horrendous year. How I wish that it would be possible to express my overwhelming gratitude to these angels of mercy! Alas, it is too late! They are no more. Yet they will remain forever in my heart.

It was during that fateful year that I made the most crucial and momentous decision of my whole life. It was a decision that was to have formidable repercussions, changing the entire course of my destiny. It was a decision that had not been given enough analytical and judicious thought; consequently it was imprudent, rash, ill-advised. In the spring of that year, I got married. He was a twin, John, (Mike was his twin brother,) and was hopelessly ingrained in the traditional Ukrainian culture. Alas it may well be that I was also hopelessly ingrained (brain-washed) into the French culture; a situation that was indeed beyond the realm of reconciliation. I was troubled, skeptical, unconvinced that such differences could be reconciled. Yet he was so confident that these differences could be resolved and that the major issues could be worked out that I was persuaded. Having been brought up in a very traditional family with severe moral values which had been irrevocably inculcated upon my psyche since childhood, wild licentious behavior was unacceptable to me. Gambling, drinking, immorality, obscenities and all such conduct violated the dignity and self-respect that is attributed to the human species. Such abandon and freedom from moral restraint contradicts acceptable conventions, propriety, and suitable decorum. (Or so I thought.) Yet to many, such highfaluting ideals can be interpreted as pretentious, even pedantic! That was indeed the impression that the residents of that district seemed to deduce from my demeanor. Although, God forbid, that was the furthest thing from my mind. As a matter of fact the BEAST was still pursuing me, as ferocious as ever! And that is to the only logical explanation that I can possibly and reasonably suggest for my irrational, illogical decision to enter into a relationship that was beyond the bounds of possibility. (Even so, I still cannot rationalize the motive of that rash, impulsive decision!) Love cannot hope to reconcile or even mediate the differences between two people whose aspirations diverge drastically in opposite directions. Destiny using its deceptive chicanery must have whirled me in such a spin that I was unable to think at all, much less think logically!

Be that as it may the marriage did take place. We were married in Yorkton near the end of the year. In spite of our differences, I was convinced that we could sort things out and make the relationship a success providing that we had entered into this partnership in good faith and straightforward intent. (My gullibility was beyond all redemption!). It is and was beyond my power to know with certainty how dedicated and honorable my husband's motives were. Yet judging from his continual persistence and persuasiveness, it certainly appeared that his commitment to the union was sincere and honorable. He also had many positive attributes in his favor. He belonged to an honorable industrious family. He was reputed to be an exceptionally skillful worker. Besides, his spirited and dashing nature made him very popular with the youth in the entourage.

Whether or not John, my husband, had firmly resolved to make this relationship a success is irrelevant for I on the other hand was determined, doggedly unflinchingly determined that it would, come hell or perdition. I was willing to sacrifice everything of no major importance, trifles (bagatelles as they are referred to in French) in order to attain harmony in this partnership. Indeed, inconsequential trivialities meant very little to me. Petty frivolous habits could easily be abandoned and negligible details such as ethnic methods of meal preparation, or for that matter ethnic cuisines, were all immaterial to me. These details were however very important to my husband. Therefore I made every effort to conform to his cultural customs. This, however, is sooner said than done and often my efforts were a complete disaster. It is utterly incomprehensible to many newly married husbands that their recently espoused wife cannot prepare a meal "the way my mother did". How could I adapt to the ways of his people when these ways were oblivious to me. Indeed my incompetence soon manifested itself as inadequacy (of which I was constantly reminded) and teamed up with " la bête noire" to plunge me into the abyss of unworthiness. Yet all these minor inconveniences were tolerable. It was, however, the disparity between his and my concept of right and wrong that was crucially problematic. What was prohibited in my moral code of ethics was accepted as a matter of course by his moral standards. Moral values and conduct were the issues that were irreconcilable. These were the cause of all our disagreements and distress.

In retrospect, it seems incredible that I did not stand up for my beliefs, my moral values. Perhaps I was still gyrating in a daze from the violent pirouette destiny had inflicted upon me. On the other hand, I felt that perhaps the guilt for all the conflicts lay upon my shoulders. Consequently, I endured the tirades in silence. But I was miserable! Meditating about that episode, it seems likely that I was becoming an anonymity, or in other words, a robot. Without the liberty to express my feelings, my thoughts, or my convictions, my individuality had been utterly wiped out. It is of little wonder that people referred to me, not as a separate entity, but as John's wife. And that is one of the world's most despicable calamities, as its occurrence is rampart wherever the human race exists. In a frantic attempt to live in peace, or at least attain some sort of harmony, many prefer to relinquish their individual rights gradually almost without being aware of what is happening, until it is too late. Unfortunately, their personalities become void, bland, and inconsequential. Indeed, they become mere shadows of their spouses and are known only as someone's wife or husband. Some reluctantly resign themselves to accept being subservient to their domineering partner forever. (But that was not my intent at least not when the future of my loved ones was involved.)

While meditating seriously and profoundly along this line of thought (perhaps straying somewhat from my theme) it occurred to me that the whole world is ruled by this oppressing phenomena. On the international scene supremacy lies in the hands of a few powerful nations. Supposedly autonomous nations are under the yoke of these giants and must acquiesce to their dictates under threat of disciplinary action. In order to maintain peaceful relations lesser nations must yield to the demands of the strong. How exorbitant is the price one must pay for peace! Yet the alternative is too ghastly to even be considered.

Yet, when I contemplate and meditate about this situation, trying to analyze the grave repercussions that ensued from this most irresponsible decision, I realize that the culpability was mine. In the first place, it was glaringly evident that two individuals with such incompatible aspirations and personalities could ever be reconciled. Secondly, it is purely wishful thinking to assume that a person can suddenly abandon his life style and be transformed into someone that will meet someone else's specifications or standards. And I, being most gullible, firmly believed that these hopeless obstacles could be overcome. Besides, being tenaciously determined to make our marriage a success I was willing to make any kind of concessions, therefore I never insisted that my rights be respected. Looking back, I honestly believe that my fiancée was sincere and that he also hoped that our marriage would succeed. After all these years, it has finally occurred to me that my husband did not have a clue, not even an inkling as to the cause of my distress. According to his standards our relationship should have been out-of-this-world.

For many years we made a desperate attempt to reconcile our differences. These years were years of misery. Not only were we unable to agree on the most crucial issues and aspects of life but we couldn't even come to terms concerning paltry immaterial trifles. We struggled on through what seemed an eternity during which there were several separations followed by desperate attempts at reconciliation.

When, at last, that most difficult year was over, we decided to visit my folks in Leoville. My sister Hélène had celebrated her marriage to Herbert Jansen in the spring. I was unable to attend. John found it extremely difficult to accept the simple small town ways, especially the fact that most people spoke French. Although most were courteous and mannerly enough not to speak French when English people were present, often the conversation reverted back to the vernacular. In spite of the fact that it was not done intentionally, my husband found this offensive. (It was perfectly justifiable.)

While visiting my parents in Leoville some major incidents transpired, incidents that were to significantly alter the plans that I had envisioned for the future. These changes were contingent upon the fact that I became convinced beyond any doubt that I was pregnant. It had been indeed obvious for some time, but I as always living in a world of fantasy hoped that by some miracle it wasn't so, thinking that perhaps some major problems could be solved before assuming such an enormous responsibility. I was torn between feelings of joy and apprehension; the joy of becoming a mother mixed with the fear for the well being of the child. To make matters worse, I had accepted a teaching position in the southern part of Saskatchewan. There was no way under any circumstances that anyone could have persuaded me to venture into an unfamiliar environment and dare to assume a new position in my condition. I was full of misgivings and the summer was nearly over before I could muster up enough courage to write that school board a letter of apology. That was after my mother's anxiety concerning the urgency of the matter prompted her to pressurize me to do so. It is most regrettable that my problem caused such inconveniences to so many. Alas it is too late to make amends.

It was great to be with my own people and in my own environment, but the problems that ensued emanating from the (would be) ideal situation were most complicated. It seemed that I was always coerced to assume the role of a mediator, trying desperately to maintain peace and reach some semblance of a compromise that would assuage the disagreements that emerged from controversial and delicate issues. Being in the middle between dissenting parties is a most vulnerable position indeed. It means being assaulted, buffeted from all sides. There is no possible escape.

It all started with the language issue! Although they made a sincere effort to do so, it was almost unreasonable to expect my parents to revert to a language that was foreign to them. French was their maternal language and had always been spoken in the home. Then there was the firewood problem! But that is another story. Be that as it may, I always felt squashed between extremely controversial forces.

It was indeed a blessing, considering the circumstances, that I was able to get a teaching position close to Leoville. The small rural school was about five miles (as the crow flies) from home with an enrolment of approximately twenty-five students, mostly native children. These children were just amazing! They were highly motivated, cooperative, and didn't have any discipline problems. After that first brutal teaching experience it felt like being released from the lions' mouth into paradise.

The problems that existed were not related to my teaching assignment, but were rather personal problems. It had been understood that I would lodge (along with my husband) at the home of the local storekeeper's family. It was a perfect arrangement. Unfortunately, I imagined that that most gracious lady was flirting with my husband and I became insanely jealous. It may have been just an assumption as being pregnant I may have been over sensitive. However, I mused, should there be one grain of faithlessness in their badinage, it would not be flaunted under my very nose. So I decided to find lodging somewhere else. There was a small one-roomed log cabin on the premises that would serve the purpose. Consequently I began at once to clean the cabin, wallpaper the walls, and make the place a temporary shelter. In fact, in a quaint sort of fashion it was almost cozy! Indeed in spite of its modesty, it was my own, a home where the privacy I desired abounded.

It was that secluded little niche that got me into a great deal of trouble. Of course there was no electricity or central gas heating. Light was provided by a kerosene lamp and heat by a wood burning furnace or heater. It was the homeowner's responsibility to provide enough fuel for his needs. This fuel or firewood was from the woods that surrounds every village and farm in the vicinity. Of course the trees had to be felled, the logs sawed into appropriate lengths and split before it could be used for fuel. For some reason my husband insisted that it was the responsibility of the local farmers to provide this service. I, of course thought this was utterly unreasonable. Nevertheless after many altercations, I was coerced to make this requisition at a special school board meeting. The board came to the conclusion that such a request was preposterous (that had been my opinion all along, I considered myself fortunate indeed to be employed!) and it was denied. The humiliation that I suffered emanating from that incidence was excruciating. Allowing yourself to be persuaded in performing something that is against your better judgment is most unwise. Throughout my life the wisdom of this truth has been constantly reiterated, yet I have repeatedly fallen in the same error. No wonder wise men (like Bob Dillon) sing, "When will we ever learn, when will we ever learn?"

Many joyful events occurred at the school during that term. The children put on a school concert, there was a school picnic, and a field day, all of which proved to be very successful and appreciated by the residents of the district. There was, however, one shocking episode that has tormented my soul with anguish ever since. Its horrific image flashes back in my mind's eye. (Woodward would say.) On that memorable October evening, the evening when the natives got their treaty money, their tepees were pitched in the woods near the store close to the school grounds. All the adults in the camp were celebrating. They apparently had used their newly found riches to buy extracts in lieu of food for their unfortunate children. There was pandemonium everywhere as the merrymakers, overcome with liquor, danced and sang all around the buildings, even around my tiny shack. I was scared to death, fearing that they might try to come in. It was the plight of the children that filled my heart with dread, transcending the fear for my own safety. Cold, hungry, miserable, these pitiful creatures were walking barefooted in the snow and weeping mournfully. I still feel their suffering, hear their cries as that image flashes back continually before me.

All these events however appear utterly insignificant in comparison to the miracle that transpired during the early months of that year. For it was in February of that year in the tiny hospital of Meadow Lake that my first child was born. I was so overjoyed that it was a boy so I could name him Walter, after the boy who had so generously given us his high school books, thus enabling both my sister and I to graduate. When I held the child in my arms I was filled with wonder. It was incredible that this amazing miraculous new life could be my own. The nurse was exasperated when she was tormented by a barrage of questions. "Was the child normal? Did he have all ten fingers and ten toes?" Etcetera.

It wasn't all a garden of roses however. To begin with, it had been a very difficult birth. For the first time in my life I really thought that death was at the door. I woke up reciting the Lord's Prayer. The anesthetic they had given me must have been very strong because either from its after effects or from weakness I lost my ability to see for almost a whole week. It was a frightening experience! Besides, the medical staff was feuding; consequently everyone was under a great deal of stress, including the patients. Indeed the head nurse decided to push me around when she was making my bed soon after the delivery. Her behavior was intolerable and I refused to be treated that way. "If you don't feel like helping me, or that you are doing it reluctantly, please let me be. I am fine and do not need you, so please go away." I said. Apparently that simple rebuke was all that nurse needed. She quit bullying the rest of the staff around, including the doctor. It is not surprising that the rest of the staff was most grateful and thanked me profusely.

Then my husband decided to celebrate the birth of his son. Not with ice cream and cake mind you, but by drowning himself in a barrel of alcohol. Thus, he was intoxicated when he arrived at the hospital. Consequently his behavior, his speech and his demeanor in general lacked a great deal of polish. I was so embarrassed, so humiliated! On the other hand, the birth of a child is indeed an irrefutable justification to celebrate. Unfortunately, partying was the furthest thing from my mind at the moment. It was a blessing when all the commotion was over and I was finally allowed to rest in peace. The hospital staff made light of the whole thing telling me that it was typical for a first time father to celebrate boisterously. But that did not make me feel any better.

I resumed my teaching duties at the school soon after Walter was born. A local girl named Rose, agreed to care for the baby during the day. She was an absolute angel. She was devoted to the baby, and did minor household chores without making any commotion.

Her calm accommodating nature created a relaxed and tranquil ambience in that modest adobe. Many years later, I learned that she had been the victim of a heinous crime. She was murdered by one of her grandchildren, which makes it more horrendous. "Why" one wonders, "must such a tragedy be the destiny of the innocent." Her tragic fate has caused me a great deal of sorrow. Wherever she may be, she will always be a jewel in my heart.

Ensuing from the firewood incident and a few other glitches, it is not surprising that the school board did not renew my contract for the following year. Teachers were in great demand as many had enlisted to go overseas during the war. I soon had a position further south near the Manitoba border in the community of White Beach. Although Porcupine School was a one-room rural school it was more modern and better equipped than most. For instance, it had a well-stocked library, and the children were adequately provided with textbooks and supplies. There was a neat little cabin on the grounds for the teacher's convenience. The residents were accommodating in every possible way, offering their assistance when it was needed or generously donating their farm products to the local teacher. Although the challenge that the situation demanded was rather stringent, (that is teaching students from grade one to grade ten in one room) the cooperation and good will of the parents made it all worthwhile. It also gave the teachers (me for one) the initiative to devote themselves entirely and with enthusiasm to the children entrusted in their care.

Perhaps that impish destiny decided to give me a break and stop temporarily spinning me around; using me as the butt of its shenanigans; its razzle-dazzle for its own diversion. Be that as it may, I was delighted to find a most auspicious family in the district. It is true that most of the residents were cordial and neighborly but that family was unique. At first I thought that their kindness to me derived from the fact that we were of the same national origin, but soon it became quite apparent that every one in that family lived by the golden rule, always ready to help a neighbor regardless of the inconveniences involved. As soon as it became known in the community that I was alone with a small child with no means of transportation, they adopted me and Walter as their own. They always made sure that we were provided with our needs. We were welcomed to celebrate holidays such as Christmas and Easter with the family, sharing the special festive meals with them. Although there were many in that household, each member was, and will always be, a treasured brother or sister. I will always cherish the memory of each one of them in my heart.

Elizabeth Assoignon with holding Walter and David

It was Elizabeth, the third oldest girl in the family that volunteered to care for Walter. That girl must have been a veritable angel sent straight from heaven, complete with celestial wings, to assist me in my need. She was out-of-this-world. She showered that child with love and affection. She read to him, told him stories, and taught him the myriad of concepts that every child learns in childhood including acceptable social behavior. She treated him as solicitously as if he had been her very own. Wherever she may dwell in the heavenly kingdom, I hope that she knows that I will always treasure her memory and forever be grateful to her for the devotion and care she gave my son. Along this endless journey upon which we tread, Providence sometimes smiles upon us, bestowing upon our path the blessing of one such as Elizabeth. Then a feeling of warmth and wonder engulfs the soul, an illuminating revelation that it was all worthwhile.

The saying "it was too good to be true" has some merits. Indeed Elizabeth was too good to be true or to be taken for granted. Soon a local boy came courting and stole her away from me after she was married (both Walter and I were miserable when she left) her sister Mary mercifully came to help me. She also was a wonderful person. This is not surprising considering her background; the superior caliber of the home where she was raised and the nobility of her parents.

The four years that I taught at Porcupine School were happy years. The children were well behaved and most were quite intelligent. There were a few Doukhobor families but a large majority of the residents were of Ukrainian origin, with the exception of my friends, who were from France. Some of the parents did not speak English but the children that were of school age all did, therefore there was no language problem in the classroom. This was indeed a blessing as it is difficult enough to teach all ten levels, from grade one to grade ten in one classroom! I was becoming more experienced; learning by trial and error, from my mistakes, and by experimenting with new improved teaching methods. It was difficult to achieve excellence in the circumstances involved.

Jeannette Romaniuk

There were too many obstacles. The most serious of these was the creation of a program and a schedule that would keep the children at all levels of achievement gainfully employed while the teacher taught a specific group. Besides, all working equipment was so outmoded that all seatwork assignment had to be duplicated by hand. There was a form of duplicating gadget in the school, but it worked so poorly that it was more advantageous to copy each sheet by hand. It is not surprising that before an examination the teacher had to work all night in order to duplicate enough papers for each student. Modern machines and equipment would have made teaching so much easier. Be that as it may, I enjoyed my work so unconditionally that none of these obstacles appeared to be particularly problematic. I was determined to succeed.

It was during these four years that many outstandingly significant developments transpired, events that may have been instrumental in the path my future destiny proceeded. At the end of the first year, during the summer vacation, I went back to the University of Saskatoon for the second six-week session of my teacher-training course. It was a summer filled with poignant and stirring events. It was then that my parents visited me as they were on their way to the coast. They had planned to relocate, making Toxedo Island their home. It was a very emotional reunion as it was unexpected and they had very little time. It was the last time that I saw my mother. I was utterly devastated when I beheld what fate had decreed upon them. It broke my heart. There they were in their declining years, without any resources whatsoever, leaving their home, and going to an unknown environment, in an effort to hack out a living and subside in a strange and disadvantageous manner. How tragic is the fate of the unfortunate whom destiny has singled out to vent its wrath. Yet all these years in my sub-conscious I have been haunted by an excruciating burden of guilt, an obsession that somehow I should have been there for them. It is no wonder night after night my dreams are filled with a never ending search, a fruitless search for a decent home for my parents. In these nightmares, one building after another is discarded as unsuitable, yet though the search continues throughout the night it is always hopeless.

It was also during that summer that I discovered that I was pregnant with my second child. Although the birth of a child is a blessed event, I could not rejoice. The future seemed so uncertain, and my unhappiness was too real. My room mate must have sensed the confusion that troubled me for she offered to adopt my unborn child. Her husband was an Anglican minister thus the child would have had a good and stable home. However it was beyond my moral values to gamble with a child's destiny. Yet there was a constant nagging premonition in the back of my mind that these children were to be my responsibility, and mine alone. The future proved to be undeniable verification that my premonition was indeed valid.

David was born on the fifteenth of March in Benito, Manitoba during my second year of teaching at Porcupine School. As usual, I was alone and someone else had to take me to the nursing home in that town as the nearest hospital was probably in Yorkton. It had been a severe winter and the snowplows were kept busy maintaining the roads. In some sections of the highway, the snow was piled nearly fifteen feet high on either side of the road. It was amazing! In fact the snow was so deep that some of the roofs crumpled under its crushing weight.

My husband and I decided to buy a half section of land in the district. We had planned to make it our home when I quit teaching. There was a little house on the property that with some renovations would have made a comfortable home for our family. We bought a small tractor, an Alis Chalmer, and for a time it seemed that we would become local farmers. It was very exciting. I learned how to drive the tractor. On holidays I enjoyed doing work in the fields such as disking, plowing, or harrowing. Later, the boys were ecstatic about their newly found freedom. One day they decided to try their hand at driving the tractor. Both of them were sitting on the seat and managed to start the engine. They were aiming straight for the garage. The doors of the garage were open; therefore they would have gone straight through had I not seen what was happening. My heart skipped a beat. I let out a most ungodly screech which alerted everyone on the premises then dashed to the rescue. But it was the boys' father that got there first just in time to save the day. The boys? Well they were not too keen about driving the tractor for a long time.

The boys and I were thrilled about the prospect of living on the farm. We'd live there during the summer even though we had to walk to school, then we'd move back to the teacher's residence in the fall. We hoped that some day we might make it our home. But again unforeseen circumstances intervened.

During my fourth year at the school my third child was born. We were delighted that it was a little girl. We named her Juliette after her aunt and a dear friend of mine. She was born on the third of December, at home. A local woman delivered her. She was indeed little, but from the moment she was born her strength of character was evident. She was baptized on Christmas Eve and my friends became the godparents.

After Juliette was born, it became evident that teaching would be difficult so John and I decided that we should try to make a go of it at the farm. I gave the school board my resignation. A crop of wheat was in the process of being harvested promising sufficient funds to provide for our needs. But it was not to be! Things began to happen; things that left me disillusioned and utterly devastated. For one thing the mortgage payment on the land was not made, although I had made the provisions to have it effectuated. Then the crop was supposed to be so poor that it would certainly not be sufficient to provide for our needs. At least that was the information that was disclosed to me which was not so. And there was more! It went on and on. As I uncovered each one of these fabrications, I became more and more apprehensive. My anxiety escalated until it became almost intolerable.

"What was the rationale behind all this bogus, this misrepresentation of the truth? " I asked myself." Was it a gimmick that would inconspicuously facilitate the accumulation of a nest egg, a reserve fund, that could be used to gratify one's pleasure, or was it that I was supposedly too stupid to uncover the truth and that no one would ever be the wiser?" Be that as it may, the truth always did surface, somehow or other. It is indeed very strange that when one is intent on destroying another he/she tries to do it furtively, behind closed doors, trying desperately to conceal the deed. This makes it doubly painful, a double whammy, for not only is there the agony of being crushed, but the victim is being told that he's too stupid to know what's happening.

Well, after all these shenanigans, it was evident that if we were to survive it would through my efforts. I had handed in my resignation, consequently it was too late to resume my duties as a teacher in the local school, or in any other district for that matter as it was already late in September and the fall term was well on its way. Fortunately, some schools in British Columbia had started the term later that fall and I was able to get a position in the northern part of that province. I was to teach in a rural school just north of Vanderhoof in a district that was predominately of Dutch origin.

The departure was somewhat difficult. It meant that a vehicle had to be purchased in order to take our belongings and of course the kids. Leaving the children with some friends, we went to Winnipeg to purchase a second hand car. Then we loaded it with all our earthly possessions including the canned fruit and vegetables, and we were off. I will never forget that journey! It was my first trip across the mountains. The car was unreliable, dangerously overloaded and many times it did not have enough power to make it all the way up a steep incline, then it would slide all the way back to the foot of the hill. It was terrifying!

All the way across these mountains I was frantic with terror, a fear for the safety of the children that was so overwhelming that the magnificent splendor, the breath-taking beauty of these lofty elevations remained unobserved and unappreciated. My thoughts were exclusively (heart and soul) consumed in prayer, imploring the Blessed Virgin to pray for us. Although there were several unpleasant incidences on the way before we reached our destination, we finally arrived safe and sound.

There was a modest but comfortable residence for the convenience of the teacher. It was situated near one of the local resident's home. This was a safety precaution, as the school was surrounded by a dense growth of tall trees which provided a veritable sanctuary for all kinds of wild animals. Most of these animals did not pose a threat to humans but some species of bears like the grizzly and black bears have been known to attack anything or anyone that appears to invade or trespass on their territory. Cougars also had been seen in the vicinity. Therefore no chances were being taken when safety was involved. Had the teacher's residence been located near the school the lone occupant would have been beyond help. It is astonishing however that the local people seemed unconcerned about my safety for I had to walk approximately a mile and a half through that thickly wooded area to and from the school building. Those woods were the moose's alleged paradise for they strolled through the area with the majesty that pertains to the proprietor (or the lord of the manor) only. Although I felt somewhat intimidated by the hordes of these huge animals, I was fascinated by the beauty of these noble creatures. Fortunately, they paid no attention to me, accepting me as one of their own.

Most of the residents were of Dutch origin. They spoke what they referred to as low German. They lived by the dictates of a severe moral code following the criterion of a strictly puritanical religious belief. The children were well behaved conforming cheerfully to acceptable routines and attending to their schoolwork with dedication. I really enjoyed working with these children.

There were a few unpleasant incidents, but all in all the year we spent in Vanderhoof would have been a success had things remained normal. But alas that was not to be. David complained that he had a pain in the lower part of his body. At first, it did not seem to be too serious, so I hoped that it would go away, but as the pain persisted and kept getting worse, it became evident that the child needed to see a doctor. As usual, I was on my own with no means of transportation, and the nearest town was fifteen miles away. The situation demanded immediate action. So I asked my neighbor to take the child to the hospital. Now this neighbor had his nose out of joint because my husband had left me in an hopeless situation and he refused to help. I didn't know what to do. David's illness was getting desperate. He moaned day and night with intolerable pain. It appeared that no one else in that district had a vehicle. Frantic with anxiety, I approached my neighbor again. "Sir" I said, "If you don't find it in your heart to take a child who is critically ill to see a doctor, and no one else is able or willing to help me, this district is not an environment suitable for me. My resignation will be forwarded followed by my departure". The man's wife then came to my rescue. "If you don't take that child who is critically ill to the hospital," she said, "you are a monster." That did it. That very day David was taken to the hospital in Vanderhoof.

As soon as the doctor examined David, he knew that the child would need immediate surgery as his condition was critical. Indeed his condition was so serious that he was on the operating table for four hours. The doctor later said that he was doubtful about the success of the procedure although he did his utmost to repair the damages to the internal tissues. David did recover however due mostly to the dedication and competence of this skillful doctor and partly to the strength of his physical health.

A friend of mine tells me that she cannot write the story of her life or even think about it because it is too painful. I understand how she feels, for there are certain events in my life so devastating that they are best forgotten. This episode of my life is impregnated with anguish and recriminations, events that mercifully should remain buried under the deepest bowels of the earth, and forgotten into the abyss of time never to be unearthed.

Subsequent to David's near fatal illness and the fact that I was pregnant, I made a most crucial decision. It was a decision that was to have significant implications on the future of the family. It was evident that the situation was untenable, so I made up my mind to stay home and take care of my children. Amazingly John, my husband agreed that in the future he would provide for his family. At the time he worked in Penny, a mill town in the north of British Columbia. The company provided living accommodations for their employees, so the family settled in a company house upon arrival. It seemed that our lives w to be, at least for the time being, normal.

Two major events occurred while we were in that town. Carol was born in the fall of that year, on September the sixth. She was born at home, but a registered nurse delivered her and came to help with her care every day for some time afterwards. Her father chose the name Caroline. She brought a great deal of joy to the household.

The other incident was outrageous. It is an incidence that occurred in the community, without involving anyone in my family. However, because it involved the abuse of a child, it has left a bad taste in my mouth. It happened that a young man in his twenties molested a four year old child while babysitting. The case was brought to court and the young man was sentenced to a year in prison. Although the sentence was an abomination in itself, the reaction of the residents in the district transcendent the malpractice of the judicial system. For in the courts of law, it is a well known that justice is often interpreted in terms of who has the best lawyer which is in turn contingent on who has the most money. Therefore the leniency of the sentence did not surprise anyone. The young man's family belonged to the most prestigious, elite circle in town. What was despicable indeed was the fact that instead of sympathizing with the victim's family the whole town turned against them. They were ostracized and were compelled to sell their home and move away. Again the victim was penalized for the transgressor's crime.

I cannot recall the catastrophic incident that transpired soon after Carol was born. It is a complete blank. Perhaps it is so painful that my subconscious has buried it forever. It must have been irreconcilable indeed to have prompted such inordinate reaction on my part. Be that as it may, I packed my children, all my belongings, the whole kit and caboodle and left.

For a short time I stayed with my sister Germaine in Big River, a town in northern Saskatchewan. Then I stayed with my other sister Yvonne who lived in Bodmin, a district not far from Big River. Soon after I arrived, I got a teaching position in a remote district of northern Saskatchewan called Sled Lake.

There were many complications. I could not take the children with me of course, and their welfare was my primary concern. Fortunately, Yvonne agreed to care for the three youngest ones. (The terms of this agreement are also buried in the past.) Walter was to come with me. I will forever be grateful to my sisters, Yvonne and Germaine for the help and support they gave me during that precarious time. They opened their doors to my family and helped me care for my children. They assisted me in every way possible. I will forever be grateful to them.

Sled Lake is in the remote wilderness of northern Saskatchewan. The Forest Rangers must have taken me as there was little means of transportation. The school was situated near the lake in a district that was predominantly native. It was the school building that was particularly spectacular about this neck of the woods. It was a log shack. Not the common run of the mill log shack, but a dilapidated hastily put together log shack. The teacher's living quarters were part of this monstrosity and were even in a worst condition than the main part of the building, if that were possible. The roof was not waterproof and when it rained everything was soaking wet. The worst problem was the lack of safe drinking water. The residents used the lake water for all their needs, but that I refused to do, as the people threw all their trash in it. I had been fortunate in finding a spring in the deep woods about a mile away and used that source as our water supply. It was dangerous to venture alone in the woods as Sled Lake is the home of many wild animals. I was terrified of coming face to face with a bear.

There were on the other hand many positive aspects to consider. For one thing, I was positively enchanted by the beauty of the lake. It was surrounded by great majestic trees and its waters stretched endlessly, as far as the eye could see. Once a student took Walter and me for a boat ride across that great lake. We were both fascinated by the reflection of the setting sun in the waters. It was an unforgettable moment.

Perhaps the most spectacular aspect about that milieu was that there lived in that far remote wilderness, a man that was a master craftsman. He had married a native woman, and it is possible that he had learned the craft from her people. Be that as it may, he fashioned the most exquisite birch bark canoes I have ever seen, even in the movies. Every detail was meticulously constructed and assembled. The finished product was a work of art, a chef d'oeuvre. It is not clear what he did with these masterpieces, but he probably had many clients.

I was greatly impressed by this man's wife. She was the embodiment of grace and good manners. It seemed strange to meet a lady of such refinement in such a remote area.

A family lived not far from the school. The husband hated city life and had decided to live a secluded existence away from civilization. The couple depended mostly on hunting and fishing for their needs. That man probably saved my life. One of the students had taken Walter and me for a ride on the lake and although both of us enjoyed ourselves tremendously, we had failed to dress appropriately. As a consequence I came down with a severe case of pneumonia. I could hardly breathe! Fortunately that gentleman had a third of a bottle of brandy which he most generously sent me. When I couldn't get my breath I'd take a tablespoon of brandy and it helped. Finally the Forest Rangers had to take me to Big River for treatment. With antibiotics and rest I was able to recuperate.

The summer following the sojourn in Sled Lake is a complete blank except for an isolated spasmodic glimpse that flashes back and forth in the murky shadows. Often I see myself, late at night when the children are in bed, sitting at the table and studying till the wee hours of the morning. Then there is the cookie baking flash back, when Louis and Charles (my nephews) joined my crew and the cookies were all gone as soon as they came out of the oven. There are some incidents that are so blurred that the exact time in which they occurred cannot be ascertained. For instance, at first the children and I lived with Yvonne and her family. It soon occurred to me that we were imposing on their privacy. Again Providence intervened. Germaine had a vacant cabin in Big River that was available. It was moved to Bodmin near Yvonne's home and completely renovated. It is uncertain what agreement had been made for the use of the cabin. The cabin was right in the midst of an area teeming with a dense growth of gigantic spruce trees. The movers had placed the cabin on government land; therefore my situation was a little bit precarious, "iffy" at best. But my father insisted that in our country, squatters had inalienable rights and that the law would protect me. Be that as it may, a government inspector came to inspect the premises. After assessing the situation, he shook his head, shrugged his shoulders and without saying one word, left. I was in my seventh heaven, living in a comfortable little cabin situated in the woods (just where my heart longed to be) safe with my loved ones, and free from constant persecution.

I did not go back to the school in Sled Lake. In September I taught in a rural school called Winter Lake situated close to my sister's house in Bodmin. It was about two miles from the cabin. Every morning the four of us, Lorraine, Joe, Walter, and I walked to the school, rain or shine. The children or students in that district were amazing. Their academic development was excellent and because of their co-operation disciplinary problems were none existent. The superintendent was impressed by the academic performance of the students, especially of those in grade one who were performing at a second year level. It broke my heart when this gentleman asked me if he (and his wife) could adopt my unborn child.

Lucille was born on November nineteenth, in Prince Albert, Saskatchewan. She was very precious, even though my concern for the welfare of these children was indeed a continual worry.

In spite of the enormous responsibilities, the endless workload, and ever-present anxiety for the well being of the children, I felt that there might be some hope for us in the future. Actually we were happy in our little woodland kingdom. But it was not to be. My husband found out where we were and came for us. I did not want to go back. Once you have had a taste of paradise it is an ordeal to go back to perdition, in fact, it is a regular nightmare! It was the same old story, things were going to be different, gambling and drinking were in the past, and my husband was going to be a good father and provider for his family. Ultimately, I let myself be persuaded to go back. But I had serious misgivings.

It is unfathomable that I have never been able to stand up in my own defense. What makes it even more incomprehensible is the fact that when standing up in protest when someone else's rights have been infringed upon, I am undaunted. With threatening claws and baring fangs I charge with the ferocity of a banshee warrior, a fury that would intimidate the bravest of the brave. Many times, the validity and justification of my argument has been recognized in that manner. (These incidences will be related further on in this narrative). It is only in my own defense that cowardice assails me, or perhaps it is the mischief of la bète noire that is incessantly tormenting me.

Little had changed in Penny. At first, John tried to keep his promises. We kept pretty much to ourselves, although the next-door neighbor and I often had coffee together. We were good friends. She had two boys and a girl who played with my children all the time.

Then all hell broke loose! I was pregnant again. When I told my husband he began to laugh. Something in my head must have snapped for I went hysterical, completely berserk! This inferno was intolerable and it seemed that there was no way out. There was only one thing in my mind. "This is the end. I cannot go on like this." Distraught and beside myself with desperation, I rushed madly out the door, aiming straight for the river where I was going to drown myself. This madness would be over, forever. What would have happened if John had not stopped me is questionable for I was freaked out, completely out of control. At that moment, I was insane, stark raving mad. There is truth in the theory of temporary moments of insanity claiming that in a moment of extreme agitation, an individual will commit actions that are inordinate and are inconsistent with their personality.

Shortly after this episode, John bought a house in Willow River, a town not far from Penny. It was a comfortable though modest dwelling with adequate space and facilities to meet our needs. For a time the comfort of living in my own home with the children sort of placated the horrible premonition of peril that troubled me constantly. The people in the immediate neighborhood were friendly, many of them went out of their way to make us feel welcome in their midst. One of these ladies, a Mrs. Brown, would come and help with the laundry every week, which was no minor undertaking. Doing the laundry for six kids and two adults is an all day affair, no less. Nevertheless this dedicated lady came every week without fail. On one of these occasions, she couldn't open a bleach bottle and after struggling for some time to open it she decided to use a more drastic measure. She put the top of the bottle between the open door and the frame and closed the door, or at least she tried to close it. At once the bottle exploded; the bleach splashing in all directions, all over her clothes, on her face, and most regrettably into her eyes. I was frantic! In spite of our extreme fright, we did not let our panic prevent us from rushing into immediate action. She and I kept splashing water in her eyes while someone else provided us with pail after pail of water. When the burning eased, I phoned her daughter. The doctor in the emergency ward at the hospital said that we had acted judiciously, and that our clear thinking had saved Mrs. Brown's eyesight.

Our next-door neighbor was a widow who had recently lost her husband. Every aspect of that lady's personality was exceptional. She was indeed a most unique individual. She had been endowed with a remarkable gift, she could feel things and had premonitions about situations and events that were far away from her immediate surroundings. She was in fact a clairvoyant. Sometimes that six sense she possessed was so powerful it extorted her to do the most extraordinary quest. The following is an account that relates one of these strange adventures.

"I was going for a walk one day," she said, " when I felt a sudden urgency to follow a path that led through woods. As I walked along this trail, I wondered where it was taking me, thinking that it was time to go back home. Yet the compulsion to go on was so powerful (it was as if someone had been pushing me from behind) that I kept on walking. At last I came to an abandoned building. Again I felt that urge to go in. As soon as I entered the building I called out but no one answered. There was however a weird sound, like the sound of the wind in the woods during a storm. It was eerie, low and moaning. It gave me the creeps. In spite of my apprehension I began to search the building trying to find out where the sound was coming from. My search led me to a room where a woman lay moaning with the last throes of death, and there beside her lay an infant child. I did everything that could possibly be done under the circumstances. Then, as fast as my legs could go, literally flew to get help. Afterwards I kept wondering constantly if God had inspired me or coercively driven me along that unbeaten path leading to the building where help was so crucially needed. Surely only He has the power to do so!"

There were countless other instances when this magnanimous woman's intuition led her to situations where someone was in a crisis and she mercifully assisted them in their moment of dire need. She said that when she had a premonition, or a feeling of apprehension, she felt that it was a warning that someone was in trouble and needed help. She would open the Bible randomly and the scripture would guide her to the source of the problem besides giving her the insight relative to its solution. She was indeed a saintly woman, spending most of her days in prayer. On many occasions, she invited me to pray with her. We would kneel together, each one talking to the Lord in her own way, for we did not belong to the same religious traditions. But that is of course immaterial, for the Lord is impartial, thus He does not restrict the direction from which we approach Him.

This exceptional lady was unique in many ways, so many that it is impossible to do justice to all her meritorious characteristics. In the short time that I associated with her it was impossible to make a complete analysis of her personality. There are many things about her that have, however remained deeply rooted in my memory. For instance, she lived in a very tiny house. On every wall of that tiny, tiny house she had taped every card, every souvenir that her loved ones had sent her through the years. She claimed that when she looked at each item it made her feel that the one who had sent it was there in person with her. She will always be in my heart.

An incident that transpired while we were in Willow River is most distressing. A two-year-old child lived across the river from his grandparents' house. The grandparents, especially the grandfather, adored that child. During the winter months when the river was covered with ice, the grandfather would go back and forth across the frozen water to get the child and take him back home. Unfortunately, one day the child decided to go across on his own. It was late in the spring and the ice was not safe. Consequently the poor child fell through the thin ice. It was a tragedy that rocked the whole town. Every able-bodied man, woman, and child in the town were out searching for the poor little mite except John. My husband did not join the search. He claimed that it did not concern us. Yet my heart ached for the family. When the child was found it was too late. The funeral for that toddler was one of the most heart breaking incidences I have ever experienced.

The boys remember one event that took place before we left, an event that frightened them and could have had serious consequences. There was a small storage shed beside the house used to store miscellaneous items. At the time it was more than half full of beer bottles. The boys must have sneaked some matches and brought them to the shed. Apparently they wanted to have a fire in the shed, but neither of them realized the danger that can emanate from fire that is not controlled. Be that as it may, when the adults noticed it the flames had already engulfed the building and everyone was on the alert for the safety of the house. By this time both boys realized the gravity of their mischief and feared the consequences. Walter told me later that although it was David who stole the matches and started the fire, he was the one who was punished.

Things went from bad to worse. Although the constant partying and carousing ceased to be a problem for me as my house was out of bounds mercifully. It didn't bother me in the least until I was urged in no uncertain terms to join the merry-making in spite of fact that I had a house full of children. That I refused to do, insisting that when you have children, the party is over. That, of course, did not go over too well.

Then Lucille had an abscess on her seat. She cried continually day and night. I kept insisting that she be taken to the doctor. But no matter how much I begged and stormed, it fell on deaf ears. This had been going on for some time when in desperation I asked my husband's friend (one of those he had been partying with, no less) to take me. To my surprise, he took the child to the hospital at once. The doctor kept Lucille in the hospital for a week and did not release her until there was no danger of infection after he had lanced the abscess. It appears that Lucille became a celebrity in the children's ward.

The most spectacular event and the highlight of our sojourn in Willow River was during the year Charles was born. He was born in Prince George on the twenty-fifth of November (just one day before my birthday) after a mad rush to the hospital. It was "Zero-hour" but the receptionist was unaware of this so she assaulted me with a barrage of questions that seemed completely irrelevant. At that point I didn't even know my own name." Why doesn't someone answer these questions?" I thought to myself mournfully. Mercifully a staff member realizing my plight came to my rescue and rushed me upstairs to the delivery room.

Charles was special in many different ways. Physically, perhaps due to the fact that he was premature, he had a heart murmur which according to the doctors was not serious. He also had double pupils and webbed toes. The most significant factor concerning his physical condition was the fact that he was starving all the time. He could never get enough food, at least not enough to satisfy his extraordinary appetite. Providing sufficient nourishment for him was such an endless occupation that at times I did not have the opportunity to have a decent meal which did not bother me in the least. My sister once told me that when he lived at her house, after he had finished his meal, he would make himself a potato sandwich which he devoured as if it had been the rarest of delicacy. His physical traits were not what made him stand out. His siblings referred to him as the "brain" of the family. He was indeed an intellectual. Truly he was one of those who are born with a book in their hands, or more specifically born reading a book. .

As time went on, I realized that staying home with my children was a fantasy, something that was too good to be true. There were things that were intolerable. For instance, leaving the children alone unsupervised while carousing with the rest of the "madding crowd" was utterly out of my league. Besides, the gentleman who had sold us the house expected to live with us. I suspected that his intentions were not aboveboard or that he had ulterior motives, therefore I wouldn't even let him come in the house when my husband was not home. The predominant factor however was the grocery bills. These bills were never paid and kept escalating. The storekeeper was supporting the family. I was embarrassed when it was essential to shop for groceries on credit. Yet the children had to eat.

At last, in desperation, I answered an advertisement in the paper requesting the services of a teacher in a Saskatchewan rural school. My application was accepted immediately. There was a problem however, in fact, a major problem. I didn't have a cent to my name and such an experience would be expensive. It goes without saying that John would not consent to my leaving, let alone pay the expenses. What was I to do? I pondered over this problem for many days, racking my brains. After a great deal of consideration I decided to ask the storekeeper for the money. That was indeed a most phenomenal incident; in fact it was one of the most astounding incident of my entire life. I had gathered up all my courage before I ventured out and felt very apprehensive concerning his reply to my request for a loan.

"Lend" he shouted waving his arms emphatically and repeating the word." My dear lady, I will not lend you the money. I will GIVE you the money."

And that was his astonishing reply.

As it was early in the season we went to visit my dad in Leoville before we set out to go to Minton, the district where the school was located. As usual the family welcomed us with open arms and I wondered how everyone could put themselves out and be so kind to such a crowd. My dad was shocked at my appearance. "Isn't there anything to eat in British Columbia," he said, "you look like a skeleton." Little did he know that it wasn't the food that was lacking but the time to eat. I borrowed more money from my dad before we left. Yvonne, who had relocated in Domremy agreed to care for the three younger children. (I will always be thankful to her for the help she gave me.)

When we arrived at Herald School I was most thankful to discover that the teacher was provided with adequate living accommodation. In fact, the building was spacious enough for all four of us. The residents in the district were very friendly. It was almost incredible that by a stroke of good luck a French Canadian family lived in that district also. As in previous school districts, the Assoignons felt that we had a common heritage and we were treated like family. The children were good students, the parents amiable, and all in all it was an ideal situation.

Herald School – Teacher - Jeannette Romaniuk - Front row Juliette second and Carol third David: row two second child from left; Walter from top second row on right.

The most outstanding and remarkable thing about that school was the fact that although it was a small rural school it had an invincible softball team. Indeed no team in the whole area had ever been able to win a game against them. It wasn't surprising that they were able to win against the teams from the country or rural areas, but they also beat the teams from the village and even city schools. Needless to say our team was not very popular among the local softball teams. Furthermore I could not claim any of the credit for the team's success, for to say that sports is not my forte is putting it mildly and it would be more accurate to say that I am hopeless. It would be appropriate to say that the pitcher, May, and her brother, Emile, the catcher, deserved the credit, and to those two all the merit of the team was due. These two must have been in cahoots with each other, giving each other signals, (a wink perhaps) for no sooner had the ball left the catcher's mitt, whizzing through air, that "bang" it was in the catcher's glove! It was as if they had been playing catch with each other, for the ball went swooshing through the air in such a flash that no batter had time to see the ball let alone hit it. Besides the team had a strong back up. Most of the players were sturdy farm boys that could send the ball sailing sky high when hit. There were two small players, Walter and David, but they were so swift no one could outrun them around the ball diamond or in the field. It is not surprising that Herald School became known for its invincible ball team. I hope these players confronted the joys and trials of their journey throughout their lives with as much courage and animation as they did when playing those remarkable games.

During the first part of the year, Yvonne had cared for the younger children. It may have been too strenuous for her. Unfortunately she became ill. It became necessary for me to take the children with me. Mercifully Cecile, my younger sister, decided to come and help me. She took full responsibility for the household duties and the care of the children, making sure that everything was done to perfection. She even scrubbed the six pairs of shoes every week. I was concerned about her health and about the fact that she was overworked, therefore I assumed some of the tasks that could be done on Saturdays. Cecile did not like my contribution however. She preferred to do everything herself.

It wasn't long before Cecile met one of the local boys and married him. Again Providence came to my assistance. My niece Simone, John's oldest daughter, came to help me. She also assumed all the responsibility for the management of the household. But lo and behold, she started dating Cecile's brother-in-law and soon she too was gone. Although I ransack my mind it seems impossible to recall how I managed after Simone was gone.

Many significant incidents occurred during those years in Minton. During the summer vacations after the first year was over I went back to Saskatoon for the third session of my teacher's course. Cecile stayed with the children. Fortunately her boy friend, Clement, made sure that all was well with them while I was away. There was one alarming incident however (thank goodness there was only one). During the warm summer days the children loved to take off their shoes and play barefooted in the yard. On one of these occasions Carol stepped on the sharp edge of a can and made a deep gash on her foot. The wound was bleeding alarmingly. Cecile was frightened! Mercifully Clement happened to show up just in time to take the child to the hospital. The version of the story would have it that Clement did not drive to the hospital, he flew!

In the spring of the fourth and last year that we were in Minton John came to the school. He had found out where we were and was bent on taking us back with him. Again! He was determined that if he persisted long enough he could persuade me to make another attempt to reconcile our differences. He had sought the advice of the local priest who had strongly recommended a reconciliation for the welfare of the children. All these assertions were perfectly logical had they been unfeigned or wholeheartedly sincere. The longer he stayed and the more he persisted the more I feared that I would let myself be inveigled, hopelessly ensnared in the same ambush. (He stayed for three or four days.) It is little wonder that he was so confident and sure of my inability to stand up for my rights as it had happened myriad of times before. I was terrified that I would acquiesce to his scheme. Mercifully, Providence stepped in. He informed me at the last minute that I was to continue to teach because it was impossible for him to support all of us. Well, I had been hoping for such a break. A clincher! Many years before I had vowed that if I had to support the family it would be on my own terms. Being on my own I would know that the money was being spent for the benefit of the family and not for other purposes. Therefore on no circumstances would I have agreed to go back on these terms. Although those few days had been most horrendous, permeated with doubt and apprehension, at least I had not let myself be persuaded into doing something that I would regret the rest of my life.

All the residents in the district were wonderful. Two of the families were exceptional. One of these was the French Canadian family who had befriended me and treated me as one of their own, the other a most reputable and dependable family of German descent. It would be difficult to say which of the two was more thoughtful; for each made sure that we were not deprived of the essentials necessary for survival. Neither Cecile, Simone, or I had any means of transportation; therefore we relied on the generosity of these kind people to shop for groceries or any other emergency occurring in the household. Church of course was out of the question, as we did not want to impose unless it was absolutely necessary.

As I mentioned previously, Cecile and Simone married boys from the same family during that year. Simone's sister, Jeannine, also married in the same family. All these weddings were occasions for joyous celebrations.

In the other friend's family, one of the girl's weddings had been planned and was soon to transpire. It was indeed most regrettable that the girl's mother, who was suffering from cancer, died before the wedding. The family was devastated of course, but as the death was rather sudden, all the preparations had been made for the wedding, all the invitations had been sent, therefore they had to go on with the celebration. It was a very emotional event for the family. For although they rejoiced because of the festive occasion, their hearts still grieved for the one who had been so dear to them.

After all these events life became normal again. Teaching during the day, preparation of lessons for the next school day, the evening meal, and bath before bed kept both Simone and I occupied with little time for relaxation. Besides we had been given two strips of land to plant a garden in two different locations. The land in southern Saskatchewan is very fertile and the vegetables growing in those small gardens were unreal. Planting, weeding, and hoeing were never ending but enjoyable tasks. Although I was responsible for the main tasks involved in gardening, it was Walter who did most of the weeding. Whenever that child had a minute to himself, he was in the garden weeding. He never had to be persuaded; it was something he enjoyed and wanted to do. Not only was Walter born with a book in his hands (for he read continually) but he must also have been born a farmer. From his earliest childhood he manifested a passion for the freedom of the wide-open spaces and he hoped to become a farmer.

Time went by very quickly in our household; in fact we never had enough of that precious commodity to do everything we wanted to do. Boredom or loneliness were words that did not exist in our vocabulary. But our neighbor was not as fortunate. The loss of his mate had left him inconsolable. His loneliness was intolerable. He began to seek companionship by visiting people in the neighborhood. He eventually turned up at our house. This was indeed a good antidote or solution for loneliness, for our house was forever bubbling with activity; absolute pandemonium! At first the commotion plus the playful chatter of the children seemed to distract him, but soon he longed for the friendship and companionship of adults, someone to talk to. That is how our relationship started. At first we'd all sit together and talk, even late into the night after the children were in bed. This went on for a considerable time, but I assumed these associations were nothing more than a need for friendship.

It seems that I was wrong! After a time my friend declared that his intentions were serious and that he wanted to have a permanent relationship with me. A relationship (permanent or temporary) was the last thing on my mind at this point of time and I expressed this to my friend in no uncertain terms. (By some impish shenanigan of fate his name happened to be John!) I had just got out of an intolerable situation and above everything else was my desire to be free. On the other hand, his marriage had been a happy relationship and he couldn't understand my apprehension. He envisioned marriage as a joyous relationship, while I on the other hand, envisioned it as being confined in a chamber of horrors. Yet he was a righteous person, his intentions were honorable, and he would have helped me with the children. It is almost incredible that anyone would have the courage to assume such a tremendous responsibility. He must have been a magnanimous person indeed to undertake a task of this magnitude. Yet he wasn't the one who was reluctant to tackle his share of the commitment, I was! Yet I had faith in this man and respected him as a person with integrity and honor. He would have been considerable support and assistance with the impossible responsibilities that the future held for me. But there was a problem unresolved nagging me that was still unsettled when we left Minton.

Juliette and Carol

Walter and his cat.

There were several considerations or determinants that eventuated in my decision to find employment in an urban center. To begin with my husband had been informed as to our whereabouts and he would be constantly at my doorstep trying to persuade me to make another attempt at reconciliation. He had convinced me many times to my chagrin and I did not want to be placed in that situation again. For under no circumstances was I to imperil the future of the children. Yet under constant badgering I feared that he would be able to persuade me again. (I certainly had a lousy track record.) Besides, every time he came there was always hell to pay. Consequently I decided to run away. This time however I made sure that my relatives did not divulge my whereabouts to anyone.

There were other reasons. I did not have any means of transportation and consequently the neighbors had to take us do all our errands and our shopping. Although most of them did this very graciously I wanted to be independent. It was my responsibility to provide for my family's needs and to have to rely on others good will was humiliating indeed. Besides, we had not been able to go to church for ages as it would have been an additional imposition on these worthy people.

Consequently I applied for a teaching position in Edmonton. My application was accepted. The superintendent of the school district tried to persuade me to remain but I thought it was the right thing to do for the welfare of the children. Besides the desire to become independent had become an obsession.

Part V

New Beginnings

So the dye was cast. I made the arrangements, packed my children with what little belongings we possessed and we were off.

Meandering leisurely along, trudging slowly forward on my daily wanderings around the lake, I reminisce as the events of that most sensational episode flashes before my eyes. As I gaze upon the wonders spread out before me, it occurs to me that these scenic rambles is the screen upon which the drama of my life have been illustrated and captured in my mind's eye. This morning, as this glorious panorama unfolds, I am delighted to behold the water again, the water that was so long imprisoned and locked in a deadly grasp under Jack Frost's strangulating grip. These waters so long buried under a thick mantel of ice and snow, have finally been set free. Once again the lake is a sea of sparkling glistening crystals scintillating and dancing in the breeze. Oh that I could keep but one of these precious crystals to cherish forever! It is then, absorbed and immersed in all this magic that I am able to pick up the thread of my story.

The entire proceedings proved to be quite an adventure. The shift from country to city life is rather remarkable. The children (and even I) had difficulty adapting to the many rules and restrictions that metropolitan living necessitates.

Immediately upon our arrival, I was confronted with the colossal obstacle of procuring suitable lodgings or living accommodations for my family. This proved to be an insurmountable problem, a problem that I had not anticipated and for which there was no visible solution. Indeed there were absolutely no vacancies available at a reasonable cost, and the few that were available were beyond my means as the rent was exorbitant. Besides, none of the landlords who were proprietors of these cushy establishments accepted children. It was a desperate situation! Mercifully Providence intervened as it had on numerous occasions.

It may have been through the Catholic Social Services that a generous family heard of my plight. Be that as it may they came to my assistance. At first they referred me to an agency whose manager was supposed to be able to perform magic for someone in desperate need. The interview was a disaster! Not only was he unable to help but he was abusive. "You people come in our town", he chided, "and you expect to get what little accommodations there are, thus taking priority over the permanent residents. You should stay where you are until you've made arrangements for lodgings." he went on and on. He likely told me to go back where I'd come from or something to that effect. I was devastated; not because he had been unable to help me as it was evident that the housing situation in the fifties was critical, but by his injurious tirade. It is true that that man was in an impossible position, however he, on the other hand, should have realized that those who sought his assistance were desperate. If he was unable to offer them any assistance, he could at least have spared them from his tyrannical abuse. On the way to the hotel I was sobbing so violently that the cab driver asked me if someone in the family had died.

It is true that drastic situations demand drastic cures. The solution to my critical situation was indeed drastic. The family who were generously helping me knew of a congregation of Catholic priests who took boys camping during the summer vacation. So it was arranged that the two boys, Walter and David, would go with them. They also knew that the Sisters of Charity took homeless girls in their convent. So it was arranged that the girls, Juliette, Carol, and Lucille, would stay at the convent until I had found suitable lodging for the family. Fortunately, I knew about the Sisters of Service from my experience in Vancouver and the good sisters agreed to take me in. They also agreed to let Charlie stay with me at the hostel. Although it was unbearable to be separated from the children it gave me the opportunity to look for suitable accommodation before September. To rent an apartment was out of the question! Vacancies were non-existent and besides landlords did not allow children in their tenements. There was only one alternative and that was to buy a house. It was an exciting prospect and I looked forward to it with great anticipation. Fortunately, during the years that we were in Minton I had saved fifty dollars a month which had accumulated to a grand total of two thousand dollars. During the fifties it was a sufficient amount for a down payment on a modest house.

I had never had a home of my own and had absolutely no experience concerning the knowledge that is essential in order to achieve a suitable transaction. Therefore it was not surprising that my first attempt was unsuccessful. The house was in a good location in the lake district (no less) but although it must have been beautiful once it was badly in need of repair. Being alone I had neither the resources nor the power to make the necessary restoration and eventually the deal fell through. My benefactors referred me to a real estate agent who was more perceptive and therefore more sensitive to my needs. Through him I bought a wartime house. It was not a mansion, but it was spacious, comfortable, and within my financial means. It was a home for my children, where the family could be together at last. That indeed was the very first thing on the agenda and as soon as the keys were in my hands I brought the children home. It had been a long summer, a summer that will never be forgotten!

Indeed it was a summer that left many painful scars on all of us. The girls were most fortunate as the sisters at the convent treated them with compassion and understanding. As they had never been separated from their mother in the past the loneliness they suffered was excruciating. Carol especially did not fare very well. She could not eat the food that was served to the children and no matter how her sisters tried to comfort her, she cried from morning till night. Mercifully, one of the sisters, Sister Good Counsel, took

Carol under her wing. That compassionate sister shared her own food with the child and took her to bed with her at night. Carol and I will never forget the generosity and kindliness of that magnanimous sister.

The boys did not fare as well. Apparently the good Fathers were overwhelmed by the enormous number of boys that had been entrusted in their care. They did not have the resources nor sufficient caregivers to accommodate so many. Besides some of the boys had problems which further complicated the situation. It appears that at times the Fathers had to use strong disciplinary measures in order to maintain some sort of equanimity. These harsh punishments traumatized the timid, frightened boys who were already devastated with loneliness. To make matters worse, due to the lack of transportation facilities, I was unable to visit them all summer. Those unfortunate lads must have thought they had been forsaken. The joy of being reunited with the rest of their family was fascinating to behold.

After taking possession of the house and our baggage had arrived we settled in to a normal (semi-normal that is) style of living. There were many difficulties to be overcome, but our joy at being together compensated for all the hardship we had to endure. Our first how-do-you-do or welcoming incident was on the first night we arrived in the district and was somewhat intolerable. The two boys, Walter and David, each had a brand new bicycle. These bicycles were their most priced possession. During the night a hard-core delinquent from the neighborhood stole both bikes and sold them. There was no doubt about the identity of the thief, everyone knew who the culprit was. So with the conviction that it is a parent's duty to guide their children in the path of righteousness and the naivety of someone who has faith in mankind, I proceeded to go straight to the parents' house. The father answered the door staring at me sternly he asked, "Yes."

"Do you know, sir" I blurted out, "that your son has taken both of my sons' bicycles?"

"Well," said he,"if he is smart enough to get away with it, good for him." And he slammed the door in my face.

I was appalled. In fact I was so stunned that I just stood there, frozen! Had I lived in the city's rough districts previously, this man's behavior would not have surprised me in the least, in fact I would have saved myself a trip to his house and called the police. This type of parent was unknown to me, a bird of a different feather, and I was too flabbergasted to pursue the matter further. The incident did teach all of us a lesson, however. In the city you must always be vigilant, for your own personal safety and for the safety of your property.

Soon the children were enrolled in St. Marguerite Separate School. Many adjustments had to be made as rural schools function on a different basis from schools in the city. For instance, in most rural schools students at different grade levels congregate in a one-room school with only one instructor teaching all levels. In city schools, there is a separate classroom and teacher for each grade level. It goes without saying that the level of achievement is far superior in urban centers as the teacher can devote all her\his time for the benefit of one level of instruction. Subsequently my children had a lot of difficulty catching up with their classmates. There was also the dress code that had to be reckoned with. In the separate schools the girls were not allowed to wear slacks or shorts to school, even in winter. Consequently a whole new wardrobe had to be provided for the three girls.

My first assignment involved teaching junior high in the south side of Edmonton. It proved to be a disaster. There is such an enormous difference between city and country children that they do not appear to belong to the same species of creatures.

Unfortunately I was unaware of this fact and totally unprepared to deal with its ramifications. In rural areas discipline is not a problem, students co-operate with the teacher, even those at the senior high level. In fact these students are an asset to the school as during competitions their skills and expertise often offset the balance in their team's favor. There is, however, a disadvantage. During the busy season on the farm such as seeding and harvesting it is necessary for the older boys to help their parents. Sometimes these students are absent for a considerable length of time. It is difficult for them to do all the work they missed during the time they were absent plus their regular assignments. These students are kept busy at all times; consequently they have no time to get into trouble. Indeed, there in lies the dilemma. Adolescents in urban centers have little to do to occupy their leisure time, therefore many resort to negative behavior in order to attract attention. The blame for this situation cannot be attributed to any particular class of individuals. It is, of course, a social problem, a problem so complex that it would take more than the likes of me to find a solution to its intrinsic ambiguity. But the real victims are those who are coerced to deal with these lamentable situations: parents, teachers, and particularly those who are led astray due to the fallible social system in which they are compelled to exist.

I managed with great difficulty and by hook and by crook to carry on until Christmas. There were days when I was too sick to work; besides it was evident that I did not belong in the junior high section. Mercifully the school board realized that the transition from a rural to urban school system plus being assigned to the most problematic level was too overwhelming for anyone to tackle. Consequently I was transferred to the primary division teaching grade one in St. Kevin School on the south side. It solved the problem. I was very happy working with the little ones and felt that with them was where I belonged.

There were other problems however, major problems! I began to wonder if my husband had finally had his way and placed us in an insurmountable situation, beyond the realms of all possibility. True I had escaped, hiding into the depths of the complex labyrinth of the city. But buried into that intricate maze of streets and avenues, was it possible for anyone in my position to survive, in spite of the obstacles? Yes, it is true that we had escaped, but at what price. To begin with, it was impossible to find someone reliable to care for Lucille and Charles. After several unsuccessful attempts, Hélène agreed to care for them. Although I knew that they would get the best of care, it was heartbreaking to be coerced into sending two small children so far away from their home.

And it was right in the midst of all this turmoil that Keith was born, on the last day of the year 1956. Although the child brought a great deal of joy to all of us, the problem of finding someone to care for him was unthinkable. My benefactors wanted to adopt him, but when they sensed that it broke my heart to part with him, they thought it unwise. Providence came to the rescue again! My sister Juliette, who was visiting at the time, offered to care for him until I could find a reliable caregiver. So she took Keith with her to Leoville. I had hoped to keep the family together, yet circumstances had necessitated that it be torn apart, one child three hundred miles east of us and two others twice that distance in the opposite direction, near Vancouver. Although these arrangements were temporary I could not help being plagued by feeling of despair, as I kept thinking, "How brutal are the exhortations of destiny, and how exorbitant the price one must pay for errors of judgment."

Keith

Be that as it may, this arrangement enabled the rest of the family to carry on with some semblance of a normal routine. I hoped that once we were established in the community having made the adaptation to living in the city, it would be possible to be reunited as a family. The children were enrolled in school and since my transfer to St. Kevin School I enjoyed my work. The other grade one teacher, Sister Good Counsel, was straight from heaven. She did everything possible to help me adjust to the new situation, not only in the classroom but with my personal problems. In fact, without her support and her encouragement, I doubt if I would have been able to carry on. When she sensed that things were at their worst, she would distract me by changing the subject. She would say in the most cheerful manner, "Isn't it a beautiful day today?" Well, who could be sad after such a comment? (Who could on old sorrows dwell... Shakespeare?)

There was a Mrs. Falkenburg, a grade two teacher, who did everything in her power to help me through those rough times. Perhaps those two magnanimous colleagues of mine pulled me through when I stumbled, each holding me by the hand. May

God's light shine upon them in Paradise, as my humble gratitude will never compensate for the nobility of their generosity towards me. Alas it is too late to express that profound gratitude, as both my benefactors are no more. Too late! Always too late!

It was before the second semester started that my friend from Saskatchewan came to visit us. He wanted to keep in contact with us but when he realized that I had managed to solve the most urgent problems, he went back home.

I am unable to form a clear mental picture of the developments during the next six months. It is evident that with the help of my colleagues I was successful in my professional duties. Besides I loved working with children in the primary level, especially those in grade one. The household management was more difficult. The difficulty was undeniably, irrefutably, beyond all doubts of my own making. There were housekeeping rituals that I had learned at home and that had to be observed. It seems that what is instilled in childhood becomes the essence of one's personality. The whole house in which we lived had hardwood floors, upstairs and downstairs, all four bedrooms, kitchen, and living room. Every week, without fail, all these floors had to be washed, waxed, and polished. We had no polisher so the children would put on some old woolen stockings and go back and forth polishing that floor until it shone like a mirror. Then there was the week's laundry which was usually done on Friday night after school. At first the clothes had to be hung on the clothesline. That was fine during the warm weather, but during the winter the clothes had to be brought in frozen, ironed to get some of the moisture out, then hung on an indoor line to dry. It was a never-ending job. When we finally got a dryer, I thought it was too good to be true. After the laundry was done, the house immaculately clean, there was the baking to be done. I usually baked a huge batch of bread on Saturday night while I did the ironing. In the morning the children gorged themselves on the scones made from raw dough fried in butter (they still have fond memories of these incidents). Somewhere in between I would make a batch of doughnuts, my grandmother's doughnuts that is, and these were out of this world. Indeed my doughnuts had quite a reputation in the neighborhood. All the kids in the neighbourhood would gather at the house to feast on those delicious delicacies. It goes without saying that many times after a weekend I would go back to school on Monday completely exhausted.

It is true that some of those weekend tasks were imperative and unavoidable like for instance the laundry. There were, however, those which were not absolutely required for the well being of the family. For instance, it is still a mystery to me why all these floors had to be stripped of the wax, washed, waxed, and polished every single week. It was an obsession. Like one non compos mentis I would make a frantic production, rushing madly about until the job was done. But why? It must be because it had been a weekly ritual when I was a child and it had been so solidly ingrained in my psyche that I was powerless to stop, even though it didn't make any sense. Another unnecessary task, which I performed religiously every week, was ironing every blessed item in the weekly laundry from sheets to dishtowels. Incredible! Would I repeat these outlandish stupidities today? Who knows!

During that year, shortly after Christmas, I received a letter from a lawyer in Ontario with the news that my husband had been in a serious accident and had suffered severe injuries. The lawyer maintained that because my husband was not responsible for the accident, I would gain a considerably amount of money if the matter was brought to court. It may have been a legitimate claim and perhaps the family would have benefited from these proceedings, but at the time I was still torn with bitterness from past experiences. Money did not seem important. Freedom was what I treasured the most, it took precedence over all other concerns; being away from all the tribulations, the heartache, the constant struggle to survive. The letter was disregarded. I had only one outstanding priority, and that was to provide for those children in a safe and peaceful environment.

As soon as the school term was over the first item on the agenda was going to Maple Ridge to get Lucille and Charlie. Hélène's property consisted of thirteen acres of land. Gigantic spruce trees surrounded the house. Two of these colossal giants were especially magnificent at the entrance of the property. Besides these there were cherry, apple, pear, and plum trees scattered everywhere. On the eastern side, a precipice culminated into a deep ravine into which flowed a river. But the most amazing of all was the waterfall whose roaring waters cascaded into the river below. That waterfall fascinated the children, they were captivated by the magic of its beauty and awed by the force of its plunging waters.

Although our mission had been to get the children, Hélène insisted that we spend most of the vacation at her house. (I hope we didn't outlast our welcome. We probably did!) Hélène was and is generous to the core. She is the embodiment of the word. The fact that she was able to cope with all of us throughout the summer is incredible. She wanted us to enjoy the freedom and wonders of life away from the city. The girls, Muriel, Babe, and Susan had a couple of horses which they rode with delight. On Sundays we 'd pack up a lunch and go to Stanley Park for a picnic. Then we'd go exploring. That park is a little bit of heaven, or a miniature replica of the Garden of Eden! The marvels and variety of plant and animal life is astounding. But the park's proximity to the ocean transcends all. The grandeur and mysterious facet of the ocean bewitches me and fills me with wonder and enchantment. During those early years my dad lived in a little cabin near Hélène's house and on her property. The children enjoyed visiting him. He always had candies for them. My dad's proximity was an unexpected bonus that complemented the happiness we experienced during those visits. It enabled me to spend many hours of quality time with the father that I had previously never really known or understood. It was while he told stories of the past or hilariously comical tales depicting the distinctive characteristics of the French Canadian culture that I began to comprehend the essence of his inner feelings, his aspirations, and the hopes he had sacrificed for the one he loved.

It was during these wonderful summers that the children got to know their Uncle Nick, Aunt Beth and their cousins. Nick (John's youngest brother) and Beth were fantastic people. They had a gorgeous home in Vancouver which was surrounded by fruit trees of all sorts: apple, cherry, pear, plum, and countless others. Whenever the children visited their aunt and uncle, they were treated the same as the rest of the family. They, especially Carol, cherish the memories of these most gracious kinfolk.

In contrast, John's twin bother Mike, who also lived in Vancouver, did not want to have anything to do with his nieces and nephews, except David. It is amazing that David was welcomed into the house and treated cordially while the others couldn't even set foot in the door. It isn't any wonder that they were unable to comprehend their uncle's strange behavior.

Hélène's ability to cope with all of us every summer is indeed unfathomable. Her generosity and unselfishness is beyond comprehension, in fact it is beyond the scope of all human imagination. Not only did she keep us all summer, but she kept and cared for Lucille and Charles for two years because I was unable to find a reliable daycare for them in Edmonton. Later Charles and David went back and lived with her family for a considerable length of time. I will be everlastingly indebted to my sister and her husband for the sacrifices they endured for the benefit of my family. Yet when I try to express my gratitude, the words will not manifest themselves. Indeed, there are no words that can do justice to the magnanimous succor they contributed to the survival of my family during a critical episode in our lives. When I meditate and digress about these difficult years and people keep wondering how we were able to struggle through those times, I must say that I didn't do it alone. It was the manifestation of Providence working through the spirit of all these caring individuals: Sister Good Counsel, Hélène and Herbert, Yvonne, Juliette, Cecile, Marie-Anne, and the Sisters of Service, my benefactors in the city. I could go on and on forever. They are the valorous heroic angels who are worthy of all the praise, for they wove a mystical web that held and sustained us throughout these crucial years. To them the credit is due. To them these righteous men and women of today, my family, owe their very existence. Without them the family could not have survived.

Although life seemed to have attained some degree of normalcy the following year, it soon became crammed with tragic events. Once again the tempestuous winds of capricious destiny violently pirouetted the hopes for the untroubled tranquility we had so fervently anticipated and in its unbridled fury launched a raging hurricane. The fall term had started amazingly well. The children were registered at school, Lucille was admitted in grade one at the same school, and the year's supplies had been duly purchased. I was looking forward with anticipation to the commencement of the school term. The saying, "It was too good to be true," may have some truth in it after all for all our routine was proceeding along harmoniously for some time. Then disaster struck! I had been tormented with a serious cough for some time before I decided to see a doctor. The initial diagnosis of my condition was that it was a smoker's cough and nothing to worry about. (My doctor was absent at the moment.) That was most unlikely as a smoker's cough afflicts only those who are addicted to cigarette smoke. Mercifully as soon as my doctor saw me, he decided to take further tests and consequently after taking an x-ray his diagnosis differed entirely from that of his assistant. According to the x-ray I had a severe case of pneumonia. The doctor prescribed antibiotic medication and sent me home. But even after taking the pills until the prescription was finished my condition was becoming worse. My doctor attributed this to the fact that the medication was ineffective without accompanying rest. Yet how can you rest with a houseful of kids? So he insisted that I be hospitalized at once. That was sooner said than done. It was out of the question to leave the children unattended. Yet the doctor warned that it was a matter of life and death. For a short time the children managed on their own, but as soon as the Sisters Of Service became aware of the situation, three of the good sisters went to the house and took charge; supervising, cooking, cleaning, and even teaching the children artistic skills like making things out of leather. It is little wonder that the children adored these providential angels who had so graciously come to their assistance. Apparently the sisters also enjoyed working with the children for subsequent to this incidence, one of the sisters went back to university and became a teacher. After the sisters left, a friend who had been a neighbor of the family in Penny, B.C. agreed to care for the family until I was released from the hospital. Even though the situation at home was in competent hands I was tormented with anxiety, wondering and fretting constantly about the welfare of my family. It's a wonder that I didn't go stark raving mad as I was in the hospital for six long weeks.

There were repercussions ensuing from my illness, excessively expensive repercussions! As my teaching contract was still on a probationary basis, the school board was not required to pay my salary while I was on sick leave. Consequently during the time I was in the hospital, besides all the time it took to recuperate, the family was without any source of income whatsoever. How we survived is beyond me! Perhaps providence came to the rescue again throwing together some mystical scheme, improvising as usual in times of emergency, even as a last resort summoning manna directly from the heavens. But we did survive because we're still all here. How? The answer is buried deep in the past.

Whether I was able to go back to work before Christmas is another issue which has not survived the passage of time.

Subsequent to the family's depleted financial situation, the children and I had accepted the fact that our meager resources would not permit elaborate Christmas celebrations. Even the negligible cost of a tree had been prohibitive. To spend Christmas without a Christmas tree was, to the children, intolerable! Indeed it was unheard of, entirely unacceptable. Especially to Carol and Lucille! So these two intrepid characters who were barely seven years old decided to take matters in their own hands. With the humongous sum of ten cents they made their way to the tree lot and began bargaining for a tree. The owner of the lot upon contemplating the size of his clients and the enormous amount of their finances was completely dumbfounded. He took the ten cents and gave the girls the most beautiful tree on the lot. Needless to say the tree was bigger than both girls put together and getting that gigantic tree home presented a major problem. But they were bound and determined that we would have a tree. So they tugged and they pulled and they pushed and they pulled and they tugged until finally, by hook and by crook they got their prize home. But lo and behold the tree was too tall! Fortunately we had a saw! Walter and David took turns sawing off the extra length and soon, to the girl's great joy, the tree was up and decorated. The whole family was filled with wonder and joy. Lacking all the amenities necessary to celebrate the festive season in proper style we considered ourselves fortunate to possess the most magnificent of all trees.

After the excitement had died down on that Christmas Eve everything was in readiness, that is as far as our resources would permit. The children were in the living room watching TV and I was in the kitchen preparing something or other for the morrow. There was a knock at the door and someone answered it. Lo and behold, who should step in but Good Old Saint Nick himself, complete with red suit, black boots, white beard, sack, and all. We all stood there dumbfounded, staring, our eyes popping out of our heads, too flabbergasted to at least welcome him. "Ho, Ho, Ho," said he, "and a Merry Christmas to you all." And popping his sack on the floor he began emptying its contents. Well the Ho, Ho, Ho, did it. It brought all of us back to our senses and we realized that this was indeed Santa Claus and that he had come to wish us a Merry Christmas. Our amazement intensified as we watched Santa pulling more and more items out of his bag. There was everything imaginable in that fantastic sack; Christmas dinner, including turkey with all the trimmings, candy and nuts for the children, dishes, linen, and a gift for each of the children. It was incredible! My only wish as this most extraordinary and wonderful incident is reenacted in my mind's eye is that I was able to express my profound gratitude, for even now as the memory of this phenomenal event flashes back into my mind, my heart is filled with joy and wonder.

My husband passed away at the beginning of that year. The letter was forwarded to me by Cecile from Minton as no one except my family knew my address and I had left strict instructions that it should not be divulged to anyone. When I received the news my feelings were in a turmoil of conflicting emotions. I was deeply disturbed. A sense of lose and extreme regret possessed me; regret considering his children who had to grow up without the love, the support, and the pride of a devoted father. Yet even then I could not suppress my bitterness, a bitterness festering in the pith of my soul. I kept reiterating to myself over and over again, "It should not have been this way." But it was too late.

The staff at the school was very compassionate. In fact, one of the teachers spent the nights with the family for a whole week. I really appreciated the staff's thoughtfulness, especially the generosity of the teacher who sacrificed her evenings for a whole week to commiserate with us. In retrospect, due to the emotional turmoil I was experiencing, I sincerely hope that I was able to express my profound gratitude.

Soon after the death of my husband my loyal friend from Minton came to visit us. He hoped that I would have changed my mind and would agree to marry him. It made a lot of sense. He was very lonely and even though it was a tremendous responsibility, he was prepared to challenge the struggles and sacrifices that such a commitment involves. Besides, I needed help so desperately. With his support the Herculean task ahead would have been so much lighter. But I was afraid! Having just escaped an intolerable relationship, all I could discern was negative or the things that could go wrong. I trusted him implicitly, but I did not trust myself. In the event of a conflict there was no doubt in my mind, right or wrong, I would stand up for the children. How could such behavior be justified? It would be against all my moral principles or standards. Yet being human, the animal instinct sometimes prevails over reason or justice. Mothers especially tend to be culpable of this frailty; the instinct to defend their young is beyond their ability to control. "Do I have the right" I asked myself, "to ask this man who is willing to sacrifice his life for us to be treated in such a shameful manner?" Therefore I decided that it was best not to embark on an adventure that might prove untenable for both of us and especially intolerable for my friend.

When school reopened, in the fall of the year 1957, Lucille and Charles were with us. Both were registered at St. Marguerite School along with their brothers and sisters. Keith was still with Juliette in Leoville. The fact that I no longer had to be concerned about childcare was indeed a great reprieve. There were other problems however! I had to take the bus to work, and had to leave the house earlier than the children. Consequently the older members of the family were responsible for the final preparations before they left the house. Making sure that everyone was ready to go to school on time was a nightmare. Lunches, keys; and in winter mitts, scarves, toques all had to be accounted for. Poor Juliette, who because she was the oldest of the girls, felt responsible for all the supervision of her siblings when it was impossible for me to do so. Many times she was called into the principle's office and reprimanded severely because someone had lost his/her mittens or toque or what not. Carol had taken over the cooking (that is when my duties kept me later than usual after school) and she did it with a vengeance. On these occasions, without fail, she'd make a huge pot of spaghetti. She'd cook the noodles until tender and just dump a can of tomatoes in the pot and that was it. It goes without saying that it became very tedious and unappetizing.

One day David, who was extremely finicky about his food, piped up and said, "Why don't you cook something else for a change. I'm getting very tired of eating the same thing day after day."

"Well," retorted Carol, " that's the only thing I know how to cook." What could David say? There was no alternative but to settle for spaghetti or starve until I got home.

My family and friends often wonder how we managed to survive financially and otherwise during those first years in Edmonton. Even I do not know by what miracle we managed to scrape through these difficult times. Surely providence intervened and assigned an angel to watch over us, for so it seemed at the time. After I was accepted on the permanent staff, a Good Samaritan on the school board insisted that my salary be on par with that of the male teachers. He maintained that as the head of the household and the sole provider my status was equivalent to that of the men. This was unfair to the female staff of course, but it proved to be our salvation.

At the end of the school year, the board's policy was to pay the teachers on a three month basis in order to cover their salary for the summer months. As it was my only source of income it was imperative that the mortgage and the utilities be prepaid for those three months. That end of the year cheque barely covered these expenses and there was nothing left for the family's subsistence during July and August. At first we spent most of the summers with my sister Hélène in Maple Ridge. Then being determined to get my degree I took courses at the University during the summer months. How we managed to survive during these two months is beyond me.

Exasperated and at my wits end with this penny pinching and living from hand to mouth, always wondering whether we were going to make it from one day to the next, I decided to work in the evenings and during the summer holidays. I had worked at the "Y" for a short time when we first arrived in the city and had rather enjoyed it. Subsequently I tried to work the evening shift at a small café. I was getting the enormous salary of fifty cents an hour and was treated like a scullery maid. Needless to say the situation was intolerable and I soon quit. Then I was hired by a dry cleaning plant for the evening shift. I enjoyed my work. The manager noticed that I was very meticulous and wouldn't trust anyone else in the plant to iron his boys' white shirts. It was not to be. There was trouble at home and I had to quit. There were various short term ventures, but none that were suitable. Then fate smiled upon me and I got a position in the diet kitchen at the Royal Alexandra Hospital. Although I enjoyed the work, I lived in fear that somehow the teachers would discover that I was "moonlighting" And so they did! One evening the principal of St. Kevin School and another teacher came to the table while I was serving the evening meal. That I was embarrassed doesn't begin to describe my feelings at the moment. I practically melted into the soup.

I worked quite a few years at the hospital. One day fortune again smiled upon me and my application was accepted to work the evening shift at the post office. Sorting mail and working in the area of communication seemed to be more consistent with teaching. It seemed less demeaning than working in a restaurant. I did this for quite a few years, in fact until the family's finances had stabilized and it was no longer imperative.

And that, although I refuse to torment my friends with all the gory details, is how the family survived! A miracle, no less!

Although it had been quite obvious from the very beginning it became more and more evident that each individual in the family had a distinct and unique personality. It is indeed amazing considering the fact that all of them have the same genetic background. Yet each member manifests (then and now) such outstanding character differences. But in spite of these differences, they had some similar characteristics, for instance in times of trouble they rallied together and pooled their resources in order to help one another. Besides everyone of them showed a remarkable resourcefulness in critical situations or even in solving every day problems. But most outstandingly gratifying is that each child was gifted with his or her own special attributes.

Endowed with a superior intelligence, Walter had a practical insight enabling him to react instantly in an emergency or in a critical situation. When we first moved from Penny to Leoville, we had to transfer in Prince Albert. I had to leave the children in the station to get our baggage transferred. There was some problem with the transfer and it had to be resolved. Meanwhile the passenger train was leaving without us as I was still arguing with the freight train clerk. Walter went to the conductor and told him about our predicament, that it was impossible for the children, who had already boarded the train, to go without me and begged him to wait. Subsequently the conductor stopped the train and waited for me to get on. There is no doubt in my mind that he choose the lesser of two evils, for what on earth would he have done with all these kids when the train arrived at the other end of the line. That incident was indeed phenomenal. It has remained ineradicable in my memory. Not only did Walter manage to get us out of an extremely perilous circumstance but he also supervised his brother and sisters while I was making arrangements to have our baggage transferred. Perhaps the most incredible aspect about this incidence is that the child was not yet six years old.

As soon as he learned to read Walter spent every available moment reading, and when he had his nose in a book he was oblivious to the world around him. It was frustrating at times, for regardless of what was happening around him, (even pandemonium) he was incognizant of any implications. He was so deeply absorbed in the contents of his readings that he, along with the characters, actively participated in the drama of whatever story he happened to be reading at the time. It was impossible to get his attention then, and I remember being so impatient. How unwittingly heedless and insensitive we are at times to the needs of those around us, and how painful it is when, years afterwards, we become aware of our blunders! How I regret the times when I impatiently distracted those moments of pure ecstasy, moments of exaltation. How many blunders must one commit before realizing their incredible irrationality and regrettable consequences.

There was yet another characteristic of Walter's personality that was indisputably perceptible from his earliest childhood. He was fascinated by the wonders of the open spaces, the freedom and the proximity to nature these boundless expanses provide. He delighted in watching things grow. Even when we lived in Saskatchewan, he'd spend hours in the a little patch of land we had been allotted to grow our vegetables, constantly weeding and watering. In the wee hours of the morning he'd make his way to that garden and work most of the day. He never had to be told, he did this because it was something he wanted to do. The neighbors were amazed (I was overwhelmed). To see one so young being so utterly dedicated was unbelievable. The whole thing was very

simple according to Walter. "When I grow up I will be a farmer."
And that said it all. True to his word he made his dream a reality.

David was and is still to this day entirely different. Indeed the two
brothers were so different that it didn't seem possible that they
could be related at all. Yet in some ways they are similar, for
instance in their unshakable loyalty to each other and to the rest of
the family besides the dynamism, and the vigorous manner by
which they both challenge every aspect of their lives, whether it is
a business enterprise, a diversion, or the task of providing for their
own survival and those of their families. In the impetus and
intensity by which they confront trials and challenges they are
identical. However in other aspects they are totally opposite.
Walter is very practical and cautious while David lives on the edge
and believes in taking chances, confident that in the end things will
always turn out right. He is a dreamer. Probably never had his foot
on the solid ground of reality, always existing in a world of
fantasy. (Guess who is calling the kettle black.) David's most
outstanding quality however, the characteristic that distinguishes
him from every one, and sets him apart as unique is his generosity.
He is the embodiment of the term generosity! In fact he is generous
to a fault. It has been the instrument that has entangled him into
some precarious predicaments on many occasions.

RAMBLIN NATIVE

Northlands Park, Edmonton August 9, 2000

Larry The Longshot (2nd)

Richard Currie & Dave Romaniuk, Owners

Purse $4,800   6 1/2 Furlongs   1:20:0

Ron Blinston Up

Barrier Lake (3rd)

Don Gilkyson, Trainer

$10.10 4.80 3.50

There I go again! When I set out to describe each of the children's personality, the description was to be brief. As a matter of fact it was supposed to be a concise outline of each child's most striking conspicuous character trait that was unmistakable from the cradle. It was meant to be a very brief perception of each individual's personality as it manifested itself even from infancy. But I have strayed from my intent and will try to conform to my original intentions subsequently. I will try to make each person's personality come to life by the role they perform in this drama, by their actions and their relationship to the members of their family and friends.

Juliette, from the time she first opened her eyes, was a little mother. She was bound and determined that it was her duty to tend to and care for everyone within her entourage. Besides she had an uncanny ability to handle difficult situations, resourcefulness few individuals possess.

Carol has always been a perfectionist. From the day she was born she has always wanted things to be right. Her life has been a continual struggle to achieve excellence in whatever endeavor she pursued at that particular time. She has never been able to accept anything but excellence, and mediocrity and slovenliness have always driven her frantic. This characteristic has driven her to a life of endless toil and torment. (Sister of Good Counsel would say that she lives "hard".)

It is almost impossible to pinpoint any particular trait predominant in Lucille's character as her personality has always been so complex. When she was very young she had all the attributes of a typical tomboy. As a matter of fact if there was a mud puddle anywhere around Lucille was bound to be in it up to her neck wallowing gleefully into its cool sleazy slush. But all this is in the past. Besides, she wasn't successful academically during her first years at school, yet later, she proved to be an honor student. Indeed her personality as a child as compared to what she became as an adult is a paradox. She went from one extreme to another. For instance, as a child she was disorganized and disorderly in her personal habits, her clothes and personal effects scattered all over the place. As an adult she is meticulous in every detail and in every aspect of her life.

From the very beginning Charles displayed characteristics which distinguished him as a unique and distinct individual, characteristics remarkably different from the rest of the family. Even in his earliest childhood it was evident that Charles was an intellectual. He spent most of his time seeking the works of literary geniuses and listening to the music of the great masters. In later years the depth of his wisdom, his keen insight, and superior ability to analyze a situation became apparent. These traits made him very popular with his nieces and nephews who sought his advise before making any major decisions.

Charles

Besides his intellectual wisdom, Charles had many distinguishing physical characteristics. Perhaps because he had been born premature he had a heart murmur, double pupils, and webbed fingers and toes. These physical characteristics singularity did not seem to trouble him in the least. His problem was hunger. He was hungry all the time. He was never able to get enough food to satisfy his enormous appetite. From the time he was born I was busy trying to make sure Charles had enough to eat and on many occasions did not have the opportunity to have a proper meal.

"When we were little we never had enough to eat," he said one day while reminiscing about the past, "I was always starving." Indeed he was, but not the rest of the family, and in fact they thought that comment was hilarious.

Then of coarse there was Keith. Hélène has described Keith as my Golden Boy and that description fits him to a 'T'. He has always been a treasure. It goes without saying that the others were also very precious. Keith, however, seemed to grow up without causing any commotion or major problem. It was weird but I felt as if he would always do what is the logical thing to do. He just seemed to grow up without anyone catering to him. My concerns must have been manifested in my subconscious however for I kept having this recurring dream or nightmare tormenting my restless sleep. In that dream, all of us were struggling to climb a colossal precipice, a precipice that was pure transparent ice through and through. The ice was slippery and the children were struggling on all fours taking one step forward and slipping back two in an effort to ascend the forbidding elevation. So one by one I would go down and pull each one of them to the top. But when it was Keith's turn I just stood there watching him struggle frantically. I was unable to move, frozen with horror. And I wondered "I pulled all the others up, why am I unable to help him, especially as he is the youngest." Are dreams an omen predicting the future?

In June of the year nineteen hundred and fifty seven David, Juliette, and Carol made their first communion and were confirmed at the same time. It was unusual to allow children to receive both sacraments at the same time. However, because of the circumstances, a special concession was granted.

First Communion: Carol, David, and Juliette

In the fall of fifty-eight Charles was old enough to start school. He had been at Hélène's for two years. Sometimes during the year Yvonne brought Keith home. Charles wasn't a problem. He was enrolled in school and didn't need care while I was working. Even then, his very first day was a manifestation of his personality, an expression of the manner in which he would confront any undertaking in his future. As soon as he walked in the door he announced, "I don't have to go to school tomorrow." That was indeed a most bewildering statement. Subsequently someone asked, "How come?" "Well," he retorted jauntily, "I learned everything the teacher knew."

First Communion: Charles and Lucille

Keith was a different enigma. He stubbornly, flatly refused to go to daycare, any daycare. And when Keith made up his mind about something it was incontrovertible, an open and shut case. I tried every means imaginable in an effort to make him change his mind,

but it was to no avail, Keith had spoken! I didn't have a prayer and should have admitted that I had lost the battle without further ado. I was desperate! It was evident that the child had some horrifying illusions about going to daycare and was petrified, but on the other hand what was I to do. Mercifully, I had an invincible ally on my team (always rooting for my side) who never failed to rescue me in times of crisis when the situation appeared irreconcilable. This proved to be no exception. True to form, not one but two of the neighbors volunteered to care for Keith during the day. Lo and behold, our hero was quite in agreement with these arrangements, as he would have the opportunity to spend the day with his friends. Both families had children his age and they had been playmates ever since he had come back home. Again I breathed a sigh of relief. Another obstacle had been surmounted! Again, and on my knees I thanked merciful Providence for its intervention on my behalf.

It was sometime during that episode that a young German couple came to live with us. They also must have descended straight from the skies for they were just perfect; amazing! Their son was exactly the same age as Keith; in fact Mary and I had been in the same ward at the hospital at the same time. They were new Canadians and were in desperate need of a place to stay, and I was in desperate need of someone to help me. They settled in a spare bedroom on the main floor. Although the accommodation was very modest, it was the best we had and the couple seemed to be most grateful for our hospitality. As for me, grateful did not even begin to express the appreciation I felt towards that couple. He was a wonderful person and she was an absolute angel. The children adored her. She took care of the two boys, prepared the evening meal for the children, and did all the housework. It was as if the heavens had suddenly decided to smile upon us. Everything was running so smoothly and we did everything in our power to persuade the couple to remain with us forever. But alas, it was too good to be true. The husband worked at the university, and soon they had saved enough to buy a farm. We missed them desperately when they were gone.

When Keith first came to the city, he couldn't understand that he had to stay in his own yard. In the country he had had the freedom to wander in much less restricted confines. Consequently he had to be supervised constantly or he'd be on the street. No matter how vigilant we were he always managed to escape. In the blink of an eye he would disappear. One day he was found on seventy-sixth Avenue, one of the busiest thoroughfares in the city. It is little wonder that the neighbors thought we were careless. The whole family was scared to death for his safety, and every one of us was on constant alert, unable to relax for a second. This situation went on and on and I was becoming frantic. So one day after I had rescued him from one of his most precarious escapades, I began to chastise him in a most unrelenting manner. I pointed out to him the dangers of the traffic, the fact that he might not be able to find his way home etcetera. I went on and on and on in an endless tirade. At last while I was right in the middle of ranting and raving, Keith cried out in a loud voice, "You can stop now Mom, I'll never do it again." Whereupon I stopped dead utterly dumbfounded. The child was not even two years old! Well that was the end of that, for lo and behold, true to his word, he never did run away again.

Juliette, Charles, Keith, David, Walter, Carol, and Lucille shortly after all reunited.

Some of the events that occurred during these first years in Edmonton have become vague, masked with the misty shadows of the years, therefore the stage at which they transpired cannot be determined with any degree of precision. For instance it was either in the first or second year that my nephew Louis came to stay with us. It was rather nice. Bits and pieces of his sojourn at our house flashback in my mind's eye. It gave me an incentive to prepare decent full-coarse meals, meat, potatoes, vegetables, and a dessert. I appreciated the change as my kids 'diet consisted mostly of wieners, hamburgers, tomatoes, and fast foods'. A premium roast beef dinner usually went in the garbage. He did various maintenance jobs around the house; tasks that I did not have time to do and were beyond my expertise. He went out of his way to help and be congenial. He even took us to the beach one Sunday afternoon to please the children. Before he left, I helped him to buy a car.

During the time he was with us Lorraine, his sister, and Fern, Marie-Anne's daughter, came to work in the city. Unfortunately, the only employment they could find was cleaning windows at a construction site. The girls found this work too strenuous and they soon were on their way back home.

The nine years at St. Kevin were filled with many momentous events. It is indeed regrettable that only the most spectacular incidences have remained instilled in my memory. Of course the habitual daily schedule and the associates or fellow workers will live in my heart forever. Sister Good Counsel, the grade two teacher, Mrs. Falkenburg were as constant as the northern star, always there to assist and give me the support I so desperately needed at the time. Due to their assistance I was able to make the transition involved in teaching from country to city schools.

During the first year and many years afterwards, I was teaching a grade one and two split, the advanced grade one students and the lower grade two students. When the enrollment increased however, my class consisted of straight grade one students. A split grade is manageable when there are a reasonable number of students and when the students are selected with care.

One year, there were eleven grade two and twenty-one grade one students in my class. The grade two children were very low. To make matters worse, two of the first graders were exceptional children. One child had been afflicted with a serious disease and was very emotional. He would become hysterical at the slightest variation in the routine and cry out in alarm, whereupon he had to be reassured and pacified. It was a process which demanded a great deal of compassion, patience, and unscheduled class time. The other child had been over protected. Apparently her mother was able to anticipate her slightest need before she requested it. Consequently she had never learned to speak. Besides, her mother was compelled to sit with her in the classroom because she felt dreadfully insecure in an unfamiliar situation. When she wanted something she'd hank at my skirt and mumble an unfamiliar jargon like "hm...hm.. hm..". It drove me out of my mind. Yet it was a situation that demanded self-control and empathy. I was astounded when at the end of the year with my help and that of her classmates, she was not only able to speak fluently but she had learned to read as well as her classmates.

St. Kevin was surrounded by the elite and the well to do: Doctors, lawyers, and businessmen. These families who lived in the district possessed all the amenities affiliated with the rich. Consequently most of the students who attended this school were from people with affluence; that was with the exception of the children who came from the "flats". Apparently families with very restricted means resided in the district at the foot of the hill. Obviously the contrast between the students from these two districts was quite indisputable. The difference was usually manifested in the behavior or the attitude of the children but what was glaringly perceptible was the quality of their clothing, the nutritious value of their lunches, their personal health habits and countless other factors. For example, the children from upper echelon of society came to school with the appearance of someone who has just emerged from a beauty salon, whereas those of restricted means wore patches and many with snags in their hair.

On several occasions my thoughts wander into the past and I experience illusive visions of these precious little angels. One year it seemed that they had rained down from the skies, they were virtual cherubs. During gym classes I had taught them a dance to the music of "Hanky Doodle" and a clap dance which they performed at the Christmas concert. They were out of this world. Veritable dancing dolls!

There are many other incidences that have remained with me throughout the years. Although these may seem trivial to someone who hasn't been directly involved in similar circumstances they are part of who I am. All those who have been so dear to me and at some crossroad along my long earthly voyage, have walked along with me, shared the joys and tears of my journey, the players in the eventful drama of my chaotic life, will forever be with me as I trudge along to the end. The spirits of all those, benefactors, parents, brothers and sisters, my children, students and dear friends, I ferry with me wherever capricious destiny points the way.

Although it is difficult to pinpoint the exact time it occurred an unforgettable yet rather remarkable event transpired during those early years in Edmonton. Carol and one of her classmates, Bridget, had become very close friends. The two girls spent a great deal of time together, visiting, doing homework, etcetera. Carol spent a lot of time at her house. As Bridget was an only child the girl's parents were glad that their daughter had such a good friend as Carol. The family had planned a trip to Europe and they wanted Carol to accompany their daughter while they visited their relatives in Germany. Although I was afraid that Carol might be homesick it seemed unreasonable not to allow her to take advantage of such a wonderful opportunity. The girl's parents were upstanding citizens and they were paying all the expenses. Subsequently I made all the arrangements for her to go.

The family was to come for Carol while I was at school. Naturally I did not expect her to be there when I came home that evening.

However she had panicked when it came time to leave and fearing that I would be upset, she had hidden in the attic. Apparently the other children, who had conspired in this shenanigan, were bringing her food! How long she stayed up there is a complete mystery, but she did come down eventually and confessed. She thought I would be mad, but that was a false assumption. It was a relief! She was home safe and sound and I thanked my lucky stars.

It was during my second year at St. Kevin School the principal had a heart attack and passed away. Although he was a very strict adherent to rules and regulations, he was fair and everyone mourned his demise. It was when Mr. O'Coffey died that another extraterrestrial experience occurred to me. It seems utterly incredible, in fact completely beyond all reasonable explanation but although great distances separated us, I actually witnessed his death. It is so weird, so bizarre that if it had not occurred to me I would seriously doubt its authenticity. I saw him sitting in his rocking chair, smoking his pipe. Suddenly something struck me with such force that it felt as if I had been clobbered with a sledgehammer. At that moment I knew that it was Mr. O's spirit who had come to warn me of his death. Lo and behold, the circumstances and the time coincided in every respect with the extraordinary supernatural encounter I had experienced. The reason why these strange, unfathomable events occur is beyond comprehension.

It was also while I was at St. Kevin that Carol's friend Bridget invited her to go with her to visit her Grandparents and her father in Germany. At first, I was apprehensive. The two girls, who were young, would be traveling alone. Besides I was not familiar with the friend's family. And on top of everything else there was the financial aspect to be considered. But that was the least of my worries as with my faithful ally, Providence, and a little bit of resourcefulness, there are always ways and means or schemes of scraping together the funds required for such an adventure. As soon as I had ascertained myself as to the safety of the girls during the journey and while they were in Germany (the reputation of the friend's relatives was impeccable and Carol was dependable) I began to make the necessary arrangements for the trip. Plane and U-Rail tickets, luggage, suitable clothing, and lodging accommodations had to be secured. Again Carol's personality manifested itself in no uncertain terms. She was so tormented with anxiety and apprehension that it was almost an obsession. She feared that it would be impossible for me to make the necessary arrangements in time. Therefore, being well aware of the severity of her angst, I decided to have everything in readiness months before the date of departure, to Carol's intense relief. Be that as it may, it was the only way the family could resume the normal routine of confronting and tackling the daily tasks at hand in tranquility.

One of the teachers from the school (in fact the same one who had spent some time with us when my husband passed away) helped Carol chose an appropriate wardrobe and gave her valuable advice concerning ways to facilitate traveling frustrations. She insisted that it is very important to travel light leaving anything that is not absolutely essential at home. She also insisted that if the girls purchased gifts they should ship those immediately rather than lug them wherever they went. This proved to be sound advice, as the girls were not burdened with the weight of these numerous purchases. I treasure a pair of exquisite and delicate lamps that Carol sent me from Holland.

There was another beneficent soul in that school staff. She was the school nurse. My financial dilemma must have been a well-known fact because all the teachers seemed to be aware that I was struggling desperately to make ends meet. Subsequently, this benign soul came to my rescue. She was a competent seamstress therefore she decided to use her expertise in order to increase my rather meager wardrobe. She spent numerous evenings sewing and remodeling several garments that were appropriate for classroom wear. I was indeed most grateful to her and wore these garments with pride.

I taught at St. Kevin School for nine years, years overflowing with moments of great rejoicing interspersed by moments of heartbreaks and tribulations. Joy engendered by the virtue and the righteousness of the people who surrounded me and my children, the essence of my existence. I will forever cherish the goodwill, the support, and the gifts showered upon me by those providential angels as I struggled along the way. Besides, it was such a blessing to have the children with me and to know that their well-being transcended all other priorities. Indeed the children's well-being, their safety, and their needs had become an obsession, a fixation! I was scared to death that they would be deprived of the essential needs (justifiably so as the task that I had tackled was insurmountable) that nothing else mattered. I had one object, one goal, and towards that end there was only one inflexible path. Fixated single-mindedly on the straight and narrow, the unrelenting route. I was incapable of straying from that idée fix (that mad compulsion) or even to set foot out from the well-beaten inexorable tract. I was driven like one possessed, madly pursuing one single perspective, one unique achievement, and the survival of those that God had entrusted in my care. (A one-tract mind? It could well be.)

It was during these early years that some significant developments began to manifest themselves in our lives. The most dramatic and problematic of these was the tribulations and the responsibilities involved in raising a family as a single working parent. Besides, in an effort to improve our living conditions we decided to sell our wartime house and buy a more convenient and modern home. Thus began what for lack of a better expression a long series of house hopping or bouncing from one dwelling to another in search of the one that would be right for us. This was a tremendous undertaking indeed for the family needed a house that was spacious with at least four bedrooms and it had to require relatively minimal up keep. It goes without saying that our search seemed to be hopeless and never ending. Fortunately, and after many long years, we did find the home of our dreams.

Although it is impossible for me to recall the exact duration of our sojourn in our first Edmonton home, that episode turned out to have had a prolonged and almost irreversible significance in the lives of the family. For it was during that period of time that the stage was set and our fate was predetermined for the immediate future. For the events that transpired then changed the whole course of our destiny. To begin with I set about frantically in search of someone to care for the children. It was a futile undertaking. The sisters had recommended a girl who appeared to be suitable. She needed a home and I needed someone to supervise the children. Unfortunately she was sick constantly and I spent most of my time taking her to the doctor; time that should have been spent with my family. She claimed that the boys would not listen to her (no wonder! And she was very unhappy). She was gone when I came home one day along with quite a few of my personal possession. No matter. Following that incidence, I had made arrangements with a young family that should have been advantageous to both parties. He was a policeman and he and his wife had two beautiful little girls with blond hair. They were to live with us, share the groceries, and she was to care for Lucille and Charlie during the day. That didn't work out either. Their youngest child had to be taken to Calgary for medical care and naturally they had to leave. At this point I had given up. Mercifully Hélène agreed to take Lucille and Charlie and care for them until they were old enough to go to school.

These early years were prophetical years. Years that were foreshadowing impending disasters looming in the not too distant horizon. When tragedy strikes one usually wonders how it could have been averted or more significantly what were the incidents that caused the tragedy to happen in the first place. In my case, a thousand and one circumstances or incidents that might have been instrumental or led to such an excruciatingly painful catastrophe kept whirling around in my mind and tormenting me. Dwelling on what lay at the root of the family's calamity drove me to the point of insanity. In the last analysis it was evidently a combination of many factors. We had landed in a district of low income families and it was, as a consequence of the parents' financial struggles a rough entourage. Besides, my teaching duties plus the management of the household prevented me from spending enough time with the children and they were often on their own. Or the boys may have been angry because they had to grow up without the emotional and financial support of a dedicated father. Be that as it may be, and for whatever reason, they began to rebel. At this point it is questionable whether their anger was directed at me, at their father, their circumstances, or all these factors combined. It is obvious that being a single parent I was at the brunt of it all.

Although I found the boys' behavior very unacceptable through this whole period, at first, their transgressions were not terribly serious according to society's norms. They were simply minor adventurous infractions common to adolescents in that age group. For instance, David began to assert his mad passion for freedom. This obsession was unmistakably manifested in his wild reckless and fearless behavior. Every now and then he would sneak out of the house with a friend and disappear for a week at a time. It goes without saying that on those occasions I would go snake with anxiety. The friend's mother and I would spend hours on end searching all over kingdom come for those two. It was, needless to say, a futile endeavor. When, at the end of their escapades, they finally came sneaking in, they simply said, "Oh, we were only camping in the bushes by Mill Creek. It was fun." Fun for them maybe! The anxiety we had endured plus the fact that the clothes and shoes they had worn were ruined were evidently the least of their concerns!

Later (but not very much later) there were the car episodes. Not one car but a zillion cars! The first one was what the younger generation calls an "old clunker." David paid a measly one hundred dollars for it. Mercifully the thing never did work and David was too young to get a driver's license. Soon it was traded in for something else. There were many of those incidences; one car followed another, all landing in the junkyard one after another. David did not believe in loitering on the road and that's putting it mildly! He drove at the speed of a flying bullet, passing every vehicle on the highway. It goes without saying that he was in numerous accidents, some of which were dangerously hazardous. David's worst problem was that fear was a sensation that was unknown to him. Consequently he could be as much of a daredevil and as reckless as he pleased without becoming alarmed or being in a state of panic. He simply threw caution to the winds.

Walter had different problems. Although there were some situations when his behavior was seriously questionable, it was during his eleventh year at school that he began to openly exhibit signs of the animosity and the bitterness that festered at the very depth of his soul. And his protests were so formidable that they shook the very foundation of our supposedly well-established existence. (It rocked the boat!)

The first crucial sign of Walter's malcontent was his continual absenteeism from school followed by his downright refusal to attend classes under any circumstances. He had several excuses, none of which made any sense. That was totally unacceptable to me. Obviously I used every means at my disposal to persuade him to persevere until he graduated from high school. I pleaded, I scolded, I raved and ranted, but to no avail. At last, out of desperation, I enrolled him in a private institution that was operated by Catholic priests. He seemed to be willing to attend that facility and I thought that the crisis had been solved. Even though the monthly fees severely strained the family budget, the education of the children took precedence over everything else. I was unfortunately deluding myself. Some time later, I had a meeting with the superior of the school. He commended me for my good intentions but declared that I was wasting my money, as Walter was not only wasting his time but that he was a disturbance to the others in the classroom. I was devastated! To have given these children a fortune was an impossibility considering my meager budget, but I had set my heart on giving them the opportunity of getting an education. Subsequent to my meeting with the superior, I knew that at this point belaboring the issue was hopeless, like beating a dead horse. Although I had put up a tempestuous fight, I had lost the battle. All my ambitious provisions for Walter's future collapsed. All the hopes and aspirations I had cherished for him lay shattered at my feet. Or so it appeared at that dismal moment. I felt at the moment, an irretrievable loss; the death of a fragment in my soul.

Looking back over all these long years it has finally dawned on me at long last that parents expect too much from their children. It has also struck me like a bombshell that I was the most culpable, the worst of them all. Because they were mine, 'they ought to be perfect', was my way-out erratic notion. There are innumerable mistakes, an inordinate magnitude of blunders parents make while in the process of raising their children. I rank at the top of the list. It is little wonder. They are entrusted with the most precious of all treasures, and saddled with the most formidable occupation imaginable, an occupation that demands the expertise and skills of all professions rolled into one. Yet parents are expected to tackle the most complex of all tasks without the slightest amount of training or preparation. Success under these circumstances would require a miracle.

At this point in my story I reminisce about the depth and poignancy of my friend's words as she reflected upon the distressing episodes of her dramatic life. "I could never write my bibliography," she exclaimed as I was endeavoring to persuade her to write the tale of her most extraordinary life. "I would be reliving all the struggles, the anguish, and the humiliations again. It is too painful, I cannot bear to walk through that miserable torment a second time." And at this point in my narrative, I know exactly what she meant, understand the turmoil of her feelings, and deeply empathize with her misgivings. For it is with the same dread that I am about to relate the next episode in the journey of my most chaotic life. At the moment, to skip or to avoid awakening the memories of the most painful and thorny stretch along the way is my ultimate desire. Indeed to cite these agonizing recollections in print is to bear the anguish all over again. It is insufferable. And I am tempted to abandon the project altogether. It is, as my friend so apply put it, too tragic. Yet to omit these unfortunate episodes in the story of my life would give it a Polly-Anna aspect and deprive it of its credibility. For my life is anything or everything but a facsimile of that aspect, nor is there the slightest resemblance between the two. My existence has been a series of contradictions, my experiences continually shifting from the enjoyment of heavenly bliss to the torment of hell's scorching fire. A veritable paradox!

At this point in time it is difficult to specify with any degree of precision exactly when the serious problems started. There had been a lot of quarrelling, bickering, and so forth among the children but though it was irritating and extremely nerve wracking, it was tolerable. It seems to me that the real trouble began when a friend brought liquor into the house without my knowledge or my permission. I had been specific regarding the use of alcohol. "Not one drop of alcohol will ever cross the threshold of this home." I declared. And so it was until someone came with several bottles of whiskey (the devil's brew) and convinced the boys that there was no harm in consuming it when it is done in moderation. Reluctantly, and not to offend our guest, I let it go by. That was a most grievous mistake! That blunder or failure to be more tenacious and to cling to my parental rights was a disaster. As a consequence I lost another battle.

After the episode with the accursed spirits things went from bad to worse. I had a tragic foreboding premonition of impending doom and I was frantic with the fear that my boys had chosen the path that would lead them to their ruin. Alas, at that most fatal moment, when my parental authority and even my moral values had been questioned and challenged, they had taken the first step toward perdition. For once they had had a taste of Satan's brew, they sought the company of those who indulge in this infernal habit. Often their new friends had undesirable even dangerous habits. "Tell me with whom you associate and I will tell you who you are," is irrefutable as a statement of unvarnished truth, for it is indeed infallible. Soon my boys joined their friends in the pursuit of their rash and inappropriate conduct. The use of foul language, the drinking, the wild carousing and partying, the continual fighting, and the reckless driving were all part of this mad jamboree. Besides every one of these boys was a petty thief!

I couldn't cope with any of this mad behavior, but the fighting and stealing drove me insane. It didn't seem to make sense. I descended from a family whose integrity was impeccable; in fact my dad was over zealous and had to pay his debts to the last cent. "How can a son of mine take anything belonging to someone else?" I asked myself over and over again.

At first I tried to lure the whole gang (the boys and all their friends) into my house where they could do their shenanigans and stay out of trouble. It was unmitigated pandemonium! The blaring music (Wake Up Little Susie" How I hated that song!); the loud talk, and everything else teenage boys do, sent me over the edge.

But it was better than having them on the street doing mischief. Many dramatic events transpired while the gang gathered at my house. It goes without saying that teenage boys are always starving. I remember making sandwiches by the truckload to feed them, a process most detrimental to my meager budget. On another occasion, one of them put a loaded shell on a stove burner while it was on and it exploded with an ear-splitting bang. It goes without saying that the culprit vowed up and down that he didn't do it, even after he had been caught red-handed. The parents ignored my plea when I requested them to keep their son at home. In fact this boy was bent on mischief. He'd sit on a tire in the middle of a busy street and dare the traffic to stop or go around him. On other occasions, he'd get in an elevator in the C.N. building downtown and go up and down without allowing any passengers in. Apparently this boy was way too much for me and for his parents to handle! It is almost incredible that the other boys were good and did not cause any trouble while they were at my house. During the interval, the boys started collecting pigeons. They built a little shelter for them in the back yard and had gathered a whole stack of them. One morning, to the boys' grievous chagrin, the pigeons were all gone. They had been stolen in the night. Although the boys never tried to retrieve their lose, David, fearless as usual, sold the ones he caught as he hung from a rafter under the high level bridge to buy food for a friend who had run away from home.

In spite of all my efforts, the boys were getting deeper and deeper in trouble. At the beginning the material they took was inexpensive, like candy and items of little value. Soon, however things got more serious and on several occasions they were caught. I was going out of my mind! Finally out of desperation, I asked John, my brother to take Walter on the farm and send him to school in Leoville. Away from the temptations of the city and his friends I hoped that Walter might make a new start, reverting back to be the creditable and dependable individual of the past. It was a viable but temporary solution, as my brother, with a family of his own, was unable to keep Walter on a permanent basis.

It was somewhere in that time period that my sister Germaine came to live with us. She had recently lost her husband and had been left with very little income or financial security. In order to make ends meet she tried various kinds of employment without success. It is unfortunate that she did not seek employment in a car dealership, as she was an expert in that field. Be that as it may, Germaine's daughter, Evelyn, found her mother doing extremely strenuous and demeaning labor and brought her to the city. She and her two children, Paul and Paulette, were to live with us. We were glad to welcome them into our home. It was a perfect arrangement. There was someone at home with the children during the day and my sister's family became part of the household. Germaine was a meticulous housekeeper and she kept the house immaculately clean. Besides, she took excellent care of Keith. It was great! As I try to conjure up the past I get the impression that every effort was made in order to make my sister and her family feel at home. I had made arrangements for Paulette and Juliette to go to a private school in Edmonton. They were getting French and religious instructions besides the regular subjects.

It was too good to be true. There may have been several explanations for the fact that Germaine was feeling more and more discontented and frustrated - things that, because of my hectic schedule I had failed to appreciate. For one thing, my sister was unable to understand my life-style. She also thought the household budget was frugal. She had never had to economize on groceries or household items before and it sent her over the edge to be chintzy when buying groceries. And to make matters worse a conflict emerged between her and Walter. In an effort to solve this problem, I asked George if he would be able to get Walter a job at his worksite, which he did. This did not solve all the problems however. Soon Germaine found herself a job selling auto parts and she decided to establish a home of her own. She bought a neat little trailer (I lent her the down payment) and she moved away. Apparently she felt that she had been maltreated at my house and she was outraged. She didn't mince her words when she vented her fury during one of David's visit. I was also very hurt because she didn't trust me enough to tell me the truth concerning certain financial agreements we had undertaken. She must have thought that I would never find out. It was an insult to my intelligence.

Not long after she left she was in a serious car accident and although she was almost fatally injured I was not notified. My nephew (my sister's son) told me about the accident much later. The car my sister had been driving was his brand new vehicle and it had been a complete write-off as a result of the accident. My nephew was devastated! He had been working for ages to purchase the automobile of his dreams and when he had finally paid for it in full someone else wrote it off before he had had a chance to drive it. After that incidence the family moved to Surrey, British Columbia and I lost tract of their whereabouts.

After living in Ritchie for five years, I decided to buy a duplex in the Kensington district. The duplex was brand new and was therefore very comfortable, convenient and easy to keep clean. When we first moved in all the children were living at home. Walter was back from the coast. He should never have gone there in the first place. However, under great pressure one often makes wrong decisions. He had been involved in some kind of trouble and George decided to send him home.

As soon as we were settled in our new home the old cycle of habitual activities began to repeat themselves. The house was inundated with friends, boy friends, girl friends, friends of every description and temperament. And there was music, music of every kind except classical, music that reverberate from one end of the house to another, in fact even the walls pulsated to the beat of its mighty rhythm. Then there was the food, the continual sandwich making. However none of these factors were on par or even held a candle to the intensity of the ear-splitting, rambunctious hullabaloo that continually rocked the premises. Absolute pandemonium! But, although all this was enough to drive anybody to the madhouse, and that at times I went completely berserk, I was glad that the friends gathered at my house. At least I knew where my children were and what they were doing. In spite of all the shenanigans and the headaches, the children's safety was all that mattered.

Then I began making one mistake after another. As soon as the boys became teen-agers the car mania emerged. From morning till night the main, in fact the only topic of the conversation was," If only I had a car." and, "All our friends have a car", are very convincing arguments, especially if you hear it non-stop. At any rate I gave in. Walter had found a 1956 Ford in mint shape and he talked me into buying it. I thought that if he had something of his own, something he could be proud of, it would give him a positive perspective and make him happy. Cars, however, come all wrapped up, part and parcel, with a baggage of problems all their own. Money for gas and repairs, traffic regulations, etc. were major concerns. These factors created complications that should have been anticipated. Yet under pressure, one is likely to make rash decisions. The boys never did tell me how they managed to buy gas and repairs for the car, it was a deep dark secret that they kept well hidden from me. I was very concerned and should have been, for that got them into one jam after another.

After struggling with all these problems (questionable car maintenance) the boys had an accident and the car was almost a write-off. Fortunately a skilled mechanic who lived in the neighborhood took over the difficult task of repairing the wreck. This man had a full time job however and could only work on the car at night. Needless to say it was a long drawn out process.

Walter was not about to wait forever for his car. So one evening he went to the man's garage, took his car that was still in need of repair and away he went! The mechanic was livid! Mercifully he did not press charges, but he insisted that I pay for the complete project, which was understandable.

As I reminisce over this madness, these idiotic incidents, I find myself unable to comprehend the motives that could have possibly been the rationalization powerful enough to justify the continual repetition of my misguided blunders. For no sooner had I been raked over the coals and put through the wringer in retribution for the last error I had committed that I fell hook line and sinker into another hazardous snare. On and on, one boo-boo after another! It was inconceivable! No wonder Bob Dillon cries out, lamenting mankind's perpetual frailty, "When will they ever learn, when will they ever learn." How wise, how applicable are these words to the human species! As for myself, Bob may as well have been addressing them directly to me, for they fit me to a tee. Incessantly I keep lecturing myself, "when will I ever learn, oh God, when will I ever learn!"

It didn't take long before the 1956 ford was out of commission again. So what did this misguided Einstein do but trade the Ford for a luxurious Pontiac Parisienne convertible. That was a boner, in fact on a scale of one to ten, it scored at the top of the scale. For one thing, the cost was way above my means, and besides it was much too fancy a car for a teenager. The boys got into all kinds of trouble trying to raise funds in order to operate that expensive vehicle. Eventually it was in an accident (I hate to say that I was driving at the time) and after it was repaired we were fortunate enough to sell it. It solved one problem. But there were a whole slew of others that were not as easily handled.

Subsequent to all these negative circumstances the members of the family were bound to suffer disadvantageous and grievous consequences. The boys' problematic associations, my misguided solutions to the problems, the family's economic status, etc. all contributed and led to the catastrophic events that ensued

At this point I envisage the most chaotic and painful stretch in the dramatic path I have tread along the long and sensational journey of my life. It is a stretch I dare not go. For I have tread that path before, it is a path strewn with thorns and whose prickly thorns threaten to pierce the heart. Many hours have I spent puzzling over the way that this episode could be told in the least painful way. Yet it felt like the reopening of an old wound, or revisiting the depths of the inferno when once you have been exonerated and have tasted the wonders of redeeming light. To that depth I dare not go, for in despair I would lack the courage to find my way back across that treacherous thorny path and would dwell in the abyss of anguish and wretchedness for all eternity.

In lieu of relating the painful details of the events that transpired during that most problematic episode of our lives, and considering the fact that I lack the fortitude to do so, I will endeavor to evade the issue by using the ruse employed by our honorable politicians. It is a well-known fact that these noble gentlemen have mastered the art of beating about the bush, going around and around an issue without ever reaching a definite conclusion. The simple words yes and no in answer to a direct question are considered lethal weapons that could well cause embarrassment and discredit the speaker. My intentions however, are not to mislead the reader but to avoid reliving the tribulations and heartaches afflicting the family during those dreadful years. As the boys (in fact all the teenage boys of the district seemed to be in the same boat) got deeper and deeper in trouble the consequences became more and more serious. In spite of my efforts to atone for their misdeeds, the situation was beyond my control and I was desperate. The repercussions were disastrous! Indeed because of catastrophic gravity of these consequences the family's future was in jeopardy. In fact the whole family was

Jeannette Romaniuk

ostracized by everyone in their midst, branded as the untouchables and every member as a persona non grata. Even the members of my family became appalled by the enormity of the tales that were related to them. As usual the magnitude and the monstrosity of the stories accumulated with every mile, therefore it is not surprising that across that far-off distance, they would be colossal. Amazingly my colleagues, instead of rising against me in condemnation, stood by me and supported me all through that dreadful ordeal.

My reaction to the crisis was, however, alarming! I could not accept or cope with the situation. I felt that it was impossible for me to go on. Millions of recriminations assailed my thoughts. Shame, guilt and what I could have done to prevent the situation from happening kept spinning around in my head on and on until I was on the verge of becoming a raving maniac! The courage, fortitude, determination, and obsessions possessing me at the onset of this venture went flying out the window. How I wished that I could have ended it all, yet such a cop out was unthinkable. If I lacked the courage to carry on for myself, then I had to carry on for the children. So in the light of this predicament, I devised a survival strategy. In psychology it's called displacement, a method by which a habit is abandoned and replaced by another. I became the mechanical woman. In my robotic state I continued to function normally, attending meticulously to all my responsibilities but refused to allow myself to think. For as soon as my mind began to drift or wander I was overcome with misery and would sink deeply into the depths of despair. I became a machine, as being human was too perilous, too painful! And it worked! I'd wind myself up in the morning, take the bus, teach all day, take the bus home after school, feed and bath the children and then correct my book till all hours of the night. But of course in school it was a little easier because as soon as the children arrived in the classroom I became so involved with them that everything else was temporarily obliterated, completely blanked out of my mind. And that was that! Of course, thinking was taboo, utterly off limits. Thinking would have been too painful, overwhelming my entire essence, and superseding my most urgent responsibilities. It would have been the vehicle leading me down the path of destruction.

My friend, Mr. Hall kept quoting words of wisdom, words that have often sustained me in times of trouble, "All this will pass," he would say, "and be forgotten forever." How this wise statement has proved its infallibility and wisdom in the years that followed I cannot rightfully say, but it has taken me past many harrowing hurdles. Eventually, after years of heartbreak and tribulations, things gradually began to ease into some semblance of rationality. A calm after the storm? Walter was soon gainfully employed and earning a reputation as a valuable employee. Indeed, he performed his duty with such speed and competence that he was highly recommended by his employers. His superior intelligence plus the ability and facility of learning new techniques and skills made it possible for him to gain an expertise in many fields and thus to be promoted to higher levels in the occupation at which he happened to be working at the time. David on the other hand decided to apprentice as a welder. It seemed to be a good decision at the time, as he had no interest or desire to improve his educational standards yet demonstrated a remarkable ability and aptitude in learning the techniques and skills that other occupations demand. Thus, as fate would have it, he was apprenticed as a welder and became a master technician in that field. Had I known the phenomenal implications and consequences involved in welding, I would have moved heaven and earth to dissuade him from that course, and would have directed him into another less strenuous field. How exorbitant is the cost of ignorance and how excessive the penalty David had to endure because of such a misinformed, misguided decision. (Another crucial blunder!) Alas it is too late to rectify.

Soon after Walter had established himself in his occupation and had become independent, he and his girl friend decided to get married. They were both terribly young to assume such a

Jeannette Romaniuk

tremendous responsibility. Consequently the girl's parents and I would have preferred them to wait until they were more mature and understood the serious implications of their decision. An incident occurred however that made it obvious to both parents that the couple had irrevocably made up their minds. If they could not get the parents consent they would elope! And elope they did, that is almost! They were gone half-way to Timbuktu when the parents, in desperation, knew that they had lost the battle. They, as parents usually do when there is no other recourse, yielded. They urged their children to come home and promised to give their blessing to the marriage. And so the wedding took place. I would like to repeat the phrase, "and they lived happily ever after," but the circumstances do not permit me to do so. That is a story that remains to be told later in this drama.

I did it again! Over and over again I have strayed and rambled away from the logical sequence of my tale. I am indeed incorrigible! For this time I have bungled things up in the most ostentatious manner! Not only have I failed to maintain the natural sequence but even the natural order of the events as they occurred has been distorted. Again I ask the reader to bear with me.

As a matter of fact it was Juliette who was the first to venture into the bond of marriage. Although her fiancée was a young man of good repute and integrity, I was indeed very apprehensive for both were too young to undertake such a grave commitment. On the other hand, the couple seemed to be devoted to one another, so the wedding took place with the parents' blessing. The ceremony which took place at St. Edmund Church was followed by a modest reception at the house. We were living in the duplex at the time. It was not an elaborate celebration as the guests were mostly family members. Actually, close family celebrations are more intimate thus much more enjoyable, and the expenditures are far less prohibitive. Again it would be unrealistic and wishful thinking to say, "and they lived happily ever after," for this is not a fairytale but a story that relates the sober, down-to-earth, and sometimes cruel facts of the hand one is dealt down here in God's supreme kingdom. Only if it were a fairytale!

David had been intermittently courting many different girls. None of these relationships seem to be very serious however as most lasted only a very short time. David had excellent taste and some of the girls he dated were absolutely stunning! One of them dyed her hair a different color every time she went out. It was impossible to tell whether she was a blonde, a brunette or a redhead. She was gorgeous. Besides she had a remarkably refined and pleasant personality. Another one of his heartthrobs was a dazzling beauty. David was captivated by that girl's ravishing charm, yet a serious relationship was never established between them. There were many others. None however were significant. That is until he met the girl of his dreams and then he changed completely. Whereas he had previously been a carefree daredevil caring for little but wild uproarious revelry, he became devoted to his sweetheart and she was the girl he married.

The wedding was held in a Catholic church of coarse. There was some controversy concerning the ceremony as the Ukrainian Priest insisted that as David was of Ukrainian origin he should perform the ritual according to the Ukrainian Church rites. This did not sit too well with me as David had been brought up according to the rites of the Roman Catholic Church. After a great deal of negotiation it was agreed that both priests would officiate. It was a wise decision as it created an ambience of elegance and sophistication to the ceremony. It was at David's wedding that I was overcome with panic. As the couple was professing their vows, it occurred to me that soon all the children would be on their own and that one by one they were leaving their home. I was overwhelmed with desolation. It was then that I realized that soon all my loved ones would be gone. Unlike so many parents who cannot wait for their children to be on their own, to be relieved of the responsibility of their care, and to live in peace, I wanted mine to be with me forever. They had been my anchor, the core of my being. Yet fate demanded that I let them go! One by one! And I to be left forsaken, isolated, drifting aimlessly, upon the wide desolate, endless, and shifting sands of life.

Mind you, it must not be taken for granted that all these events occurred in one fell swoop. On the contrary somewhere in between there were the courtship days, the days when all the young people gathered at our house in Ritchie or in Kensington to have fun and enjoy being with their friends. Those were the days! At times there were as many as twenty-five kids in the house. Pandemonium! Big time! It would have been hard to say what was the loudest: the chatter, the laughter, the stories or jokes or the music. To tell the truth it must have been the music. They'd crank that phonograph up to its highest volume and play their favorite records over and over again. The volume was so formidable that the very structure of the house was hoisted upward and jolted from its very foundation as it swayed from the shear force of the vibrations. Needless to say the walls did not fare any better. They rattled and jerked while the hanging pictures crashed to the floor. It is amazing that these kids didn't all get up and dance, as usually the lilt of the music carries you away. Perhaps their whole being rocked with the beat of the music. On the other hand perhaps they did dance and I was too distracted by the loud music to notice. To this day, "Wake Up Little Susie", "Goodnight Irene", and "Mule Train" are songs that I despise with a passion. On the other hand, I preferred having the kids where they were safe, having a good time, and not getting in trouble. Most of them were good kids. There was however was one that proved to be out of my league, but he was an exception rather than the rule. He'd shoot pellets into the boys' hockey game and into my typewriter, ruining them. We're lucky he didn't set the house on fire. (It wasn't for lack of trying.) As I reminisce about those days I am amazed that my meager budget could be stretched enough to provide lunches and sandwiches for all these hungry people. Besides, it is almost incredible that the neighbors didn't sign a petition to have us evicted from the neighborhood. The racket we raised was loud enough to wake the dead.

The fact that I had to work in the evening at a different occupation in order to make ends meet was highly influential in aggravating our precarious and difficult situation. Although I did not work during the first years when the children were very young, they should not have been left unsupervised when they were adolescents. Necessity is, however, a ruthless master! Looking back it seems that there were other solutions but at the time I was too overwrought to think of the alternatives. For instance, as the provider of the household, I should have hired a full time housekeeper to take my place in the home. The children would have developed a sense of security that a stable and normal household routine provides. No stones should have been left unturned until the right person had been found and I deeply regret my failure to do so. The second alternative would have been to live according to our meager budget. This is almost impossible with a house full of teenagers.

As soon as we arrived in Edmonton I started taking courses at the university (and some by correspondence) in order to obtain my Bachelor of Education Degree. It was very difficult as Saskatchewan and Alberta have different educational standards. The Department of Education in Alberta would not accept my high school diploma; therefore I had to take an additional science course in order to register at the university. Besides the ambience or general atmosphere was different. While the professors at the University of Saskatchewan did everything in their power to help the students to succeed I had the impression it was the exact opposite in Alberta. Perhaps it was in my imagination but it sure felt that way. A first year music course was required to qualify for a first class teaching certificate. When I registered in that course I thought it would be a piece of cake as my mother had taught us all the rudiments of musical theory. It was not as simple as that, however, as the professor had his own version of what musical theory should be. He twisted and turned that theory inside out until what had previously been simple factual data became a jumble of confusion. Indeed, I wondered if my mother's teaching could have been in error. Be that as it may, my confusion and his boorish attitude made me so nervous that I failed the exam. (One of the students almost had a nervous breakdown as a result of this course.) The next year with another professor I passed the course with flying colors. In retrospect, all my first classes were less than enjoyable.

As time went on it seems that the contents of the courses became more familiar. My major was French and my minor was psychology. French was easy for me and psychology has always been a subject of great interest to me. I managed to complete my third year taking evening classes. I was taking two courses which meant four evening classes each week. After teaching all day, I'd take the bus to the university, attend the classes, and upon getting home late in the evening attempt to do whatever essays assigned and prepare my lessons for the next day. It was grueling! I remember being exhausted to the point of being disoriented. At times while on my way to the university I found myself wondering for a brief moment where and what I was doing on these crowded buses. Mercifully for the fourth and final year I decided to take a sabbatical leave of absence from my teaching duties. It was a blessing to be able to attend classes during the day and not have to worry about lessons for the next day. It was difficult enough to do all the assignments involved as a fourth year student. In retrospect, it seems to have been a long drag and have taken an eternity to accomplish what I set out to do; yet it was nevertheless a major achievement considering the inordinate impediments and obstacles that had to be overcome. Besides, many summer holidays, instead of going to summer school we'd go and spend the summer either in

Maple Ridge with Hélène's family, or in Léoville with John's and Juliette's families.

In the year 1967, Canada's birthday, I finally got my Bachelor of Education! It was indeed awesome, as the kids would say! The Governor General of Canada, Honorable Roland Michener presented my certificate to me. It was a proud day indeed!

Two incidents concerning that certificate are constantly reoccurring in my thoughts as I reminiscent over the past. The graduates usually have their pictures professionally taken on graduation day and are expected to purchase them. Unfortunately due to our financial situation I was unable to do so. This is most regrettable. It would have been a cherished souvenir for the children. Besides I had planned to send one to my dad, as I was the first in my immediate family to graduate and get a degree from the university. But perhaps the most extraordinary thing for me was the fact that the governor general was the one who handed the graduates their certificates in 1967, the year I graduated.

The other incident is rather irrational and in retrospect doesn't make any sense whatsoever. The consequences are what comes to my mind, as the motive that drove me to such irresponsible behavior is beyond comprehension and inexcusable. For some inscrutable reason I was unable to leave the house and for a yet more mystifying and obscure reason my certificate was to be produced for verification at some institution on the same day. So, with a great deal of misgiving I was imprudent enough to send Charlie (who was then very young) to deliver the certificate. And lo and behold he lost it. He said he might have left it on the bus. I was frantic! But it was my fault as a child of that age couldn't be cognizant pertaining to the importance of such a document. Be that as it may, after making numerous inquires and at my request the university made a copy of the document.

After teaching nine years at St. Kevin School which is located in the southern section of Edmonton and traveling all the way on the bus from the north end of the city I decided to ask for a transfer. For the next two years I taught a grade one class at St. Mathew School. The atmosphere in that school was ideal; the staff being compatible and the principal very cooperative. Working in that school was a pleasant experience indeed. It was then that the school board granted me a leave of absence or a sabbatical to enable me to obtain my degree.

My next assignment was at St. Gerard School. Although there were many families that were permanent residents in the district there were also many transients. This situation greatly complicated the teacher's duties. Confronted with a situation where half the students are motivated and have the necessary foundation to proceed with their studies while the other half is entirely clueless makes it entirely hopeless in attaining any measure of progress or achievement. The teacher is desperately trying to cover the required program of studies making sure that the concepts involved have been thoroughly understood and mastered while part of the class is entirely oblivious to what is going on. The situation is absurd, absolutely ridiculous! Of course those children who are constantly on the move cannot be blamed for their lack of knowledge. They are never in one school long enough to learn or master any basic skill.

On one occasion my colleague and I (two grade one teachers) each welcomed a new student in our class, two brothers. Both had the most charming personality and were very well behaved. We soon discovered that the boys did not possess any of the basic skills that first year students have acquired at that period of the term. So both my colleague and I set about with great dedication determined to teach our new students reading and other skills. It was a formidable task as we had to start from the very beginning, and it was late in the school term. Undeterred, both of us went all out struggling until we were blue in the face. It was most discouraging! Late every morning the boys crept into their desks, unwashed, uncombed, just as if they had just got out of bed. It would have been a miracle if they had had any breakfast! Subsequently the school nurse decided to see if she could be of any assistance and paid the home a visit. There was no need for further explanations. A family with six children lived in a one-room house and they had six dogs to boot! (Surely that cannot be true!) Well be that as it may be, after slaving away for a whole month, the boys were gone! The family had moved away again. Both my colleague and I felt a sense of lose and regret that such beautiful children be subjected to deprived and unfortunate circumstances.

There is another phantasm or illusive image that is deep-rooted and ineradicable from my thoughts as I reminisce over those most fateful days. It is a mental picture of a little (nay a big-little) boy who was unique in every way. In fact even if you journeyed to the end of world it would be a miracle if an exact replica could be found. I shall call him Master P as I cannot use his real name. What made this student so remarkable is the fact that in spite of all my efforts to persuade him to do so, he refused to do any of his assignments; in fact he refused to do anything at all. Rewards, pleadings, punitive measures, nothing worked. Indeed I could have turned the heavens and the earth inside out and upside down and it would have been to no avail. Well one day by some miracle, he decided to do the work that had been assigned. And lo and behold when he handed it in, it was a masterpiece! Naturally I took advantage of the occasion to encourage him to do his work in the future. I showed the work to the class and praised him to high heavens. To my amazement one of the boys gave him a bear hug, kissed him on the cheek and exclaimed," Oh Master P. I'm so proud of you." That of course, was worth more than all my praises.

There was another memorable incident involving Master P. It is not surprising that he was bored to death as all he did was sit there and stare, his eyes agape with a look of utter bewilderment as if he had been shocked to find himself suddenly emerged in the classroom not knowing how he got there. It was quite apparent that he didn't have a clue what any of us were about. So he sat there and yawned and yawned and yawned. The yawning was tolerable, barely! But as his yawns echoed throughout the room as a replica of the Tarzan jungle call, it was unbearable! This went on and on. Not only was the noise disturbing the class but it was getting on my nerves terribly. At first I tried to ignore it hoping that if he didn't get the attention he was seeking, he would quit. It was hopeless. I kept wondering how long my patience could endure this behavior and hoping that I would find a way to discourage it until one day Tarzan's piercing call echoed throughout the room. That did it. Some thing in me snapped! Acting on an impulse, and in most domineering tone I called out slowly, emphasizing every word,

"Master P come here at once" I commanded. Startled, he looked at me as if his eyes would pop out of his head.

Master P come … here   now!" I repeated. Still no response, but his eyes were agape, incredulous!

"Master P" I ordered with great emphasis "come here at once". He decided that I was not to be put off so slowly, ever so slowly he made his way to the front of the classroom.

"Now, I said, "face the class" whereupon he turned and faced the class.

"Now," I commanded, "do that again!" The poor boy looked at me as if I had suddenly become insane.

"Do that again." I repeated. Again there was no response.

"Do... that... again." I repeated in such a dictatorial tone that Master P knew that he had to comply.

It was a cruel thing to do to a child. Yet it seemed the only recourse potent enough to solve the problem. And it worked! Tarzan decided to seek another jungle in which to replicate his ear-piercing animal call.

Reminiscing about all the fuss education authorities brew concerning individual differences, it suddenly dawns on me that Master P was a prime example of what these wise gentlemen are referring to. Oh, this child was different alright, as different as different can be. And he simply refused to be molded to society's norm. It also dawns on me that it is refreshing to encounter in this mad world, someone with a unique individuality, someone who dares to refuse to be carved; to fit the mold society exigent. Woe to that one who dares to refuse to be punched, stretched, kneaded and whipped into shape in order to be acceptable to society's norm. Yet it is regrettable that those who have the courage to do so, do not consider that in remaining true to themselves they sometimes disrupt the lives of those in their milieu.

While at St. Gerard School I was reminded of a concept basic to world peace and stability by a native resident of the district. She was devastated because some of the students were abusing her children on the way to and from school. She was hoping that together we might be able to find a solution to the problem. Acting on past experience and knowledge, my advice was rather ill advised. "A bully is usually a coward," I said, "and perhaps the children should gang up and give those bullies a dose of their own medicine."

"No" replied that judicious woman, "violence breeds violence. If we encourage our children to fight, more and more children will participate and the situation will get out of hand. If those malfeasants do not get any response and my kids don't strike back, they will get bored and stop." The principal and I were amazed at this humble woman's wisdom. It is regrettable that she couldn't share her wisdom with world leaders.

My next assignment was at St. Vladimir School. The school is situated in a middle class district and most of the residents are in the middle-income bracket financially. Subsequently the students are usually well adjusted and there are few discipline problems. It was an ideal situation. I was teaching a grade one class during the first few years but when the school board got wind of my ability to speak French, I was switched to a grade four class. One year the more advanced students were allocated to my care. It was a most stimulating experience. As these students were superior in intellectual ability I was able to try modern improved methods of teaching advocated by those who do research in the development of superior educational procedures. The new approach was very successful especially in the language arts. Teaching a foreign language demands an entirely different method of presentation, organization, and implementation than lessons taught in the vernacular therefore I found it quite challenging.

There are only two incidents that have remained with me as I recall the years I taught at St. Vladimir School. That is indeed very strange because I was there for five years. The incidents referred above are those relating to events occurring at the school. Although there were some significant developments occurring during those years in the lives of those dear to me they will be mentioned later. There were two students who remained illiterate in spite of the tremendous efforts that my colleagues and I made to teach them. One little fellow (he looked like an angel) in grade one had no desire to learn, could not be motivated to make an effort, and at the end of the year had not learned to read. The other student came to grade four class and could not recognize one word from another. The resource room teacher and I bend over backwards in an effort to solve the problem. At the end of January both of us were congratulating each other, because our student had made quite a bit of progress. Alas, in May when we tested him again, he had forgotten everything he had learned! It was unbelievable. At coffee time I jokingly asked my colleague, "What have we been doing all year?"

There was another remarkable incidence that occurred while I was at St. Vladimir which is rather weird. It was long past dismissal time and most of the teachers had gone home except me. I was trying to catch up on some of the never-ending tasks that is the lot of all teachers. The secretary called me in the office. She sounded very agitated. It was little wonder for she was at her wits end wondering how to deal with a difficult situation. A policeman was sitting in the office with two of our grade one students. He had caught them doing 'break and enters' in every house on the block. The strangest thing was that they were not looking for money or toys but for food: flour, sugar, etc. The policeman intended to take the girls to the station and wanted to notify the school. I looked at the colossal officer (he must have been six feet six inches tall) and then at the two tiny little girls and I was appalled.

"What are you going to do with them when you get to the station?" I inquired. It was late and the child welfare bureau would undoubtedly be closed.

"I haven't the slightest idea." he responded.

"Would it be more sensible to call the foster parents and let them deal with the problem?" I asked.

The officer was relieved. Indeed he didn't have a clue as to what he was going to do when he reached the station with these two would be criminals, so he agreed; whereupon the anxious parent came for the girls. Judging by the troubled expression on her face, the girls were often in trouble.

Meanwhile our family was blessed with the arrival of a baby we loved and cherished with all our hearts to this day. Cherrie brought great joy and happiness to our home. Although she was Lucille's little girl, in her childish mind she felt that she belonged with the whole family. She had decided that this was her home and here she was going to stay and that was that! Lucille made every effort to make her feel at home with her when she got a place of her own but it was useless. The child was extremely miserable and lonesome for the rest of "her" family. At last, it was unanimously agreed that she live with us. It must have been a heartbreaking decision for Lucille and I remember feeling a horrible sense of guilt, thinking perhaps it was my fault that the child had become so emotionally attached to all of us. Yet it was beyond my control.

My guilt probably emanated from the fact that Cherrie brought so much joy to our home. My self-reproach and remorse was on par with the culpability of a thief, a kidnapper, no less, yet for the well-being of the child it was the only solution that seemed feasible at the time. During the day she was at a day home and cared for by the proprietor, Ruth, an amazing lady whose devotion and dedication to the children who had been entrusted to her care was exceptional and unprecedented. In the evening, when I had to work double shift, one of the family members looked after her. None of them seemed to mind; indeed everyone seemed to enjoy it. Carol especially, as everywhere she went she took Cherrie with her. Even on dates! It was a understood that if Cherrie couldn't tag along the date was cancelled. On holidays when she went to the coast, to the beach, or any other vacationing sites, Carol always took Cherrie along with her. Keith also took his turn babysitting Cherrie and enjoying it. And Charlie? Well, Charlie was another story! He was bound and determined that he wasn't going to let any harm come to Cherrie, whatever the cost. One evening at bath time there must have been soap bubbles in the bath water for she was having a blast using the tub as a water slide slipping from the edge to the bottom. It was a dangerous thing to do, as she could have hit her head as she slipped down into the slippery bubbles. I (party pooper) asked her to stop but of course it was too much fun and she ignored me. After repeating myself for the third time, it became quite apparent that something drastic had to be done before she hurt herself. So I gave her a couple of taps on the wrist. Well! I might just as well have sounded the fire alarm! No sooner had she given a startled screech that the whole family had ambled up the stairs, three steps at a time.

"Why did you hit her?" inquired Charlie, who was evidently greatly distressed.

"I had to stop her or she most certainly would have hurt herself." I retorted.

"Well," reproached Charlie, with tears in his eyes, "did you have to hit her so hard?"

It would have been impossible to mistreat or abuse Cherrie in her sanctuary, she had too many protectors. Which was, of course as it should be.

Cherrie brought great joy to the rest of my family but it is incomparable to the moments of pleasure and happiness she brought to me. Indeed I could not believe my good fortune when she became part of our family and would live with us forever (hopefully)! She loved skating. There was a small community skating rink not far from our house on 141st Ave. and we were always the first ones there. Usually I had to clear the snow from the rink which was quite amazing to the men of the district. Then I'd help Cherrie with her skates, sit on the snow bank and watch her skate for hours on end. Looking back, that little rink was the place where she had learned to skate. It didn't take long, after a few falls she was on her way. It always amazed me that she never seemed to get tired or bored. She also loved roller-skating. On one of the school celebrations my class had gone to the roller Aerodrome to celebrate. The girls had formed a long parade joining with hands on waists and without a doubt there was Cherrie leading them all. Then there were the swimming episodes! It didn't matter if she went swimming with her classmates, friends, or if the two of us were alone, she swam and swam and swam. In fact swimming may have been the sport she preferred, although it's hard to say as she liked all sports. Indeed, Cherrie was in love with life, just the sheer joy of being alive!

One summer after he moved back to Edmonton, Danny had left his dog Hector at the house. Cherrie fell madly in love with that dog and vice versa. The bond between these two was extraordinary. Hector followed Cherrie wherever she went, played with her, and protected her. The two were soul mates. There was a large empty field not far from where we lived in Londonderry (in fact, in winter the skating was there) situated in an ideal spot and used as a place of activity by the people in the surrounding district. Many times Cherrie and Hector would wander to that field with me tagging along and just run wild. Hector would hold Cherrie's hand gently with his teeth (holding hands) and the two of them would go swooping down the hills or across the fields. These two must have been kindred spirits for they understood one another perfectly. It was a joy to behold.

Cherrie's First Communion

At this point I must pause and interrupt the gradual sequence of my tale for I have encountered an epoch in my journey in which the bottom of the world suddenly seemed to have dropped from under my feet. It is an episode in life when all preceding and crucial cares and endeavors become insignificant. Survival, success, routines, all seem to vanish into thin air. It is a time when my soul is engulfed with excruciating sorrow. I am lost again adrift in an endless dessert, with nowhere to go.

Yet I am thrilled by the radiance of the gleaming crystals upon the waters scintillating in the radiant sunlight and with these waters alive and pulsating with the flocks of wild geese resting a moment on their southern journey. Oh, that I could take wings and with them in the vast immensity and freedom of the skies, fly away far from the sadness inherent in my soul, threatening to engulf me in the depths of despair. For I am torn between the ecstasy, the wonders of the mystical panorama displayed so luxuriously before my eyes and the agony of the trauma cruel destiny has chosen to inflict upon those so dear to me. For we have been struck by a series of devastating and emotionally excruciating blows occurring one upon the heals of the other with no respite or time for the wounds to heal between. And as I go along on my way I am loath to traverse this stretch strewn with thorns, lurking with the spirits of those who are no more, and where lie the scattered remains of hearts that have been shattered.

It was early in the spring of the year when Lucille told me that her husband, Richard, had been diagnosed with the recurrence of a malignant cancer. He had been afflicted with this disease when he was in his early thirties, but it had been successfully removed, and the cancer had been in remission for over twenty years. The doctors were confident that they would be able to remove all traces of the afflicted tissues once again. Alas it was not to be! The cancer had spread rapidly and some of the cancerous cells remained undetected during the operation. As Richard was afflicted with an aggressive cancer his condition deteriorated rapidly. His oncologist recommended another operation in Calgary because one of Canada's top melanoma specialists was there. That was a very serious technical error indeed as the disease was too far advanced and it considerably added to the patient's discomfort. Lucille insisted that she would take care of her husband herself at home. Although both the members of his and her family insisted on helping, Lucille was determined that their last precious moments would spend together. Richard passed away on December the ninth of that same year. The chasm that was left in our hearts will forever remain barren. He was a good man, one of the best, and one cannot help but wonder why he was taken so young.

Meanwhile, and as we were hopelessly struggling to cope with Richard's illness and death Juliette went through two serious operations. Although these procedures were not life threatening both were extremely painful (the removal of cancerous cells on her nose and of hemorrhoids in two successive operations) and both engendered a great deal of anxiety. And lo and behold, while all this was happening, Johnny was in a serious motorcycle accident, was badly hurt, and landed in the hospital where he remained for two weeks. Of course I wasn't supposed to know about all this, that is, the accident and the operations, less I should torment myself with worry so the children always conspire to hide serious trouble from me. But trouble does not go away, and misfortune has a way of revealing itself. Although the children's intentions were commendable, I was hurt. I felt that, in times of trouble, all the members of the family should be a support to one another, whatever the cost!

Amidst all these tragedies the family was desperately trying to hold each other up. Everyone was especially concerned about Lucille. Her marriage had been seemingly the relationship construed by the angels in their celestial kingdom. Indeed it was one of the rare out-of–this-world alliances that seldom exist in this imperfect world. And for Lucille, her husband was her entire world. Subsequently her lose was inconceivable. Everyone did their utmost to distract her. Family get-togethers were constantly on the agenda and during these reunions the password was "no tears." Lucille insisted on having Christmas dinner at her place with her children, Brian, Rick's brother, and Faye in an effort to keep things as normal as possible. As usual, Danny prepared the festive meal for the rest of the family and the other members of the family were to come afterwards for tea. The dinner was absolutely magnificent! Indeed Danny was an excellent cook or chef. Carol took care of the decorations, the planning, the fine details, and the trimmings, but it was Danny who prepared the main part of the meal, e.g. the turkey, dressing and vegetables. It was also Carol who had to make sure that everyone had a gift. (How she managed to do all that is beyond me.)

Walter invited the whole family for New Year's dinner. It was wonderful to have the family together and everyone enjoyed the celebration. It was unfortunate that Cherrie wasn't there as she was the only member of the family missing.

Front: Lorraine, Walter, Keith, Dave
Back: Juliette, Danny, Lucille, Carol, Debbie

It was that evening that it became glaringly evident that Danny wasn't well. Everyone had noticed that something was wrong with him but we had all arrived at the wrong conclusions. Carol thought he was despondent and lacked energy because he was unhappy and she was quite concerned. I thought that he was beginning to feel that everyone was imposing on him for he was an excellent architect and could design and skillfully construct a building according to any specification. He had not confided in anyone but looking back it is quite evident that he had been ill for a considerable length of time and had suffered in silence. However, at the family's New Year party everyone noticed that there was something wrong with Danny. He was uncomfortable the whole evening and had to leave early. On the way home he asked Carol to take the wheel as he was suffering from severe pain in the lower part of his body and was unable to drive the rest of the way. It was then that Carol insisted that he get medical attention. The doctors were unable to diagnose his condition even after several appointments. Even the specialist was unable to locate the cause of his excruciating affliction. Carol feared that Danny's malady was cancer as his mother's death had been caused by pancreatic cancer. Although she communicated her apprehensions to the doctor, tests were unable to confirm or locate any sign of cancer. In fact Carol was told with great emphasis, "You don't have to worry. There is no cancer." Although this was somewhat reassuring, Carol was not convinced. She was still suspicious that her husband's affliction was critical. Danny's condition was rapidly deteriorating and the pain was becoming increasingly more and more intolerable. Yet when the pain was beyond human endurance, all that was ever done for him was to relieve it with a deadly drug, morphine.

Alas, when the specialists and the physicians finally diagnosed Danny's condition as pancreatic cancer, it was too late! It was medically impossible to save his life. His days were numbered! And so they were! On March the eleventh, only a matter of days after that devastating diagnostic, Danny passed away. His demise left a penetrating agony, an ineradicable emptiness in our hearts. He will live forever in the hearts of all who knew him, for he was one beyond compare and second to none.

It would be unwise at this moment to recount the events that occurred and led up to Danny's death. It is too painful, too soon! It would be too cruel to drag the reader into the abyss of misery into which my soul now dwells. Yet, how selfish it is of me to feel sorry for myself, for compared to that of his wife, Carol, and all those who were there at last and endured with him the last throes of death, my anguish is but a pebble in the sand, an insignificant trifle! For I was banned from the sick room on pretext that my frail health would not be able to endure the excruciating emotional trauma of being incapable of alleviating Danny's suffering.

It is written in the stars that when tragedy strikes, it does not strike once but trice. Perhaps it would be more accurate to say that it comes in battalions, one tragedy following on the heels of the other. For so it was in our family during that most fateful year of 2004. Fourteen days after Danny demise, on March the thirtieth, my brother John passed away. I went to the funeral with Carol and Juliette. I was so emotionally drained that it was an effort to assist at the prayers and the funeral mass. Then, immediately after the funeral, my sister Cecile became ill. Her physician was unable to diagnose her condition; consequently her illness kept getting progressively worse. Soon after she was taken to the hospital, she lost consciousness and remained on life supports most of the time. She passed away on August the eleventh. In a daze, we wondered, "When will it end?"

I felt as if nothing mattered anymore, as if lost in the vast expanse of the cosmos, there was nowhere to go, nowhere to turn. Yet after a great deal of meditation and the healing touch of time, I realized that perhaps human beings are ungrateful and selfish indeed. Not unlike King Midas and King John who horded and coveted treasures of gold and clung to them with a passion, we cling to other treasures, our loved ones. Furiously we hold on, covet, horde, and jealously guard these treasures as our own. Whereas these ancient kings locked their gold in an impenetrable fortress, we hold our treasures in our hearts. How badly our foolish hearts do err when they profess to claim these treasures as their own and will not let them go! For these treasures belong to no one but the Almighty. And although we cling to them, they are here on borrowed time. So, no matter how painful, it is imperative to remember that these treasures are not ours to keep when the Lord calls one of his own to his Kingdom. He has, in His mercy, left many here to be cherished and to comfort those who are left behind. It seems weird that after going through a traumatic experience, one sees the world in a different light. Loved ones, friends, indeed everyone seems to have a new import, a new meaning in one's eyes. Even the trees seem to have acquired more brilliant colors and stately grandeur. Could it be that we take everything we have for granted? Could it be that we are grateful for our blessings only when we are sorely tried and realize that those we cherish the most may be taken from us when we least expect it? Is it only then that we are truly grateful for what we have and truly appreciate those the Lord has, in his bounty, left to comfort us.

Although my heart is still burdened with distress and confusion, I must make an effort not to indulge in self-pity (pick up my socks) and continue recounting the rest of my story.

I was about to tell the ramifications that Cherrie had on the lives of the family. It was incredible that such a small child should bring so much happiness to every member of a household. When she was left in my care, I could not believe it. It seemed too good to be true! But although I was overjoyed, my happiness was overshadowed by pangs of conscience. It seemed so wrong to take such a beautiful child from her mother. Yet it seemed to have been written in the stars. And so it was.

Besides creating such a stir in our household, she managed to make a strong impression on the lives of her classmates, her friends, and all those in her world. Endowed with a unique and charismatic personality she always managed to be the center of attraction. Even as a child she was a philosopher and never failed to find the rational behind any sensitive situation. From the time that she was born she used her thumb as a soother, a habit that she found very difficult to break. She was teased constantly about this bad habit; she was even told that she would probably walk down the aisle on her wedding with her thumb in her mouth. All these traits contributed to set her apart or to get the attention of those around her. The girls in her class were twice her size and they treated her like a doll or as someone who needed special consideration. We were still at St. Vladimir when she made her first communion and all the family came to the church for the occasion. Even the principal of the school was proud of her.

While she was in the early grades at school she was taking lessons in ballet dancing. She seemed to enjoy it at first. She went to the weekly classes for two years. Her group gave a performance at the Jubilee Auditorium at the end of the term. Because of her size, she performed alone in the middle of the stage while the others danced in a circle around her. It was spectacular! For some reason she became disenchanted with the ballet lessons. Perhaps she found it too tiresome or she may have felt that she would never be successful as a professional dancer. And indeed it was difficult. The classes were held in the Alberta College downtown and we had to take the bus to get there and back. It was also very time consuming. Be that as it may, Cherrie decided that she didn't want to go any more. And that was that.

Cherrie had decided that she wanted to join a marching band. Her cousin, Joanne, had joined the Edmonton Girls' Marching Band and it seemed very exciting. I was a little disappointed about the ballet, but the girls' band was a positive venture, so she (more accurately, we) joined. For every week both of us went to the practice. It wasn't as difficult then because I was driving my reliable little Honda. Cherrie was playing the cymbal in the band and she was very proud of herself. Besides she was the smallest girl participating, and as usual she created quite a sensation. Besides the practice, the parents had to raise funds by making and selling crafts, having bake sales, and taking turns at being a chaperon. It was fun being with all these girls. The coach insisted that the girls work hard, sometimes keeping them overnight and making them practice in the wee hours of the morning and late at night. It meant that the girls were kept over night in a rented facility and had to sleep on foam mattresses. It also meant that the parents had to provide nourishments for all these people. I was elected to be a chaperon on several occasions. It was fun!

As it turn out the band proved to be a very positive venture. When the coach felt that the girls were ready and they had their costumes, he decided to take the band on a European tour and have them perform for several audiences in different countries. This was indeed an exciting opportunity for the girls. Those who had made the arrangements had made very precise provisions for the safety of the girls. To save money, they were billeted in the homes of responsible and reliable local families. Many chaperons went along to care for the well being of the girls. And the fee for the whole tour was a measly two hundred dollars! Although I was somewhat apprehensive at the thought of allowing Cherrie to go on her own as she was only twelve years old, the arrangements were so well organized that my concerns were somewhat dispelled. It was such an exciting adventure, it would have been despicable to ruin it for her. At first, it appeared that I would be chosen to go as a chaperon but one of the mothers made such a fuss that we had to let her take my place. As it turned out it proved to be an opportunity for me to tour Europe with my daughter Juliette without worrying about Cherrie.

By this time several members of the family had left home. In fact, Cherrie and I were the only ones left in the household for a considerable length of time. Juliette was the first to be married, then Walter, followed by David. Carol lived at home intermittently while she worked at the bank or went to university and Lucille while she was yet very young asserted her independence and with a friend established a home of her own. Charlie and Keith were living on their own in British Columbia. (But that, of course, is a long story in itself, one that I will try to relate to the best of my ability in the following paragraphs.) With a heavy heart I watched as each of them prepared to leave. It was so hard to see them go!

Keith had spent quite a lot of time in British Columbia, as almost every summer the whole family visited my sister in Maple Ridge. He simply loved that province! The mild climate, the mountains, the breathtaking scenery, and especially the ocean, fascinated him. The fact that we had chosen to settle in such a forbidden habitat in lieu of paradise was to him unfathomable and beyond the realm of reason. It is difficult for the young to understand that necessity is a brutal task master and you are reluctant to take chances when it involves the welfare and security of the family. Had I not been such a coward, I would have taken advantage of the opportunity when it presented itself. While touring the island with Hélène, we were visiting the Legislative building in Victoria when we came face to face with the Minister of Education for the province. He couldn't believe that he had, by some weird chance, met someone who was a grade one teacher and could speak French.

"Go back to Alberta and get your degree," he said, "and when you have your Bachelor of Education I will guarantee that you will have a teaching position in the province."

To quote Shakespeare, "There is a tide in the affairs of men that taken, leads to fortune, omitted, all the voyage of their lives leads to shallows and misery."

Perhaps I should have listened to that great philosopher's wisdom. Who knows? Be that as it may, I felt that such a venture was unpredictable and the fear of the unknown plus the tribulations of starting all over again in a new environment was too frightening. Besides, it meant another year at the university with no income coming in to support the family. So it was that we decided to leave well enough alone and stay where the future seemed more secure.

But that dream had not been forsaken by one member of the household, Keith. He had made up his mind. And when Keith makes up his mind, well he makes up his mind! As fate would have it, he discovered a twenty-eight acre property in Falkland that was for sale. That did it! Keith was bound and determined that we were going to buy that property. He never gave up. Day and night he paced the floor and he raved about the property's merits, trying to convince me that it was sound financial investment. At last I gave up. Although how we would manage to do that was beyond me, unless of course, Providence intervened and the money would come down from the skies. And as usual, when I am in a desperate situation it did! The down payment was reasonable and Charlie's girl friend contributed half. The owner carried the mortgage which was to be paid monthly at a low rate by the boys.

The purchase of that property proved to be an advantageous venture both financially and as a source of recreation. Situated in the midst of the mountains, the scenery is breathtaking. During the summer holidays we'd spend a lot of enjoyable days with the boys in their recluse away from the chaos of city life.

One summer Juliette's family spent some time with us at the site. While they were there Vince's brother parked his motor home in the yard. It was quite a conglomeration. There was my daughter with her four children, Ted's family, my two boys, besides myself, Cherrie and her cousin Angie. We were having a wonderful time. It was great!

It was while all these people were with us that a girl walked in on us one day. She was a little bit odd but otherwise she seemed harmless. Nonetheless, I tactfully tried to keep the children away from her for I had a premonition that something was not quite right. One afternoon she decided to take all the children for a walk. I protested strongly, but with my reputation of being over protective of the children and the fact that everyone else could not foresee any danger in a stroll in broad daylight, the children were allowed to go in spite of my misgivings. At six o'clock they still had not returned. At ten o'clock I was frantic! By this time every one was pacing up and down the road wild with anxiety. Lo and behold, when we were on the verge of calling the police she and the children came calmly marching down the road.

Some time after we had purchased the property it was subdivided. Part of it was sold and the proceeds used to pay for the remainder of the estate. By this time Charlie was living in Vancouver. Unfortunately the boys decided to sell the property and invest the money in a business enterprise located in Vancouver. I did not agree with the boys' decision as I knew that the property would be worth a great deal of money in the future. I tried to dissuade them but knew it would have been unreasonable to stop them. It was their investment and it was theirs to do as they pleased. The decision to sell was regrettably ill advised as years later the site was developed into a park. It must have been written into the stars that riches would never be our lot, for numerous times opportunity came knocking at the door and we never took advantage of it.

Part VI

Dreams Sprout Wings

Before I can get back to my story I am seduced by the enticing call of the lake, the lake whose magical power never fails to lure me to its shore. So with careless abandon, I throw caution to the winds and go for a jaunt along its path. It has snowed continually for days and although the path has been cleared, the trees are seething under a heavy mantel of snow, their branches straining, bowed by the weight of the massive burden of pristine whiteness. Some have been broken and lie prostate on the thick white cushion, praising the One who created such mystical wonders! I am hypnotized by the magic of it all, enraptured by the splendor of winter's magical charm. But enough of this reverie, this dwelling in the land of ethereal dreams, for I must return to the tangible world.

With all the members of the family gone their own way, Cherrie and I were the only ones remaining at home. I was at liberty to accompany her on all her projects, her ballet lessons, her marching band practice, skating, swimming, and numerous other activities. We spent many joyous hours doing things which had been impossible with the others regrettably. Therefore, when Cherrie went to Europe with her marching band the door was wide open and I was set free at last to follow my sensational dream.

We had planned that seemingly impossible adventure for a considerable length of time. For Juliette it was the excitement of taking a long voyage out of the country and seeing and experiencing new things that thrilled her. She looked forward with great anticipation at the prospect of being free and away from the endless responsibilities of childcare and household duties. She had married when she was very young and in her early twenties already had four children. Hopefully she would enjoy the freedom and the pleasures she had been denied in her youth. As for myself, I had always dreamed of visiting Paris, especially the Louvre and to be able to savour the famous works of art contained in that most illustrious museum. I also wanted the visit the Palace of Versailles. So we made the preparations. The boys, Kevin and Danny, were left with their grandparents, the girls, Joanne and Debbie, with Trudy, and of course Cherrie was in Europe. We were free to go! Again where the money came from for this daring adventure is beyond me. We made the arrangements through Wardair, (the best airline company that ever existed) bought a U-Rail pass and we were off!

We landed in Amsterdam. The diamond cutting factory was indeed impressive. However, we were filled with wonder when we visited the museum or factory where they create elaborate glass ornaments. The beauty and splendor of their creations was amazing. We were both fascinated with the Dutch lace manufacturing enterprise. Their handmade lace is of a remarkably delicate and exquisite quality. We were also greatly impressed by the flowers. There are flowers, flowers, flowers everywhere! And those flowers are just magnificent! Amsterdam is but a gorgeous garden of luxurious blossoms. We did visit a village where the people, to impress the tourists evidently, still wear the traditional Dutch customs. The windmills in all their grandeur are still standing there. We saw and actually touched the legendary dykes so famous in legends we read concerning that most fascinating and picturesque country. It was most interesting. We did visit the famous Van Gogh museum. Unfortunately, being disgustingly old-fashioned and ignorant about the master's type of art, both my daughter and I were unable to understand or appreciate the quality of his artistic talent.

When we landed at the airport building, the floor was covered with young travelers in sleeping bags. It is very likely that their budget did not cover hotel accommodations. It surprised both my daughter and me as it is unlikely that this would be allowed in any Canadian airports. Several policemen were on duty and there was no disorder, but to us it was most amazing.

From Amsterdam we took the U-Rail to Paris. We were quite disconcerted at the French people's attitude towards tourists. When we landed at the terminal we got a cool unfriendly reception. What was even more startling was the fact that at the information desk, we were given the cold shoulder by the clerk who pretended not to understand what I was saying. I was offended by her haughty mien and her rude manners. It is true that there is a slight difference in the pronunciation. The French put a lot more emphasis and stress on the vowels than Canadians. For instance, the 'i' sounds like the long 'e' in the Canadian rendition.

Hotel accommodation proved to be quite a problem. In July, the tourist season, all the hotels are full. After having inquired at several establishments, we were walking dejectedly along the deserted streets (it was pouring rain) of that great metropolis with our heavy suitcases. Mercifully a sister, realizing our plight, directed us to an hotel manager who soon found convenient lodgings for us. Contrary to the reception we had experienced at the airport, the owner of this establishment couldn't do enough for us. He was amazed by the fact that I could speak French fluently. "It is incredible" he said," that throughout these many centuries and the vast distance separating us you have retained the culture and the language that we share." He made special dishes for us (du café-au-lait) and gave us a complete run-down of the most illustrious tourist attractions. It took us five days to visit some of the most famous attractions in Paris. It would indeed be difficult to say which of these marvels impressed us the most. Each and every one of these marvels took our breath away and left both of us spell-bound. It seemed inconceivable that so many wonders existed. At first we got from one place to another on the Metro. But the cars were jam-packed and besides, Juliette decided that the men were flirts, so we decided to walk. Even though it rained cats and dogs all the time we were there, we tenaciously walked right through Paris. On one of these occasions the rain was coming down in torrents. We were both drenched and frozen to the bone.

Being yet quite a distance from our hotel we decided to stop at a near-by café. You can just imagine that we didn't want to attract any attention, so we sneaked quietly to the very back of the restaurant and sat down. Soon the drippings from our saturated garments formed a large pool of water all around our table. We both wanted to disappear through a crack in the floor. Soon the waiter appeared (we were expecting him to ask us to leave in no uncertain terms!) but being very professional, he did not react negatively and he had a blank expression on his face. Mercifully! The soup that he brought us was out of this world! It was the most delicious, the most luscious soup I've ever tasted! It tasted so fresh, as if the vegetables had just been picked out of the garden. It must indeed have been extraordinary for I can still taste it to this day.

To the best of my recollections the Louvre was our first stop. The art treasures held in that famous museum are inconceivable. It would require an eternity to be able to thoroughly and exhaustively savour all the magnificence and the worth of all the masterpieces contained therein. We could only spend a fleeting moment admiring each of these chef-d'oeuvre. Of course the Mona Lisa was the painting we were most anxious to see. Although it is a beauty and its excellence is indisputable, I had expected to be an immense creation but was rather amazed at its dimensions. We admired so many wonders (the sphinx for example) that it is impossible to mention them all. I could have stayed in that amazing museum for the duration of our journey but we had so many other places to visit on our itinerary.

I was most impressed by the church of the Invalids, Les Invalids. Napoleon Bonaparte's remains are entombed in that most illustrious church, The Emperor's laws have been codified and are inscribed on cement plates hanging all around the basement walls. The wisdom embodied in these laws is a direct testimony that reveals the extraordinary intelligence of this most famous man.

Indeed he was a veritable genius His ambitious and greedy character was most regrettable.

The order in which we visited these spectacular wonders has long been buried in the past. However we managed to visit most of these marvels as we toured Paris on foot and in the rain. We visited the magnificent churches, Notre Dame cathedral and the Sacré Coeur cathedral, L'arc de Triomphe, the Champs Elysées, Les Tuileries, La Place de la Concorde. We sailed on a sight-seeing cruise along the Seine River. At the Eiffel Tower, I was bound and determined that we were going to climb to the top, but Juliette didn't think it was a good idea, so we took the lift. Unfortunately because it was raining heavily the view of the city from that height was compromised. We were loathe to leave Paris for it is true that once you have been in that great city, it will remain with you forever.

The French Riviera was our next stop. The beaches are beyond any figment of the imagination. Golden sand stretching on and on as far as the eye can see. It was a little bit shocking to see young girls bathing in the nude but it appeared to be normal as no one else seemed to notice. We followed a path that led to the top of a high elevation. I was fascinated by the breathtaking scenery along the ascending path, but what was most spectacular and almost incredible was that the site was strewn with the ruins of ancient churches. Myriads of them! I was intrigue by these ruins, the history of the churches that had once stood upon them, why so many had been erected side by side, and above all, the aspirations of those who worshipped within those antiquated walls. Nice, its dazzling beauty mesmerizes and enchants with its magical charm. It was in Nice that my daughter and I were surprised when we realized that the mass, in such a modern state, was still celebrated in Latin. It was a very touching experience as the past was being reenacted before my eyes. I could see my mother at the piano directing the choir, all the hymns sung in Latin, the Credo, the

Gloria, etc. and the priest celebrating the mass exactly as it was celebrated in our parish church when I was a child. It brought tears to my eyes. It was as if I had slipped back through time, through many generations, and found myself back in my homeland where I belonged; at home! And even on the streets the people seemed to be familiar. It was weird!

From Nice we took the train to Monte Carlo. Not that we intended to gamble but we were intrigue by the romantic tales emanating from that most famous and dramatic kingdom. For from that land emanates the fairyland story of which is not "The Princess and the Pauper" but it's opposite, "Beauty and the Prince". We hoped to be able to catch a glimpse of Princess Grace, the Prince, and the children. This was not to be and justifiably so. Princess Grace insisted that the privacy of her family life be respected. The casino was also out of bounds for us. The dress code was very stringent (we were casually dressed as we were traveling,) and besides, gambling was not our intent and way out of our league. We did however tour Prince Rainier's magical kingdom, therefore we felt that the journey had been well worthwhile.

Juliette and I were like little kids who refuse to go to bed because they do not want to miss any of the action. We were intoxicated with the desire to explore the treasures encapsulated in this ancient European land. In fact my daughter did not want to take the time to eat; she felt it was a waste of time. There was too much to see, too much to do! We were both bound and determined that we would explore every nook and cranny of the many lands from whence emanated the multicultural Canadian heritage. And we only had twenty-seven days to do all this! No wonder there was no time to eat or sleep.

Versailles was our next destination. For someone who had been raised during the depression and had lived on a meager income, Versailles was an ethereal apparition, a magic illusion belonging to another world rather than to this mundane and ordinary planet. The opulence, the grandeur of the structure was dazzling! The interior was even more spectacular. In every room the furniture and the decor was of a luxuriousness and magnificence beyond one's imagination. Even the beds were fashioned of pure gold. I wondered at the time how many peasants had gone without food to allow the king such extravagant luxury. In every room and on every wall, prominently displayed was King Louis XIV's spectacular portrait. The Queen's portrait appeared in one room only. Conceit?

Rome was our next stop. Even though we had been dazed by the splendor and magnificence of Paris, we were simply thunderstruck upon arriving in that great metropolis. For, and I quote from the Encyclopedia Britannica, 1964, volume 19. "Rome is unique in its possessions of so many fine buildings spanning so many centuries. It is a city of palaces and churches, of parks and squares and statuary and fountains." All these are memorials, irrefutable testimonials of the countless sensational deeds and the phenomenal events that transpired in the nation's historical past. It was absolutely impossible to grasp the significance, the intrinsic value of its treasures, or to embrace the deep spiritual essence of this magnanimous city in one short week.

The itinerary and the schedule of our sight seeing tour has been lost in time. However, in history and in my family the Vatican was always associated with Rome, therefore, it seems logical that our tour started at that point. The Pope gave an audience from the palace balcony while we were touring the gardens. Although his presence was discernible, it was impossible to hear what he was saying because of the enormous crowd. The Sistine Chapel, situated in the Vatican Palace is one of the most impressive and extraordinary artistic creation of all times. It was regrettable that we happened to visit the chapel when a mass was being celebrated consequently my daughter insisted that we leave almost at once. It was with great difficulty that she managed to shoo me out of there as I was entirely engrossed and overwhelmed by the exquisite beauty of the artist's creation. I stared and stared in amazement, my eyes fixated upwards, admiring the chef-d'oeuvre of the great genius, Michelangelo.

The magnificent St. Peter's Cathedral was reconstructed under direction of Michelangelo, for not only was he a painter, but as an architect and a sculptor he was exceptional and the quality of his work has remained unsurpassed throughout the ages. In the cathedral the towering status of St. Peter stands, majestically guarding the entrance to the right of that monumental structure. Legends have it that prayers said while touching the feet of the statue are always granted. The famous statue, the Pieta, and numerous celebrated works of art, including the painting of Raphael, are displayed everywhere in the church. The grandeur of St. Peter's Cathedral will be with me always.

A "Roman Holiday" (as portrayed in the film) that would last a whole year, and then some, would be the time needed to see Rome. In a few days, it is barely possible to catch a fleeting glimpse at the most spectacular highlights or famous historical sites. We managed to visit the Colosseum, then in ruins, and in the process of reconstruction. Its name is appropriate, for it is indeed a colossal monument. We visited the ancient churches near the Forum, a site that was especially interesting to me because of its historical significance. The Pantheon, the stairway of the Piazza di Spagna, and the ancient walls of Rome were fascinating. We were most impressed by the numerous and the lavish magnificence of the Roman churches. In fact all the churches in Europe are exorbitantly rich in design and décor. It is unfortunate that time has erased the memory of all the wonders we admired while we toured the city. We had read and heard so much about the catacombs and therefore we were determined to visit them. Walking through those underground dungeons was weird, bizarre. The very walls seemed to be haunted by the eerie, ghostly sigh of the dead. We made haste in finding our way out of that most lugubrious passage. The city abounds with monuments that are a treasury of historical, architectural, and valuable works of art. The skill, wisdom, and resourcefulness of the ancient Romans is manifested in the aqueducts which they built to supply the city with water. The immense theatre is a manifestation of their advanced and refined cultural values. The theatre's amazing grandeur bears witness to the Roman's love for the more sophisticated aspects of life such as the theatre, music, and drama.

While in Rome we took a bus tour to the Fountains of Tivoli. En route we discovered that our guide was fluent in seven languages and was trying to learn several others. Amazingly he could switch from one language to another without any trace of an accent. The fountains were dazzlingly beautiful with sprays of colored water exploding into a brilliant mist illuminating the whole sky. Alas, too soon it was time to return to the hotel.

The Italian people are very warm and hospitable. Everywhere we went we were welcomed. The shopkeepers always gave us a generous portion of fruit at the market, especially cherries. It was a little surprising to realize that in Italy, pedestrians do not have the right-of-way enjoyed by Canadians. They cross the streets at their own risk. Motorists are driving every which way and do not seem to follow any rules whatsoever.

We had planned to spend a day visiting the museums and art centers of Florence. Regrettably it was a holiday when we arrived in the city and everything was closed. Fortunately we were able to see the world renown statue of David, one of Michelangelo's masterpieces.

Munich was our next destination. We stayed in a residential school while we visited the main tourist attractions. Both Juliette and I loved Munich. How I wish that I had kept a journal of all the interesting places we visited, the things we did and the some of our amazing experiences. Alas, it is too late and some of these fascinating events have been forgotten. While we were in Munich I made up my mind to get two admission tickets for the "Passion Play", a play performed by local actors in Oberammergau, Bavaria. We had been warned that it was impossible to get tickets at the site. Well, I bent over backwards to get those tickets, but it was hopeless. After going all over the city, from one place to another unsuccessfully, I decided to try on the black market. (That's how determined I was.) My daughter teasingly said that I was ready to exchange her for a ticket. At any rate she had abandoned the whole idea and was quite disgusted with my persistence. When all else had failed, I decided to try another tactics.

"Let's take a bus tour to the site. At least we will see the place where the play is held." I urged Juliette. But inwardly I hoped our luck might change. The scenery as we traveled along was incredible. The route took us through the Black Forest, the origin of so many Fairy Tales. Parks, lakes, and recreational play grounds dotted the landscape along the way. The road led amid a dairy farming area and at milking time the cows had the right-of-way. We thought it was amusing when the bus had to stop in the middle of the road to allow a herd of cows to go through. Our driver told us how the art of sky painting had originated in the region. It seems that a local artist decided to paint Fairies tales and religious themes, not on canvas but in bold designs on the walls outside the buildings. It was most fascinating. For there on these walls were the well-known tales, "Little Riding Hood", "The three Bears", etc.

We finally arrived. I was as determined as ever to see that play. I was obsessed with the idea. So in spite of Juliette's admonitions I went straight to the theatre and approached the master of ceremonies. Although I was shaking in my boots, and after introducing myself, told him that my daughter and I were very anxious to see the play.

"My daughter and I are from Canada," I said, "and we will never have another opportunity to come to Europe. The *Passion Play* has become famous in our country and it would be a great privilege to be able to enjoy it ourselves, so that we too could laud it to our friends."

"Be here tomorrow before eight" he said, "and I will see what I can do."

Well to be there before eight was sooner said than done. At the reception desk we were told that there was a train traveling in that direction that left at five o'clock. The train did not take us all the way however. So there we were, sitting in the station, wondering what to do next. Fortunately, another couple (mother and daughter) were in the same predicament as we were, stranded in the middle of nowhere. But mercifully a taxi offered to take us the rest of the way. I'll never forget that ride! That driver went as the crow flies across country following no roads and driving like a maniac. "This is my last ride", each one of us thought as we held our breath. And to add insult to injury he was going to take off with our luggage. There was no way that we could make that man understand what we were saying. (Or was he pretending.) At last after a great deal of sign language we managed to get him to open the trunk and we retrieved our belongings.

True to his word, the master of ceremonies managed to get us two seats. Although we were not seated together we were most grateful. The play was fantastic! Although it was performed by local actors it was superior to any rendition of the Passion performed by celebrated actors. The choir was superb, divine. Indeed, out of the skies, even the birds came down to join the singers' celestial chorales. The dramatization was so genuine that the audience was transported in time to the actual scene of the crucifixion.

That adventure proved to be worthwhile indeed! The local artists are master sculptors. The whole town was alive with life like wooden replicas of famous people especially religious and biblical characters. Sculptors of various sizes, some life sized of the last supper were displayed everywhere. In the center of the terrace there was a replica of Mary, Joseph, and the donkey on their way to Jerusalem that was so exquisite that at a distance it appeared to be real. In fact that donkey seemed to walking towards you. Besides, all the buildings were adorned with air paintings. It was extraordinary. As if we had been suddenly transported and landed in a world of magic.

The sequence of my story is again in error for our itinerary led us to Austria first. It is logical for Austria is much further East than Munich. Austria is the birthplace where so many famous people have emerged, so much of our great and classical music and songs have emanated, besides tales of its wonders that both Juliette and I felt almost at home in that fascinating land and we longed to visit all these illustrious sites. Obviously Salzburg, Mozart's birthplace, was our first destination. The great master's home is a veritable fountain of musical plenitudes. Instruments, ancient and modern were all over the premises. A spinet, an instrument that was most interesting, was, according to our guide, the contraption upon which the musician's father first learned to play the piano. Apparently Mozart had inherited his musical talent from a long line of ancestors. His father had taught and guided him from his early childhood.

The spectacular Schonbrunn palace was our next stop. The palace had all the pomp and splendor typical of castles. It was, however, the gardens surrounding the premises and the ancient coaches that impressed me so profoundly. These coaches, there were hundreds of them, were so magnificent, so elaborately decorated that their opulence surpassed even that of Cinderella's magic coach. Some represented the historical episode in which they were built, others the famous personage for whom it had been constructed. The gardens were a mass of ornate greenery and alive with the efflorescence of brilliant colors. After walking through a wooded path we went up a steep elevation upon which stood a rather impressive monument. It had been constructed to honor the soldiers who had won a brilliant battle and had been named "La Glorietta" in memory of their valiant courage.

As I gazed upon the picturesque elegance of the landscape before me, I understood the ecstasy that overwhelmed Johann Strauss as the "Blue Danube" and "Tales from Vienna Woods" poured forth in joyous rapture from his very soul. For the enchantment of these woods, the allure of these flowing waters, and majesty of these great mountains bewitches you.

Castles situated on the summit of high mountains are scattered in many regions of the continent. These castles are actually fortresses as from that position an enemy could be spotted from a distance. Besides, for extra protection the castle was usually surrounded by a moat and the only accessibility to the entrance was by means of a draw-bridge. Folktales are filled with legends emanating from these ancient castles. We were fortunate indeed to have the opportunity to explore many of these, some in Austria, Germany, and other states.

After all this excitement, Vienna was a crowning delight, the icing on the cake. The leisurely pace of the people as they stroll languidly about, the relaxed and easy-going way by which they attend to their every day duties was comforting. Motor vehicles were not allowed on the streets in the inner city and therefore pedestrians are not in constant fear of traffic. There is an aura of mysticism about the whole city that made both my daughter and me wonder if we had not been suddenly transported into Peter Pan's "Never-Never Land". Most of the city resides in water and the foundation of many buildings is bathed by the steady current of the stream upon which it is situated. Most of the transportation is carried on by boats or gondolas as these exotic barges are called. Even the garbage is taken away in these. Juliette and I were so intrigued by these gondolas that we managed to persuade one of the captains to give us a ride. We visited many shops where various articles are manufactured. Venetians are famous for their expertise in making exquisite lace. I was tempted to buy a beautiful tablecloth but feared that my budget would not allow such extravagance. It is indeed regrettable that our itinerary did not allow us to explore the magnificent churches, palaces, and museums in a city famous as a tourist's paradise, for Venice is a city unique and distinctive, with characteristic exclusively its own. There is a mysterious ambience, almost metaphysical about its setting, as it appears to have been constructed and resting on a sea of magic waters.

It was probably at this stage of our journey that we visited Bavaria and King Ludwig's dazzling Linderhof palace. Perhaps dazzling is not a term to adequately describe Ludwig's spectacular castle. It was verily resplendent with luminescent mirrors and ornaments. A fabulous terrace with a sparkling fountain graced the façade of the building. As I gazed at all the ostentatious décor, the gilded paneling, the porcelain peacock, the rug of ostrich down, and all the exorbitant luxury, I wondered if the king's realm was in reality, and if he somehow was in league and dwelt with the inhabitants of another inscrutable world. For surely he had built a domain fit for a queen, the queen of a mystical world! I was intrigue by all the legends surrounding King Ludwig. He was obsessed with a passion for building castles using Versailles as a model. His obsession was to create monuments of beauty and not weapons of destruction. That was unacceptable in the era in which Ludwig reigned. Leaders then were ambitious and had to win the approval of the masses. They had to plunder and massacre in order to enrich and expend their kingdom. Therefore, because he abhorred violence and because he wanted to build instead of destroy, his colleagues thought he was insane.

It was perhaps after we visited Ludwig's kingdom that we traversed Switzerland by rail and through the Alps. As we sped through these majestic mountains I imagined myself tending the flocks with Heidi, leisurely dreaming the hours away. At one point we stopped at a monastery, friary, where the monks are famous for the quality of their wine and jewelry.

As we traveled through Europe and explored all its marvels, I began to reminisce about my childhood fantasies. I began to bring back the days when I walked along a wooded path, or on my solitary excursions of berry or root picking. I would build these castles in the air and the images began to flash back in my mind's eye. Yet as I envisaged all these wonders, the images would flash upon my perception and a strange thought would whisper in my ear. "I have seen this marvel before in another unearthly mythological and chimerical world". All these gleaming palaces, Versailles, Linderhof, those in Vienna and Austria, the magnificent churches, the fortresses surrounded by moats I had envisioned in my dreams as I built those illusive castles in the skies. But the wonders we admired had been erected from the sweat, the tears, and the hunger of many. Mine were fashioned from gossamer cobwebs and their foundations anchored in illusive nothingness. Yet when I gazed upon these marvels, I wondered if it was all a dream, and if there was even a remote possibility that dreams could come true. I have been accused of not knowing the difference between dreams and reality, but if these wonders were a dream than I hoped that it would go on forever.

When we crossed the border into Germany after sleeping all night on the train, as we often did to save hotel bills, we were startled and somewhat alarmed when we were confronted by a group of soldier carrying machine guns who proceeded at once to interrogate us. But as soon as they saw our Canadian passport they welcomed us into their country with a smile. We were greatly relieved. Indeed everywhere we went in Europe we were treated like gold because we came from Canada. Guess Canadians' international reputation is excellent!

While we were in Germany we sailed down the Rhine River. It was then that we were given the opportunity to explore the interior of many ancient castles, torture chambers and all. It is regrettable that in trying to modernize these and to utilize them for modern conveniences, the romantic ambience of these historical monuments has been eclipsed by greed.

As the time was getting closer and closer for our vacation to end we were both reluctant to go. For once you have tasted of the felicity of paradise; you loathe to resume the hum-drum of daily living and assume the responsibilities, the problems, and whatever wiles destiny has concocted for you. I of course, was anxious to see the children, but poor Juliette, even though she did want to see her children, had serious problems awaiting her upon her arrival, problems that seemed to have no immediate solution. It is little wonder that she did not want to go back! She had no desire to face a relatively impossible situation. Mercifully, during the time she had been away from the situation she had been able to reach a logical conclusion and make a rational decision.

The sequence of events in this narrative will be a complete disaster evidently. I should have kept a daily journal had I had the faintest idea of the magnitude a project of this nature demands. Indeed it would require an elephant's memory to be able to keep all the events neatly recorded in the mind's filing system. Evidently my filing system was at best mediocre, and consequently the events in this drama are not always as they occurred in reality. The reader will have to bear with me and be cautioned against attempting such a humongous enterprise at eighty- five.

Be that as it may a major mess has occurred. I had had a previous and exciting adventure before venturing on the European tour. During the Christmas holidays in the later part of the seventies, Carol and I went to Hawaii for two weeks. I had never been out of the country before and the adventure was most exhilarating. At the time the island was not so commercialized and every effort was made to make tourists feel at home and enjoy themselves. We did indeed have a wonderful time.

While we were there the people had a folk festival on top of the famous crater, Diamond Head. A celebrated American band, Santana, was playing and there were all kinds of activities, displays, and sideshows. A local family had taken Carol and me under their wing and was taking us to all the tourist highlights and attractions. We visited a huge shopping mall, the largest in Honolulu, went to a disco, and watched dance performances on two occasions. The dancers wore their native costumes, grass skirts and all. Both an adult and a young girls' group were very graceful in their performance of the ancient Hawaiian dance, the hula. We also went to a Polynesians' Festival of Light. The performance was staged upon barges or canoes floating on a nearby river. Besides the colorful costumes of the actors, the most astonishing performers were the fire-eaters and those who walked on live coals. It was unbelievable! We attended a luau, or Hawaiian feast. The main dish is usually a whole roasted pig but it also consists of many exotic oriental dishes. On a bus tour of the island we visited a pineapple, a sugar cane, and a banana plantation. We were both fascinated by the vegetation, especially the coconut trees and the many varieties of flowers. The informality of dress is most relaxing. The women wear loose ankle length dresses called muumuu and men aloha shirts all year round.

The population is a mixture of many different cultures. This is reflected in the relaxed atmosphere and friendly public relations that exists throughout the island. Cultural, religious, and language barriers do not exist. This factor plus the island's ideal climate make Hawaii a tourist's paradise. Coming from Edmonton when the temperature was thirty below zero, Hawaii was indeed a paradise!

After St. Vladimir, my next teaching assignment was at St. Rita. It was an ideal situation. My homeroom was a mixed class of grade one and two and I taught French in grade four, five and six. There was only one significant event that occurred during that year. Although my grade five class was rated as being above average and the most proficient in all Edmonton, the grade six French class was hopelessly low. There was a clown in that class! That child had made up his mind that he wasn't going to learn French and that he wasn't going to let anyone else in the class learn French either. As my time in the grade six class was very limited, it was almost impossible to discover why that child was so belligerent and I was at the point of giving up altogether. During one of those classes, I was trying desperately to get my lesson across when I realized that it was a waste of time to continue. He was up to his shenanigans again making the class laugh at his stupid grimaces and gestures. So I stopped dead in my tracks and just stood there, and suddenly there was a dead silence as all eyes focused on me. It was my moment.

I said, "Why do you hate us so much?" Well, he was so startled that his eyes almost popped out of his head.

"I don't hate you", he protested with great emphasis.

"Oh yes you do." I insisted, "You must hate all of us with a passion! You must hate me, for you do not let me do my work, and you must hate your classmates vehemently, for you will not let them learn and they will all fail this class. Its strange that you hate us so much because I love you, we all love you, don't we class?" What a risk to take!

Instantly all hands shot up." Yes, we all love you", they shouted.

It was a revelation to see the look on that boy's face. His eyes were as big as saucers and his face was as red as a beet. Be that as it may we were able to continue our French academic work for the rest of the year without any interruptions.

Although my teaching position at St. Rita was ideal and would have stayed there for the next term, a young teacher on the staff, determined to remain in that school, persuaded me to transfer in her place. Although Bishop Savaryn School was conveniently located, the transfer proved to be a mistake. The residents in the district were not as genial as those at St. Rita and the principal was very domineering. However the students more than compensated for the disadvantages. After all these years, when by some coincidental encounter we meet at church, at the grocery store, walking around the lake, they recognize and greet me affectionately. Those are precious moments, moments that fill my soul with warmth and joy, a sensation that it was all worthwhile.

There are events in one's life that are irrefutable proof of mankind's righteousness and decency. The community in the district had built a skating rink in the school yard at Bishop Savaryn to amuse the children during the noon recess. There was a problem, however. The children were not allowed to put their skates on in the school. The older children managed to change from boots to skates quickly but the smaller children were unable to do so and most of the time their hands were frozen and recess was over by the time their skates were on. At the staff meeting, the principal claimed that if students put their skates on in the building the floor would be scratched and the teachers claimed that it would double the supervision. As far as I was concerned the skating rink was useless for most of the students were unable to use it. So I offered to be fully responsible for all the supervision that would be required if the students were allowed to change in the building. I also volunteered to help the little ones tie the laces on their skates. A heavy rug was installed at the end of the hall near the door and benches placed along the wall. It worked like a clock and was more than worth the effort because the little ones were so grateful. They could skate now without freezing on the snow bank! Besides, the older students always came to help with the younger ones. This went on for about two weeks. I was amazed and deeply gratified when a group of parents took over claiming that these were their children and that I didn't have to give up my lunch hour for them. What an amazing group these parents were!

My next position was at St. Timothy. In spite of the many problems that existed in the student population, problems emanating from the homes and permeating throughout the school, the principal and the entire staff were dedicated and devoted their efforts cooperatively in order to solve problems and assist their students.

At the time the district was a conglomeration of stable and dependable families interspersed by a mixture of dysfunctional, broken, and abusive family relationships. The children from secure family situations always bring joy to the classroom and are an inspiration to the teacher and their classmates. Unfortunately children from unhappy home situations have seemingly insurmountable problems, the most devastating of these being the feeling of rejection and insecurity.

Some of the incidences occurring in my classroom during these four years were heartbreaking. One little fellow had been rejected by his father and he decided that without his dad life was meaningless. So he sat there day after day doing nothing. Both his mother and I tried in vain to get him out of his trance, to comfort him, and to give him some reason why he should make an effort to go on with his life. Carol and I took him to movies. I suggested to his mother that she get the Uncles at Large to help but she was reluctant to trust her son to a stranger. All our efforts to help that unfortunate boy failed miserably. I often wonder what happened to him.

Then there was a boy who had been raised by his grandmother in the Philippines and was suddenly taken to Canada after his mother remarried. Not only did he long for his grandmother, but he was forced to live with a mother he barely knew and her husband who was a complete stranger to him. Besides all this he had to adapt to a new culture and a new school. It goes without saying that the child was miserable, in fact he was furious! He had violent fits of temper during which he managed to destroy anything within his reach. He'd start by tearing his scribblers, and then he'd break his crayons, his pencils, his scissors and erasers. Then he attacked his desk, shaking it furiously in an effort to smash it. It was evident that the child needed help. It was also evident that he wasn't getting any support from his mother or his classmates who were unable to understand his strange behavior. And because he was different, some were even unkind to him. The school counselor referred him to a psychiatrist. The school counselor, the mother, the child and I were present at the meeting. Apparently the child had never been told that his natural father had been killed in a car accident. What was even more incredible was that the child who was nine years old had never asked about his father. (None of this made any sense to me.) Besides all these traumatic events were being revealed to him in front of an adult audience. The psychiatrist, unable to read between the lines, blamed all the child's problems on the school situation, to the mother's great relief. It was the usual litany, the child was being discriminated against, the other children were mean to him and on and on. The moral of the story is, if you can't find anyone else to blame, blame the teacher! Looking back, I've always regretted the fact that I didn't keep trying to find someone who could have helped that poor boy. That psychiatrist didn't have a clue. The next year the boy was expelled on the grounds that he was a threat to the other students.

One of the boys in the class could not tolerate being teased. He was a great kid and had a charming personality. In sports he was a team all by himself, taking on the rest of the boys in a game and winning. It goes without saying that when his classmates found out about his paranoia, they teased him constantly, thinking that his explosive outbursts were hilarious. The consequences were as expected. Being a robust young lad and much stronger than the rest of the boys, he avenged himself with his fists, with the anticipated results. After using all my diplomacy as a peace maker with little results, the vice-principal came to my rescue. She took the boy in her office and started firing one question after another at him, without giving him any time to answer any of them. She went on and on without any reprieve. The boy must have been exhausted when she finally relented (I was) for he decided that it would be easier to stop his negative behaviour rather than to go through that again and the problem was solved. At least the problem was solved during the years he attended St. Timothy, for during that time he was an ideal student. Years later, I was devastated to hear that the problem had started all over again. Later when the student attended junior high he was expelled.

It must have been that destiny was at its old mischievous tricks again other wise similar situations would likely never have repeated themselves twice to the same person in the same location. For one fine day the principal brought a new boy into my classroom. He had beet red hair and as I found out later, a temper to match. He must have been Irish but there was no time to discuss nationalities. I had my hands full just dealing with his temper. After introducing him to the class the new student settled in and the daily routine was restored in harmony. That is until recess time! As soon as the class was dismissed, all hell broke loose! It sounded as if war had suddenly been declared. The screaming and shouting not to mention the language, which was not the sort you normally hear in within the precincts of a school, summoned the whole staff outdoors to investigate. When we finally reached the scene all we could see was a melee of bodies madly skirmishing in the dust. Flaying arms, bleeding noses, co-occurred with the blow of a punching fist. Well, when the combatants were finally separated, it was discovered that our fiery hot-tempered red head had single handedly taken on the whole school in combat. I was completely dumbfounded as my students were well behaved and usually got along well together. As can be expected the boys were severely reprimanded. New students were usually treated with kindness in order to make them feel welcome in the new situation. Apparently this boy's name was Hoolahan, the same as the nurse in the T.V. program "Mash" so the boys teased him about his name and he went berserk. Evidently this problem had to be solved. So after the others were gone, I tried to find out the reason for these outbursts.

"Usually" I began, "the students in this class get along together. I cannot understand why they were so mean to you."

Immediately he started to cry. "It is not their fault," he sobbed, "I am upset. My parents are divorced. My father's girl friend doesn't want me and my mother's boyfriend doesn't want me. I don't know what to do."

By this time I had tears rolling down my cheeks. "Well," I said, "I wish I could take you to my house, for my family and I would love to have you. My only concern would be your ability to put up with the rest of the children."

That seemed to be the answer! He was astounded that someone could actually want him and accept him. I never knew how the family problem was solved. But hereafter peace was restored and reigned in our midst.

Twice in all the thirty-seven years of my teaching career I had the courage to stand up and defend the rights of those in my profession. It must have been my mother speaking through me for the oppression of and abuse of someone's rights were intolerable to her. Throughout her life she stood up and fought with the fangs of a tiger for the rights of those who were vulnerable and had no voice in the eyes of society. Unlike my mother, I have the reputation of being timid. So I am still amazed and am completely astounded at the audacity that enabled me to speak up in favor of teachers' rights.

The school board had sent a member to inform us that hereafter someone would be allocated to spy on staff members to ascertain the fact that all teachers were performing their religious duties faithfully including the regular reception of communion. I couldn't believe my ears! Indeed I couldn't believe that anyone in this modern world would have the gall, the effrontery to even suggest such a brazen policy. I expected the principal to protest vehemently. He didn't say a word. Then I looked at all the teachers sitting around the table (there were at least twenty of them). Still not a word. I looked at all of them again. Surely someone among them would have the courage to point out the ramifications emanating from the enforcement of such a ludicrous policy. Still no one spoke. The silence was deafening! Perhaps they were too stunned to reciprocate. Were they all going to be coerced into this enslaving net without even raising any objections, like sheep led to slaughter? When freedom is threatened it should be defended even if the cost is exorbitant. Would these enlightened people sell their soul for a crust of bread I asked myself? I could not bear the silence any longer. I could not contain my outrage any longer and my fury exploded in a wild passionate outburst.

"So," I declared angrily, "we may as well be dispossessed of all our rights especially the right of privacy as the characters were in the book '*1984*' and have Big Brother spy on us every minute of our private lives. The enforcement of this policy would be a direct violation of our human rights as recorded in our Canadian Constitution. Besides, fearing the loss of their employment many teachers would feel compelled to receive communion when they are not disposed to do so. The board would be responsible for this sacrilege as it was instigated by and made compulsory by their ill advised ruling."

Then miraculously every one spoke up and there was a heated discussion. What would have happened had I not said a word is debatable. Be that as it may the policy was apparently never adopted and we never heard about it again.

The next time I defended teachers' rights was during a parent teacher meeting. A grade six student had assaulted a teacher and the mother blamed his teacher. She went on and on. The teacher involved was absent and could not defend herself. Again I was absolutely astounded that no one on the staff supported a colleague. Fortunately, the boy's sister was in my class and I knew the abuse these children were subjected to in their daily lives. So again, I stood up and told some of the events that transpired in that home before these children arrived in the classroom. Confronting the mother I asked all the parents who were present.

"When you send us a child who is emotionally distressed sobbing his heart out, the school is not responsible for your child's misery or for his behavior when he strikes out in anger as a protestation against the situation in which he has no control. In such circumstances, would you proceed with daily instructions or would you comfort and pacify the child first so he could regained his composure and hear what you were saying. Before you condemn any teacher for your child's behavior, please think about what is involved."

The principal then spoke up emphasizing the fact that the purpose of a parent-teacher meeting was to get acquainted and that problems should be handled in the privacy of his office. "Students' problems are confidential and should be respected as such," he declared. Subsequently, although the mother wasn't entirely satisfied, order was restored and the meeting was resumed in harmony.

After I had taught at St. Timothy for four years, I decided to retire. The staff, the parents, and the students organized a retirement party at the school. The teachers and parents gave me a silver tea set with the year and the name of the school inscribed on it. The students gave me a silver plate inscribed with the name of the class and year. I was deeply touched! The school board had also celebrated several teachers' retirement, but the celebration at the school was more intimate and I appreciated it so much more.

Although I knew it was the right thing to do at the time because of the teacher surplus, my feelings about retirement were mixed. It was evident that I would miss the children desperately; as they had always been such an important part of my life. Without them I would be lost!

In order to be with the children I tried to be a replacement or substitute teacher. It became quite clear to me that subbing was not for me. A substitute teacher has to be special kind of a person. He or she must be a very strict disciplinarian among other things. Being able to adapt to different situations and personalities is very important. One teacher put it this way, "You must come into the room like a tiger and not let up all day." Somehow students think they can have a field day when their teacher is absent. A relationship with students that is based on coercion was unacceptable to me. During my career, I was usually able to get the good will and the cooperation of my students, as I believed that a suitable atmosphere is crucial to the learning and well being of any child. It goes without saying that after several negative experiences, I decided never to sub again.

I missed the children however and wanted to work and play with them again. The opportunity soon presented itself. Carol was teaching at Batyrn School and she wondered if I would help the children who were having difficulties with the reading program. So I volunteered as a reading assistant. At first I had only one student, but soon the other teachers asked me to help their students. Soon I was teaching all morning and had as many as four reading groups. It was an ideal situation. My wish had been realized, the children were learning to read and the parents were delighted because their son or daughter was getting extra help. Besides, soon those parents were bringing their children to my house for extra help and I was tutoring almost full time.

At first my students were mainly students who were in the French immersion program. They needed help with the pronunciation and the understanding of the language as most of their parents did not speak French. Science was especially difficult for those students as the vocabulary alone is very challenging when it is not presented in the vernacular. Struggling with the meaning of all these formidable terms prevents the students from understanding the concepts involved. When the material was translated for them they were able to grasp its significance. Later many students needed assistance with mathematics. Then I found myself teaching a variety of subjects. Many students in high school needed help with their essays. Although this proved to be most interesting it was rather time consuming. At one point I had as many as twenty students from all levels of achievement, even a few first year university students. I enjoyed this type of teaching and found it most rewarding.

In 1984, the year of my retirement, Pope John Paul 11 came to Edmonton. In order to accommodate the huge crowds it had been arranged that he celebrated mass on the outskirts of the city in an open field. Our priest had organized a pilgrimage in which the pilgrims were to gather at St. Charles Church and walk to the site. Many of our parishioners participated forming a huge parade walking through the city. After the mass the Pope's sermon was brilliant. He reiterated his moral norms concerning the sanctity of life and stated that these issues were not optional for society. However the main theme of his sermon was a plea for social justice, a plea that was uttered with such passion and force that it sounded like thunder. He lamented the fact that the resources necessary to help those in need were employed as means of destruction. His message echoed clearly to the crowd who listened transfixed by the wisdom of his words as he proclaimed that, "This poor South will judge the rich North". Everyone knew that the truth had been spoken. Alas truth is inexorable to the delicate ear and is often unheeded till it's too late. This of course is irrelevant to many, as they wouldn't know the truth even if {or until} it hit them in the face. To others, truth is a concept that is too stringent or formidable to digest. Consequently they either steer clear or find a way around its veracity, unable to cope with the accountability it exhorts. Yet others, realizing the righteousness of the responsibilities the term dictates, promise to fulfill these obligations in a more distant and convenient future. Meanwhile they let others assume the entire burden the term exiges.

I am ever so thankful that I had the courage to go on the pilgrimage to Namao with the rest of the crowd. It has been an unforgettable event in my life. As I listened to the Pope's words I knew that he was a man of God, an emissary straight from heaven.

Unfortunately on my way home I got lost but that is not surprising. Getting lost is my trademark!

The years that followed my retirement were filled with many exciting experiences. Touring Europe and Hawaii had kindled a yearning to explore the many wonders of the earth. Indeed it had become an obsession. The children were all on their own by this time and I was free to do as I pleased. My sister Hélène was also smitten by the wandering bug so together the two of us went touring whenever the opportunity presented itself.

Our first trip was arranged by a Vancouver tourist company. It was almost a pilgrimage as we visited many of the most religious shrines in Europe. After landing in London and enjoying the hospitality of a luxurious hotel our group proceeded to Lisbon, where Priscilla, our tour guide, had chartered a bus tour for the rest of our journey. Fatima, where the Blessed Virgin appeared to three local children, was our first stop. The shrine and the cathedral erected in honor of the Blessed Virgin is most impressive. However, the most remarkable and inspiring characteristic of the Portuguese people is their faith and devotion to their religious belief. The intensity and fervor of their prayers was overwhelming. They are also very kind and hospitable hosts. It is unfortunate that many merchants insist on selling their wares as tourists wish to absorb the culture and the ambience of the country and not to be burdened with merchandize or be continually hassled by high-pressured salesmanship. However, before the onset of tourism, Portugal experienced some dire economic problems. We visited the homes where some of the peasants lived and those where the three famous children previously lived. Although the village had been abandoned at the time, the ruins reeked of poverty and deprivation.

From Lisbon we crossed the border into Spain. I remember wondering how these people survived. For miles and miles as we traveled along the highway, a sea of sand stretched endlessly before us as far as the eye could see. There seemed to be no vegetation whatsoever except a rare grove of olive trees. Even the fences separating individual properties were walls of stones.

Our tour guide had arranged a tour of Avila, a city surrounded by a formidable eight-foot thick stonewalls giving it the appearance of a fortress. St. Theresa of Avila was a novitiate at the convent within these fortified walls. Relics of the saint are prominently displayed in the reception area at the main entrance of the building. The convent has become a famous tourist attraction.

Madrid was fascinating. The Spanish culture is most interesting as it seems so different from our own. The people do things with such a flare and in such a flamboyant manner as compared to the American style. For instance the waiters in the hotel restaurant were dressed in formal attire and waited on us with a formality that was almost intimidating. Many in our group wanted to see some of the fabulous attractions unique to the Spanish culture. The flamingo dancers were first on the list. Fortunately there was a performance on the evening that we arrived in the city. We wouldn't have missed it for the world. The performance was magnificent, the dancers brilliant, and the costumes exotic. None of the ladies were interested in attending the bullfight, a sport that is very popular in Spain. The Picasso museum was very interesting to most of the group who are connoisseurs in art but the master's style is unfamiliar to me.

Our next stop was Barcelona. I have a vague memory of the city except for the luxury of the buildings and the traffic. Indeed the traffic was so heavy that you could not hear yourself think let alone sleep. The hotel where we stayed was lavishly decorated and furnished; yet it was impossible to sleep because of the noise on the street. Priscilla informed us that Lucy, the only survivor of the three children who had seen the Blessed Virgin at Fatima, lived in

Barcelona. Because of her age she was not able to have any visitors.

In France we spent more time in Lourdes than in Paris. The fountains where pilgrims bathe as an intersession for a miraculous cure are most impressive. They are situated where Bernadette, a simple peasant girl, saw the Blessed Virgin. The group visited the home where Bernadette's family lived. It is amazing that a whole family lived in such confined quarters.

It was at Lourdes that on my way to church I slipped on the marble pavement and broke my arm. At the clinic I was astounded by the devotion and the painstakingness of the doctors. There were at least five of them meticulously examining my ex-rays and discussing the results. It was evident that an operation was necessary. I decided to have the procedure in Edmonton. With a cast immobilizing the fracture there was no pain and I was able to enjoy the rest of my trip.

Back in London the group members had a few days that were unscheduled. It was a golden opportunity for adventurers to cram as much of the city as possible in such a short time. Florence, our traveling companion, just wanted to rest so Hélène and I set out to explore on our own. We sailed along the Thames River and stopped at many historical sites already familiar to us, as they were relics of the reformation period in British History. It was weird, as what had just seemed a story in a book had suddenly become real and stood right before our eyes.

Windsor Castle was next on the schedule. It proved to be a little disappointing, but of coarse, from fairy tales we have such grandiose expectations of what a castle should be and simplicity is not one of them. As one of the guards contemplated the conspicuous cast on my arm, he shook his head and remarked jokingly,"I'd hate to see the other guy!" It was refreshing to see a member of the police force join the human race!

I will never forget going to the theatre in London. It is one of the most spectacular memories of my entire life. A live production of "Les Miserables" was on at London's most prestigious theatre and although the tickets were exorbitant, nothing could have kept us away. I have seen many renditions of that play but none could even be compared to the quality and expertise of that performance. It was exquisite! I sat glued to my seat less I should miss even a bit of the action. Later, I felt guilty as Florence felt ill during the performance and Hélène had to take care of her all by herself. Yet even though I felt selfish, I was so intrigued and immersed in the development of the plot that I could not tear myself away.

We explored the mall where the queen is said to do her shopping. Neither one of us was impressed. However, the queen's doll house is displayed prominently behind a glass casing and is incredible. Every item it contains has been exquisitely fashioned and is indeed a work of art.

Hélène was supposed to meet her son-in-law's mother at the airport. She looked for her and even had her paged on the intercom but was unable to find her in the crowd. At the last minute she decided to join Florence and I in the line-up just a few minutes before the plane was scheduled to take off. I was in a panic and didn't know whether to board the plane without her or take a later flight and wait for her. Mercifully she came up just as the passengers were being ushered into the plane.

Soon after my arrival a great bone specialist, Dr. Russell, operated on my elbow and my arm was just as good as new. Fortunately for there was already another adventure brewing in the horizon, an adventure that I wouldn't have missed for the world. For once the wandering fire has laid its claim upon a restless spirit. Its smoldering desire to drift aimlessly into the unknown and distant shores will forever remain sizzling.

The next time Hélène and I sprouted wings over the Atlantic we found ourselves en route to the Holy Land. Priscilla, our trusted travel agent, had organized a tour of the historical shrines in Israel where Jesus lived. There were more than thirty in the group. We were fortunate to have three priests among us who could explain and enrich the religious aspect of the journey. Besides, there was a lady in our group who sang like a nightingale. This lady was remarkable in more ways than one. She sang in the church choir in her hometown which was the only outlet she had for her amazing talent. She lived alone on a farm not far from Edmonton as her husband had passed away about a year before this journey. She claimed that it was a miracle that she had been able to raise enough funds for this adventure. She said that a long time before he died, her husband had invested a few dollars in some stock. She had been deeply troubled because the family lived on a meager income and couldn't spare a dime. As it turned out those few dollars mushroomed into a sizable sum, a sum that covered all the expenses of her trip. It was indeed a miracle! Although she entertained us during many celebrations with her beautiful voice, on one occasion she sang way down in the pit of a Shakespearian theatre and her voice reverberate to those seated in the upper levels.

After landing in Tel Aviv we toured Israel by bus. Our tour guide and bus driver was very professional on both counts. His expertise was manifested in his dedication to the safety and comfort of the passengers and his knowledge of the Bible, e.g., the life of our Lord. He was able to tell the incidents that transpired at every site as we traveled along the path that our Lord tread during His life. His rendition of the Bible was consistent with my mother's version which she had taught us from our earliest childhood. His detailed account of every episode pertaining to the religious version of the life of Christ was astounding.

We stopped at a religious compound or commune, known as a Kabutz. It appears that these communes kabbutzing, as it is called, is a Jewish method of holding land and is not unlike compounds of the Hutterites in America. The meal they served was delicious and the sleeping accommodations were excellent. It was quite an experience!

Jerusalem was our home base during our stay in the Holy Land. Our guide had apparently planned to follow the path that led where major events in the life of Jesus transpired. Hence Bethlehem, where Jesus was born, was first on his itinerary. That was, to my utter consternation, a fact that did not coincide with what I had been taught as a child. According to my mother's teachings and everything I had read (and taught) Jesus had been born in a stable. But I was completely astounded to learn that in accordance with reality, He was born in a cave. Apparently many in these Arid lands, resorted to this type of shelter as a protection from the wandering Nomad tribes who killed and plundered everyone and everything in their path. Upon this Holy site the Emperor Constantine later erected the Church of the Nativity. There are three chambers in this cave in the center of which there is a well. One of the priests assisted by the others celebrated a solemn mass in that very confined space, a space mesmerized by a mystical, a metaphysical aura.

In Nazareth, the main attraction was the Church of the Annunciation. Other tourists were impressed by St. Joseph's workshop, Christ's table and St. Mary's well, but as the authenticity of these relics are questionable, the beauty of the church was the memorial that inspired me the most.

Jerusalem was the limelight of the tour. We walked through the sites and routes that our Lord tread during His brief existence on this earth. Walking along the route Jesus followed as he carried the cross, the Via Doloroso, our group ascended to mount Cavalry, the site of Jesus crucifixion. It is also the site of the Holy Sepulchre, the church where our Lord's Body is entombed. As we marched along that most dolorous route, I was again filled with amazement upon the realization that there were no pictures or statues depicting Christ's passion and suffering along the way. Nonetheless it was heart warming to observe people of many faiths paying tribute to the Lord both along the Via Doloroso and in the church where He is buried.

We visited the Garden of Gethsemane where Jesus and His apostles spent the night in prayer before His death, and where He was betrayed by Judas. We were also taken to the room which is supposedly the site of the last supper. The rest of the group visited the Wailing Wall but I was unable to go.

Jerusalem is the seat of many historical and spectacular treasures. Therefore it is impossible to savour all of its magnificence in such a short period of time. Indeed it would require many sojourn and time to speculate on all the wealth the city embodies. Among many other things, I was greatly impressed by the famous Dome of the Rock and the religious chanting that echo eternally throughout the city.

From Jerusalem some of us were anxious to see the Masada, King Herod's summer residence. Although Herod was reputed to be a villain he was nonetheless brilliant. The residence, built on a plateau at the summit of a towering mountain was a masterpiece in construction and design. What was so amazing was that this extraordinary marvel had been achieved without the aid of modern equipment and facilities. The complex had every facility for convenience and comfort: a safe water supply, food storage facilities, and even bathhouses.

Although the complex was amazingly spectacular, it was the transportation to the premises that evoked a lasting sensation in my memory. I will never forget that taxi ride. The driver drove like a maniac. Indeed Hélène and I had the impression that he was speeding across country heedless of roads or obstacles obstructing the way. Both my sister and I feared for our lives! Thank goodness that a lift took us to the summit of the mountain!

Rome was next on the itinerary but Hélène and I had opted to go to Athens instead. Looking back, it was indeed a wise decision. During the three days of our sojourn in that city we managed to explore the most famous tourist attractions. The Acropolis was of course our main target it being so phenomenal in the annals of history. A guide led the way through and explained the significance of the most spectacular monuments in the complex: the illustrious Parthenon, the statue of Athena, the Alter of Athena, etc. We toured the central market place, the Agora, with all the structures which are testimonials of the Greeks' ancient belief in many Gods. These alters and monuments erected to venerate and pay homage to their Gods fascinated me, especially the alters and temples that were erected to pay homage to Zeus, who was, they believed, supreme. It is little wonder for our libraries and schools are filled with myths and legends about the Greek, Roman, and Norse Mythology. Therefore we are entirely captivated by the mystical and ethereal lore these deities represent.

Situated just beneath the south side of the Acropolis is the Dionysiac Theatre. It is constructed of what appears to be pure marble columns. It is a manifestation of the skill and the ingenuity of the Greek architectural and artistic expertise. Besides this magnificent theatre, the vision of a little church situated high on the summit of a steep elevation has remained in my memory. The church of St. Michael, accessible by climbing a mountain of stairs only, has intrigued my curiosity ever since Hélène and I discovered it. Many were ascending those myriad stairs, some on their knees. How I longed to follow them, but alas, we had to leave. I've always wanted to go back to Greece, fantasizing that perhaps then there would be an opportunity to go up these stairs and visit that mysterious little church.

We crossed the channel and toured the island of Peloponnesos. Our guide led us to many fantastic attractions including the world-renowned Olympia, the birthplace of the Olympic Games. There were many other interesting sites, too many to be able to fully appreciate in such a short time. Wherever we went we were overwhelmed by the beauty of the Arts.

On the way back, we stopped at a convent nestled in a deep valley and completely surrounded by lofty mountains. I was utterly astounded when I realized that the sisters in that remote region were French and were unable to communicate in any other language. They sold various articles, souvenirs mostly. I bought a book written in French about Athens, its history and its prestigious influence on the civilizations and culture of the enlightened world.

At the airport, homebound, we were greeted with a veritable bombshell. My name was not on the passenger list and there were no vacant seats available on the departing flight. It appears that the travel agency had neglected or forgotten to add my name to the list. Neither of us knew what to do. Hélène didn't want to leave me alone; on the other hand it was imperative that she be home to explain the circumstances to my family less they become frantic with worry. After making suitable arrangements with the travel guide, I decided to stay until the next available flight. The superintendent had been informed of our plight and of the gravity of the situation. This most gracious gentleman bent over backwards to find a seat for me. Lo and behold, at the very last minute there was a cancellation and I boarded the plane. It goes without saying that both of us heaved a sigh of relief!

When we arrived at the airport in Amsterdam, we discovered that the rest of our group was stranded. Somewhere along the line the travel agency had erred. (Again!) After a great deal of red tape the tour guide managed to get the rest of the passenger on a direct flight to Vancouver. Hélène and I had our passage booked from Athens.

As I reminisce about all the voyages, and contemplate the wonders of all the lands in which I have traveled, I am filled with nostalgia. I find it impossible to decide which of these journeys I cherish the most. For every nation, every society and every culture has something unique and precious to offer to the rest of the world. A certain ambience, or nuance permeates the atmosphere and creates an exclusive sensation the instance one sets foot in that particular domain; a sensation emanating from the whispering vibes that distinct environment generates. Therefore, it is wise to conclude that every journey has been a source of ecstasy and revelation to me.

Meanwhile many changes had taken place in our family. Walter, David, and Juliette were married, Charlie was working as an accountant for a company in British Columbia, Keith was living in the house he had so strongly persuaded me to buy in Falkland B.C., and Lucille was living on her own. Carol, Cherrie and I were the only ones left at home. (Not for long however.) Carol was working about a block away as a teller for the Royal Bank when she came back from Europe she decided to go back to University and finish her Education. It was great to have her at home. She helped me take care of Cherrie a lot. She'd take her to the babysitter; watch her while I was moonlighting, and even take her on dates. It was an unwritten law unchallenged by her friends. "If you want to take me on a date, you must take Cherrie, otherwise forget it." She even took Cherrie on long holidays, wherever she went in her little red Toyota.

As mentioned above, it wasn't long before Charlie came back to Edmonton and was soon followed by Keith. Charlie worked for the Catholic School Board for many years and during those years he lived at home. It was while he was still living at home that he brought his bride, Linda to live with us. Unfortunately as soon as the couple moved out on their own, the marriage went sour. Charlie was heart broken. My reaction made things much worse. When he told me that Linda had left him I really and truly thought he was joking and I started to laugh. It is indeed strange that the expression on his face did not reveal his anguish. I will never forgive myself for this blunder. It was another, yes another blunder that will haunt me the rest of my days as I plod along the rest of the way.

Meanwhile, Lucille married a gentleman from a very well respected family, Rick Murdoch. Although he was a policeman, his integrity as a person had nothing to do with his profession. His unshakeable belief in the difference between right and wrong was a trait that I admired about him. To him there were no shades of gray in between as politicians are so apt to color. He thought his obsessive passion for excellence was a flaw in his character. He continually apologized to everyone about what he labeled as compulsive behavior which had escalated to a point beyond his control. As far as I was concerned, I secretly wished that I possessed some of Rick's alleged shortcoming. This doing things by hook and by crook is not all it was cracked up to be!

Rick and Lucille with children Johnny and Alicia

The couple had decided to have a private ceremony with as little fuss as possible. There was no wedding reception or honeymoon. As a matter of fact the family was not invited to attend the ceremony. Nevertheless the couple had a beautiful relationship. They were devoted to each other and did not allow outside influence to intervene in their relationship. Which is of course, the recipe for a happy marriage.

Soon afterwards Carol and Danny decided to get married. The wedding ceremony was a private family affair. It was followed by a simple reception and dance. Close friends and family members were the only guests. It was, however, a delightful celebration. The friendly and close relationship of those present created a ambience of warmth and affinity among the guests. Without the encumbrance of hosting an elaborate and gala affair, the family joined the festivities and celebrated the joyful occasion. Needless to say Carol and Danny, who were among their dearest friends, were enjoying themselves tremendously.

Carol and Danny

Danny was one of these great guys that everybody just loves. It didn't matter if he was at work, at a party, or with the family, his quiet demeanor and great sense of humor won the heart of everyone present. A carpenter by trade or more specifically an architect, as his ability to design a plan for any building even surpassed his skill as a construction worker. Besides, he was able to do almost anything; you name it, he was a plumber, an electrician, a good Samaritan all rolled up into one. It is not surprising that whenever there was an emergency or someone was in trouble guess who always came to the rescue? Why, Danny of course! And I was perhaps the most culpable of them all. It is not surprising that his family and all his friends wonder how they can get along without him.

Perhaps the most remarkable trait about Danny's personality was his passion and his love of music. He loved all music, modern, Irish, country, but he was simply enraptured by the works of the great masters. Whatever he was doing, whether he was driving, building, or painting, it was always to the rhythm of a melodious refrain transmitted from a radio that accompanied him wherever he went.

That two individuals with such different personalities should be attracted to one another is inconceivable; Carol whose aspirations in all aspects of being and endeavors were to be content with nothing less than excellence; excellence in every minute detail. Shooting for the stars no less! Danny however, had a different way of looking at the world. He felt that one should look only at the big picture, things that were crucial, and completely ignore things of little consequence. He must have been in league with the author of "Don't Sweat the Small Stuff." For he continually let trivial (and sometimes not so trivial) matters go right over his head. Needless to say, this didn't go over too well with Carol who insisted on perfection in every minute detail. How two individuals with such striking differences manage to reach a mutual ground is indeed amazing. Yet, intelligence and logic prevailed. They were both successful in their careers and managed to establish a luxurious home for their two daughters. Because of his extraordinary talent as an artistic architect besides his skills as a carpenter Danny was unable to keep up with the demand for his services. Carol, on the other hand, has become an excellent teacher. Her aspiration to achieve excellence and her dedication to her students is remarkable. Indeed, her preoccupation and total devotion to the welfare of those who have been entrusted to her care is beyond the call of duty.

Carol and Danny with children Nicole and Michelle

For a considerable length of time Charlie had worked for the Separate School Board. He had been promoted to a responsible position and was in charge of a department with many employees working under his supervision. Some controversy occurred concerning lax operational practices and standards of efficiency which were intolerable according to Charlie's criterion. During a board meeting, serious disagreement ensued when he, in no uncertain terms, poured out his concerns. Although Charlie tried to show his colleagues a more modern, practical, efficient and easier method of doing things, the staff was adamant. They had been doing things a certain way from the beginning and change was to them taboo, utterly beyond their perspective. So Charlie, unable to work under these circumstances, was forced to leave and find a position with another firm.

It was while he was unemployed that Charlie met and later married Linda. The couple lived alternately at the house and downtown in a rented house. Besides Charlie and Linda, David and his family had moved back home temporarily. So for a considerable length of time we had a full house and things were not exactly facile for anyone. My memory is entangled in cobwebs which cast many shadows over an episode, which although vague in my recollections, is permeated with euphoria, pathos, and tribulations. David and Trudy were having marital problems at the time. Needless to say the whole family became embroiled in the fray. Although outsiders should never interfere, it is almost impossible to remain detached when you see someone in trouble. Ensuing from these turbulent times, both Carol and Charlie were left with very painful memories.

However, many joyous episodes more than compensated for the tribulations and the heartaches. Cherrie and David's boys became very close. Indeed the children formed a brother and sister relationship, a bond that has remained unbroken through the years. As adults they still share their joys, their problems and always seek one another's counsel before making any decisions much as members of the same family do.

It was also then that Irene, my cousin, came to spend a week with us. Apparently she felt at home with us. Besides, she had a great deal of trouble with her digestion and at our house she could eat whatever she pleased. She was delightful and the children adored her. I thought they would be intimidated because she was a nun, but she was so down to earth and had such a good sense of humor that soon after she arrived everyone was exchanging jokes and having fun. The enormity of my workload soon became evident to her and it was all I could do to stop her from weeding the weed-infested garden. At the airport when she boarded her plane to leave she had tears in her eyes and a feeling of sadness filled my soul. This parting was to be our last, and a deep feeling of regret and loss settled in our home after she left. How great it was to be reunited and yet how painful so soon forever to part!

Years afterwards Irene's oldest sister Aline came to spend the night with me. She had come from High Level to visit her daughter and to see a doctor. It was wonderful to see her. We talked all night and even when her daughter came for her there was still volumes to be said. I had not seen Aline since I was a child therefore her life story was unknown to me. And that was indeed the subject of our conversation. She was working at various jobs in High Level; as a camp cook, teaching life skills to native girls, etcetera. The family had experienced many hardships farming in Northern Saskatchewan. Apparently they had survived by sheer will power and resourcefulness. Evidently when the children were grown Aline decided to find a more profitable way of making a living, which is the reason why she was all alone and working in High Level far away from her family. She told me all about her family. Her family was scattered all over, one daughter in Edmonton, two in Saskatchewan, two in Calgary, and the rest on Victoria Island. My cousin was overcome with emotion as she recounted the many trials, the joys and hardships the family had experienced while the children were growing up. Recently I was delighted to meet most of Aline's family and was able to associate a name to the right person, a person who had previously existed in my imagination only. But again I am ahead of my story.

Previously I had the opportunity to visit my Aunt Léonide who was then on the island of Victoria. Hélène had graciously asked me to go on a tour of the island. After admiring all the tourist attractions, the Butchart Gardens, the Wax Museum, etc. in Victoria, we drove North to visit my Aunt and Uncle Charlie. Driving through the majestic forest along that highway was like driving through wonderland and at the time I wondered if perhaps my fantasyland did exist somewhere on this planet. My Aunt and Uncle lived in a trailer close to their daughter's house. Both had had a severe stroke. My aunt however was in complete possession of her mental faculties and she was delighted to see us. Needless to say I was ecstatic! We spent long hours reminiscing about the old days, recalling the days when every time I'd get upset I'd walk the five miles to her place and she'd always make me feel better. Her stories about my grandparents and about my mother were delightful. Too soon it was time to leave. I never saw them again! My uncle died soon after and my aunt, who was in a wheel chair by this time went to live with her other daughter, Marie, near Montreal. How sad it is to have loved so many and to lose them forever as we follow a tortuous path along a perilous and unpredictable journey.

Again the sequence of this tale has been lost in the depth of time and the event that I have just recounted happened long before the family had left to seek fortunes of their own. In fact it happened long before Cherrie was even born. As I reminisce about this most remarkable experience, I cannot help but wonder where the children were while their mother was gallivanting unconcerned all over the country.

Until Cherrie went to Europe she was a delight to the family. Indeed everyone doted on her. She was always content with whatever was done for her, no matter how trivial. Instead of being a burden she was nothing but joy. After she came back from Europe however, she was not the same. She wasn't the carefree and jovial Cherrie of yore. She seemed troubled. Physically she was skin and bones! Apparently the girls had had great difficulty adapting to the European cuisine and had eaten very little during their sojourn abroad. Although I made every effort to find out what was troubling her, all my efforts were in vain. One thing for certain all the girls had not been able to eat the food they were served and their main diet had consisted of chocolate bars. Besides, they had had to conform to a most stringent schedule, practicing for two hours before sunrise followed by several performances each day. Sometimes the practice was repeated again late in the evening. It was no wonder the girls all came back looking like skeletons.

But Cherrie was not perturbed about food or the comfort of their living accommodations. She wasn't one to fret about trivial things and always made the best of any situation. Her problem emanated from sources more serious than physical comfort; hence the reason for my concern. At first I feared that she had encountered a traumatic experience, but as my fears proved to be groundless I was at a loss. She was not about to confide in me and tell me what was troubling her no matter how much I tried to cajole or persuade her to do so. Perhaps she felt rejected because she had been adopted. Who knows! Yet nothing was further from the truth. From the moment of her birth she was showered with affection and cherished by those in her family and anyone in her immediate surroundings.

Be that as it may the next few years proved to be very difficult indeed. Difficult for me and the rest of the family but an unmitigated nightmare for Cherrie. Undoubtedly she was trying to declare her independence, or perhaps she was making a statement, a retributive statement as a punitive measure against anyone she deemed responsible for her misery. No matter how much I tried to help her; keep her out of trouble and protect her, she kept bouncing from one predicament into another. First she refused to go to school. I thought it was a matter of adjustment and kept switching her from one school to another until she was registered in five different institutions at the beginning of the term. Although the principals and the counselors did their utmost to accommodate her she couldn't adapt to any of these situations. Besides she out- and-out refused to get out of bed in the morning. Needless to say I didn't win that round. Things kept getting from bad to worse until one day she decided that she didn't want to live at home any more so she asked child welfare to put her in "Care" That was a complete fiasco. Some of the workers in that department are so blatantly incompetent, lacking the ability to envision and discern the over-all truth of a situation and questionable judges of character, traits crucial in such a sensitive position. They fail to see the motive of a self willed child who will use any vindictive means in order to get what they want which is sometimes a detriment to their well being and their safety. A judicious parent will naturally forbid such behavior. That a professional worker will consider the parent's position abusive is beyond all logical comprehension. On the other hand the same workers fail to discern when a child is being seriously and brutally abused.

The next few years were difficult indeed. They were years in which we were back and forth like a yo-yo to the land of fire and brimstone. But no matter, I knew the way, for I had been there many times before. At times the situation seemed desperate. It seemed that we'd never emerge from the tribulations and chaos to the sanity of a normal existence. But as my friend used to say, "…all this will pass", and time is a wonderful healer.

That episode in Cherrie's life was very traumatic. She seemed to be searching for something, a haven where she belonged. She tried one thing after another yet she was forever haunted by a nagging restlessness and discontent. Her marriage ended in a divorce. It is unfathomable that although we were trying to do what we thought to be right for Cherrie and we all loved her to death, we unwittingly failed to give her what she needed the most. Her mother thought she would be happier if she stayed with the family because she always begged to be there, and I was overjoyed when that (perhaps ill-advised) decision was finalized. Yet at the time it seemed to be the only solution.

Although her marriage was not successful, her children, Chris and Victoria, brought Cherrie joy and were the treasures that brought peace to her restless spirit. Yet there are times when alone and lost in thought, the ache returns to torment her troubled past. Many of us, like Cherrie, have a can of worms festering, gnawing and crawling in the pith of our very soul, which if given free reign, threaten to destroy the essence of whoever we are. Mercifully, many, like Cherrie, in spite of the thorns cruel destiny has chosen to scatter along their path, have the courage go on and make a success of their lives. Refusing to indulge in self pity, she took the bull by the horn, made a home for her children, embarked upon and was successful in getting a career, and has succeeded in attaining a comfortable standard of living for herself and her family.

The European adventure proved to be a decisive and crucial point in Juliette's future. Detached from the situation she was able to look upon her problem in rational manner. It became evident that her marriage couldn't be saved. Vince, her husband, had allowed alcohol to become his master and he seemed to be completely helpless in its power. He had been such a wonderful person; it was heartbreaking to realize that he had allowed a demon to possess him. On the other hand it was impossible for anyone to endure the tribulations of living in an inferno. Much to Vince's chagrin, Juliette was granted her divorce papers and later an annulment which allowed her to remarry if she so desired. Being exceptionally resourceful she was able to earn a decent living for her four children. And there in lies another maneuver that I deeply regret, another one of those culpabilities to be added to a burden n of guilt whose weight accumulated steadily along the way. As Juliette was going through hell in an impossible situation and contemplated leaving Vince, I would beg her to give him another chance. He had been a good person and I hoped he might be able beat this habit. But I was sadly mistaken! As things kept getting from bad to worse it became evident that it was a losing battle requiring drastic measures.

Unfortunately Juliette's marriage wasn't the only one that did not succeed. It is almost incredible that only three of these eight couples managed to have a lasting relationship. Of course when a couple has an ineradicable deep-rooted personality contrast such as Wally and Diane, the marriage has no hope of succeeding. A lasting relationship is founded on common aspirations and not on conflicting goals and values. Unfortunately the lethal weapon used by Satan to lure souls to his bidding, the Devil's brew in my book, was the agent responsible for the destruction of the other marriages. It is indeed most lamentable that Lucifer can use his demonic curse to destroy the sanctity and magnificence of two people who consecrate their lives to each other. At this point the reason why Wally and Dianne's relationship did not succeed is uncertain.

But after many tears, many heartbreaks regretting and lamenting what might have been fate intervened. Both Walter and Juliette found some one who was more compatible to their personalities and had similar aspirations to theirs. They both found peace and harmony in their new relationship. There is a rather comical anecdote that occurred concerning Walter's new girl friend. He had gained a prestigious position at Syncrude in Ft. McMurray and was doing well financially. But I had heard some disturbing rumors relating to his courtship. I refused to accept the credibility of these rumors, at least not until I was positive that it was true. Fortunately David and Keith were working in Fort McMurray and when they came home I confronted them with the sixty-dollar question.

David beat about the bush going around the question but not answering my question directly with a plain yes or no, as evasive as a wily politician. Exasperated, I confronted Keith.
"All I want is a plain yes or no" I declared, "is it true or is it not true?"
"Well" Keith retorted, "what you have heard has been distorted and the truth has been twisted. There is absolutely no truth in those rumors." And that was that! Keith had spoken. Now this whole absurdity could be forgotten.

David, still troubled after going through a divorce, was busy comparing every girl he met with the love of his life. He did form a relationship with some one he met in Russia but the relationship is at best precarious, as neither party seems to feel secure in its success. Both are uncertain and are trying to decide whether or not to pursue a relationship that is so vulnerable. Whatever their decision, the blessings and the support of their loved ones will always be with them.

Nadia and David

I am indeed incorrigible switching from the past to the present. But although I am committed to follow the thread of the events as they transpired, the present keeps butting in relentlessly. Alas, hell thronged with those who have good intentions.

Meanwhile Juliette and I kept drifting back and forth winging our way south to Mexico. On our first trip when we landed in Puerto Vallarta, Carol and Lucille were with us. It was an amazing adventure, not only because the four of us were together but because it was our first encounter with the country's fascinating vista, its amazing beaches, and its unique culture.

The ocean has a bewitching power over me. I am mesmerized by the enchanting rumble of the incoming and receding tide whose beguiling drone seems to whispers softly to me, "Come away with me to lands of mystical and enchanting splendor." And I dream, spellbound, hypnotized by the lure of its mystical call.

As a tourist attraction most of the hotels have a special celebration which they call a Fiesta. It includes an elaborate dinner and a show that comprises various dances and performances displaying Mexican artistic talent. It was most enjoyable.

There were many attractions and activities that were most interesting, including shopping, tours and museums but what fascinated me the most was walking along the beach and gazing at the mysticism and magnitude of my beloved ocean. However, the fact that the four of us were together made this adventure delightful.

On one occasion Juliette and I traveled with Hélène and a group of other travelers. The tour had been well planned with hotel reservations and the sites where our group was to explore. I had insisted on exploring the relics of the ancient Mayan civilization and examining the monuments that are the testimonials of their sophisticated and advanced civilization. With this end in mind our tour led us to the Yucatan Peninsula. The most spectacular edifice and what has remained graven in my memory forming the limelight of the tour was the view of the Mayan pyramid temple El Castillo at Chickén-itza. I had a mad desire to climb these stairs. Perhaps the only thing that saved me from attempting this perilous and fool-hardy escapade was my injured knee. Limping along with my leg in a cast, it was all I could do to walk let alone climb. Hélène must have inwardly heaved a sigh of relief for she was apprehensive and had an aversion for these mad climbing expeditions of mine.

We were fortunate to have the opportunity of attending a Mexican ballet performance. It was out of this world! The dancers were exceptionally talented and the costumes were absolutely breathtaking, magnificent. The performers had a different elaborate costume for every dance in the performance. The cost of these alone must have been exorbitant. I bought a videotape as a souvenir of this great spectacle.

Besides the Mayan pyramid and the Mexican ballet two events have remained imprinted in my memory as I reminiscent about the tour. We were lodged at a luxurious tourist center for the night. Each group had been assigned a separate cabin on the premises. The surroundings of the numerous cabins were exotic and filled with blossoms of every color and with peacocks strutting majestically about, proudly displaying their brilliant plumage. The three of us were basking in all this luxury, counting our blessings and enjoying every minute of it. But lo and behold, in the morning we were awakened by not one but a multitude of ants. There were a few in my bed but Hélène's bed was simply crawling with ants. Indeed the sheet was black with these veracious insects. Whether or not Hélène slept that night is debatable. The whole thing was actually hilarious!

Besides the ant episode there is, I regret to say, another event that put a damper on our trip. As soon as we got out of the plane I was anxious to walk on solid ground so Juliette and I decided to go for a stroll. Hurrying along the path, I fell and injured my knee which according to the local doctor was fractured. A cumbersome cast was wrapped around my leg, a cast which considerably impeded my mobility. My two companions were not too pleased with my clumsiness.

Every year afterwards in the thickest part of winter, either in January or February we gravitated back to Mexico. Sometimes, being a globetrotter, I wished the girls would choose to explore other regions of our earth. But the warm climate, the nearness to the ocean, and the relaxing atmosphere were the attractions that always managed to lure us back.

Mazatlan however was chosen as our next destination, and it proved to be the ideal spot for a vacation. The beaches stretching as far as the eye can see are superb and the hotels compete to accommodate tourists. All the commodities are situated in a manner that facilitates easy access and convenience. Even the church stands in a central position, a short distance from any of the hotels. There are many popular restaurants serving delicious seafood. Our favorites were the Panama with its fantastic bakery, the Puncho, and the Marina. There are many attractions such as the shell factory with its fabulous decorations.

The moment Juliette discovered Mazatlan she decided that was where she would spend her vacations. She has been returning to that city every year except twice. On one occasion she and her husband traveled through the Maritime Provinces and visited Newfoundland while Walter was working there. On another occasion she went with Carol and me to Hawaii. That she considers Mazatlan a sanctuary of sorts is not surprising for it is a retreat where she can relax and rest from her grueling job at the Post Office. There are absolutely no demands made upon her. Instead of working all day, coming home exhausted and tackling another shift doing housework, she is free to sit in the sun, read a book, go for a walk or anything at all she desires.

Juliette and I returned to Mazatlan five times. Carol, Lucille, and Joanne each came with us once. The two of us were on our own the rest of the time. Although we did a lot of exploring and took many tours to get a general impression of the Mexican culture, we enjoyed and spent many delightful hours walking along the beach. The statues along the way were and are inspiring as they are a vivid manifestation of the people's hopes and aspirations. It goes without saying that I spent endless hours gazing at the ocean, just dreaming those hours away. I am mesmerized by its magnitude and hypnotized by the bewitching spell it casts upon me. And as the tides come lapping against the shore I hear its voice as it speaks to me, beckons to me. Yet although my spirit longs to do its bidding, the bonds that hold me are indestructible.

One year, Carol, Juliette and I decided to go island hopping from one island to another in Hawaii. If we had known the full implications of such an adventure, we would have thought twice before tackling it. Keith had been extolling the thrill of this venture so naturally we took it for granted he had been the first to try it. But he was playing a practical joke on us. When we came back, exhausted from all these comings and goings off and on the planes we asked Keith why he hadn't warned us concerning the enormity of such a venture.

"Oh" he replied, "That was an experiment. I wanted you to try it first and if you survived then Debbie and I would know it was okay for us to go."

Of course he thought it was hilarious. Needless to say the three of us felt like ringing his neck because he had succeeded in pulling a fast one over on us. In spite of all the fatigue we had to endure, we had enjoyed our trip immensely. Had we not explored the other islands, we would have missed what constitutes a major portion of the wonders and the beauty of the Hawaiian Islands. From Honolulu on Oahu we explored five of the islands, Maui, Molokai, Maui, Kauai, and Hawaii. Each island held a certain unique treasure of its own.

In Kauai we walked through the Waimea Canyon, which is a miniature Grand Canyon of Colorado. Half way across it began to pour. We were soaked to the gills. Indeed water dripped down in torrents from our noses coming down in sheets over our glasses, blinding us. Mercifully Juliette was able to guide us back to the car. I was never so grateful to get back into a warm dry car! Kauai is said to be the rainiest spot on earth which probably accounts for the magic greenery of its voluptuous foliage. In spite of the constant rain, we were overwhelmed by the magnificence of this picturesque island.

On the island of Molokai the promontory where there is a settlement of lepers was most astonishing news to me. I was under the impression that modern science had succeeded in wiping out this dreaded disease. Apparently dedicated and selfless men, such as Father Damien, still sacrifice their lives to care for these unfortunate invalids.

Hawaii was perhaps the island that impressed us the most. The highway extends through miles and miles of black volcanic rocks, lava from which the island was formed. It appears that this stretch of blackness is interminable. It was on this island near Hilo Bay, on Hamakua Valley that we visited Hawaii's amazing Tropical Botanical Garden. The garden is 40 acres in area encompassing 2000 different species of tropical plants, plants collected from all regions of the earth. The varieties of different trees, flowers, ornamental shrubs and plants is unparalleled. Indeed it is difficult to realize that so many different varieties of plants even existed. Needless to say the magnificence and marvels of this extraordinary garden is overwhelming!

There appears to be some confusion about the location of the Tropical Garden. Or perhaps the confusion exists only in our minds! All three of us were under the impression that we had visited the garden on the island of Kauai, but according to the Atlas it is definitely on the island of Hawaii. It may be that the garden has been expanded and that many of its rare and endangered species have been transplanted onto Kauai where it is resplendent with a magnificence of its own. The island's fertile soil and abundant rainfall certainly provides a luxurious base for the growth and successful development of plants.

My next venture took me to the Quebec, my ancestral land. Hélène had already made contact with our cousins, those who had remained in la belle province after the great exodus, when so many Quebecois dared to relocate in the west. She was bursting with tales extolling the virtues of those who had been left behind. So with great difficulty and persuasion Hélène and I managed to convince my sister Juliette to come with us. There were four of us, my two sisters, Hélène's husband, and me.

I had always wondered why so many make such a big to do about their "roots" and spend a greater part of their lives trying to establish their genealogy. I finally understood the significance of this obsession as soon as I set foot on the land of my forefathers. It was so weird, out and out bizarre but I felt that I had come home at last, that this was where I belonged! It was as if I had known these people all my life, as if I had grown up with them and that these cousins were my brothers and sisters. And I lamented the fact that distance had created such a barrier between us. Yet the sheer delight of being in their midst and sharing their lives, if only for a brief moment, was overwhelming! All of my dear cousins: The Abbey, René, Denise, Simone, and Yvette indeed will dwell forever in my heart.

John, my oldest brother, was three years old when my parents left Lake St. John. I was obsessed with the idea that he should go back to the land of his birth and get reacquainted with his cousins. In fact, some of the older cousins remembered him! Henri remembered him as a toddler stumbling along as he trudged behind his dad on the way to prepare their homestead for cultivation. Persuading Juliette was a cup of tea compared to the difficulty I had with John. He was adamant, finding every excuse in the book exonerating him. He couldn't leave Victorine, he had work to do, he couldn't afford it, etc. Well, after I had dispelled all his objections one by one, and I had begged, coaxed, got down on my knees, he finally gave in.

There were quite a few of us on that trip: Hélène and Herbert, John, Grace, a friend, Muriel, Hélène's daughter, and me. Needless to say all the members of our group were welcomed and treated with the utmost hospitality, and even though Grace did not speak a word of French, everyone managed to make her feel at home. John however was the one who was received with the greatest ovation. He was greeted with the flourish usually lavished upon a distinguished war hero returning home from the front. They literally rolled out the red carpet and rang out the bells as they welcomed him with open arms in their midst. Indeed every family insisted that his time schedule would permit him to be their guest, and he was chauffeured like a prince from one home to another. When I contemplated my brother's sheer exuberance, I was overwhelmed with delight. It goes without saying that his joy more than compensated for all the tribulations I had experienced in getting him there.

In the vague recesses of my mind I had illusions that I had gone a third time to visit my relatives in Quebec, but it seems to be just an illusion. It is little wonder that I could kick myself from here to kingdom come because of my failure to keep a journal. Memory is a very unreliable aspect of human nature that will often err and therefore cannot be depended upon for validity.

My next extravaganza was a fantasy of traveling across Canada, from coast to coast on board Via Rail. Needless to say my fantasies are never within the scope of moderation, but always outrageous, many times beyond the scope of feasibility. A pie in the sky you might say. As it turned out Hélène was also dreaming of exploring the eastern part of Canada. My sister never does things blindly or on an impulse. Every thing has to be carefully considered, reflected upon, and meticulously planned. And so it was that after much deliberation and endless discussions the two of us agreed to embark on this mad venture. But it took months of planning and redesigning with the help of a travel agency before an acceptable itinerary was put together measuring up to my diligent sister's approval. Needless to say it was a masterpiece!

That adventure turned out to be spectacular; an adventure that stands out as a bright and delightful experience. After every one of these thrilling adventures, I am tempted to assume that it was the most exciting and the greatest of all the previous expeditions. However such an assumption would indeed be erroneous as the knowledge, the new perspectives on life, the insights, and the greater appreciation and tolerance of other cultures was invaluable and in a class of its own.

Perhaps the most enjoyable part of this journey was the bus tour of the islands via the Cabot Trail. The tour was planned to a "T". We were taken to all the tourist attractions, our hotel accommodations were excellent, and the restaurants where we ate served the most exotic foods.

Part VII

My Treasures

Circling the lake just as the sun was peaking over the horizon a strange mysterious and mystical sensation possessed me. It gave me a new perspective on the meaning of all creation. It was as if my eyes had suddenly become aware for the first time of the felicity and magnificence of God's world. The trees, the waters of the lake, my beloved birds, and the stars scintillating out of the waters all took on a new aspect and became a miniature replica of Paradise. And it was in this Paradise that my feet lightly tread. Engulfed in rapture and inspired by the magnificence before me my ecstasy gushed forth into a song of joy joining the Angels' chorus of exultation in the Magnificat.

Verse 1
O Lord my God! When I in awesome wonder
Consider all the worlds thy hands have made,
I see the stars, I hear the rolling thunder,
Thy power through-out the universe displayed,

Then sings my soul, my Savior God, to thee,
How great thou art, how great thou art!
Then sings my soul, my Savior God, to thee.
How great thou art, how great thou art!

Verse 2
"When through the woods and forest glades I wander
And hear the birds sing sweetly in the trees
When I look down from lofty mountain grandeur
And hear the brook, and feel the gentle breeze,

Then sings my soul, my Savior God, to thee,
How great thou art, how great thou art!
Then sings my soul, my Savior God, to thee.
How great thou art, how great thou art!

As I speculate upon the tumultuous path along which life's journey has led me, I am assailed by so many conflicting thoughts. I do not possess any remarkable gifts such as beauty, wisdom, artistic talent, and least of all material wealth, yet lodged in the deepest abyss of my soul are treasures more precious than all of these. Treasures more precious than all the gold stored in the queen's coffers! My beloved children, my family, the myriads of students so dear to me, the kindred spirits that have always surrounded me, and the extraordinary delight I experienced along my life's adventurous journey. The intrinsic virtue of these transcends by far those of rocks frantically hacked out in the bowels of the earth. Their ecstatic merits are beyond the scope of the imagination. As their images flash and parade before my eyes, the euphoria overwhelming my spiritual-self is a sensation words cannot express. It may well be that my childhood fantasies in which I created all these beautiful people and those castles in the air have been transformed into reality! Stranger things have happened!

Even at this eleventh hour as I mosey along on my merry way, certain incidents keep materializing transporting me years back into my childhood. During those moments, I visualize a specific episode so clearly that I am actually experiencing it again in my mind's eye.

Yesterday Evelyn, my niece, called me from Winnipeg. She is trying to unearth information concerning her parents. This of course brought the memory of my sister's wedding and a vivid image of the ceremony flashed before my eyes. It also conjured up the memory of the abnormal and excruciating throes of childbirth she endured before she was finally taken to the hospital a hundred miles away.

Although the marriage ceremony is still imprinted clearly in my memory I am unaware of the circumstances that prompted the family to have it performed in our home. It may have been due to the stringent economic circumstances of the times; therefore the exorbitant expenses of a traditional wedding were out of the question. This in my opinion makes the most sense and had I been thinking clearly it would have been the logical reason that I should have suggested to my niece. There could have been a more surreptitious motive however! At that particular epoch in time and in that predominating Catholic community parents supervised their daughters' relationship with the opposite sex with an iron hand. Premarital sex was taboo. If a girl had the misfortune of becoming pregnant, not only did she become an outcast but her whole family was held in disrepute. Is it any wonder that courtships were strictly supervised. I must have been given the boot as a chaperon by then (thank goodness) as I don't recall going on dates with Germaine and her fiancée. My parents used another strategy however. Whenever a couple seemed to have a serious relationship they used every method of persuasion to advance the wedding date. Indeed they did a little bit of arm-twisting. This may well have been what happened in my sister's case.

My parents' concern plus the pressure from my Grandfather who was Catholic to the gills, culminated in a very dramatic and unique ceremony. Hopefully the couple had been alerted, for the rest of the family was apparently caught by surprise when the priest, escorted by my Grandfather, arrived at the house ready to perform the wedding ritual. This was a most unusual procedure and even as a child I wondered what had prompted such a drastic decision. My niece has been troubled by that decision and has sought to resolve its implications. Naturally I wasn't able to clarify the issue, as I am at odds with it myself. In order to understand some of the peculiar behavior of people of that era it is important to remember the conventions, the prejudices, and the mores of the times. What is considered perfectly acceptable and normal in today's society was absolutely taboo a few decades in the past.

The most obvious and logical reason was of course the financial situation of my parents and indeed of everyone in the country during that particular time. That is quite evident and had I been wearing my thinking cap, I would have given my niece an answer that would have eliminated her concerns. But I had not anticipated her call much less that most dramatic question and therefore was unable to think back and reflect clearly upon that fateful event.

My sister's marriage took place right smack in the middle of the depression when everyone squeezed their pennies until they squealed and jobs were few and far between. In fact it was impossible to get a job as money for wages was unavailable. Young men left their homes drifting here and there in search of any kind or any form of employment. After wandering all over the country in a vain attempt to find suitable work those unfortunate "drifters" found themselves in a most desperate situation. Far away from their home, and having exhausted their meager funds, they were without shelter or any means of survival. The government, in response to the emergency, was giving five dollars a month to a farmer who would employ a homeless young man. Needless to say, it was all many farmers could do to provide for their own families let alone provide for a stranger. And so it was that many of these unfortunate drifters who were victims of these harsh and cruel times, found their way to our doorstep. There were so many of them I can still count them on my fingers and remember every one of their names, Charles, Ben, etcetera, on and on. Of course our door was always open to anyone in need and as my mother always shared her last crumb they had indeed come to the right place. Don't ask me how my mother managed to feed her family, a destitute family who had taken permanent residence at our house, and all those desperate souls who found themselves at our doorstep. She must have been able to perform miracles or have assistance from a miraculous source!

Well my sister's fiancée was one of these young men, who through no fault of his own found himself in this situation. Being very young at the time, the courtship and promises he made to my sister Germaine were even then and at best vague or impervious to me. It is however obviously logical that an expensive wedding was out of the question. My parents, the groom, even my grandparents were penniless and could not afford a church ceremony or an elaborate wedding reception. It is evident that a quiet and simple ceremony in the parents home was the only sensible solution.

Someone who hasn't the faintest notion of the circumstances prevailing during the depression could not conceive, not in a million years, the hardships and difficulties endured during those harrowing times. Survival was the essence, the prime concern, and the most pressing matter on everyone's mind. Therefore all other concerns had to be organized and adapted around this crucial taskmaster. It is therefore not surprising that my niece, Evelyn, hasn't the slightest idea of what could possibly have induced her mother's parents to make such a rash decision. That of course is evidently because it is almost impossible to get a accurate concept of the situation that existed at the time in our community. Indeed for a person living in these modern times, the provincialism, mores, prejudices, and stringent rules of conduct is inconceivable.

Transcending these cultural mores was the fact that the country was in the grip of a severe economic recession. Many existed at a bare subsistence level. Needless to say celebrations were out of the question.

Considering the leisure and the abundance that technology has brought, it is not surprising that the modern generation cannot visualize the ramifications and the privations that existed during that era. Many are confused and wonder how it was possible that such drastic changes could have occurred during one generation.

Many in this modern world that revolves around scientific and technological principals wonder about the early days when electricity, running water, motor vehicles etc. did not exist or were unavailable. "What was it like without these modern conveniences," they ask, "and how did people ever manage?" In other words, they are curious about life in pioneer days. It was during that era that I was born, spent my childhood, and most of my youth. For me the contrast between now and then is astronomical. It's like existing in two different worlds. Like being born in one situation and being suddenly plunged into a foreign unfamiliar milieu; Mars for instance. Although many allusions, inferences and suggestions have been made to illustrate the differences, the advantages, and the disadvantages of these eras, perhaps the contrasts were not illustrated with sufficient precision and clarity for the reader to get the full impact of the situation as it existed then.

Subsequently, I will endeavor to highlight some of the most outstanding contrasts between these chronological stages in time. The changes that occurred during those years are closely similar in magnitude and repercussion to the changes that occurred during the "Industrial Revolution" in Europe during the eighteenth century. In the pioneer age every thing had to be done by hand. Pioneers did not have any access to electricity, running water, motor vehicles, or any modern conveniences made possible by contemporary technology, especially in remote areas. Central heating was unknown and so the homes were heated by a wood burning tin heater and the smoke was emitted along a series of pipes leading to a brick chimney. Although we lived in a well-treed area, providing an adequate winter supply of firewood sometimes posed a problem. Farmers and small town residents were compelled to get a license in order to cut down trees. Money was non-existent. Heat, of course, was crucial for survival during the severe Saskatchewan winters. So everyone, covertly and quietly, got a winter's supply of firewood in spite of that ridiculous law, hoping that no one would report the incidence. That would be most unlikely, as most were in the same boat. Even the councilors looked the other way. They realized the unfeasibility of such a law, a law that was utterly beyond the bounds of possibility. It is almost unfathomable that those who legislate these outrageous rulings are not aware of the disastrous consequences involved. The firewood saga did not end there unfortunately. After being hauled into the yard the logs had to be sawed and split into suitable lengths. Looking back, it appears that my parents hired a machine to do this huge, backbreaking project only once [to the best of my knowledge]. During the remaining years my dad assumed this grueling task. He proceeded to put the logs on a saw-horse, then with what he called a buck-saw, he sawed the log into blocks or chunks. He then placed the blocks on a huge stump to split into suitable pieces. It is indeed incredible that when my dad worked up north during the winter, my sister Hélène performed this humongous task, and that when she left it became my responsibility.

Although at the beginning of the twentieth century most large cities enjoyed the facilities of modern technology, rural areas and villages were still using antiquated, primitive tools, machinery, and appliances. Many farmers had to use oxen to do the work in the fields. Machinery such as seed drills, binders, etc. was sometimes shared among them as very few had enough money to purchase such costly items. Hay mowers and hay rakes were purchased at a later date when finances became less stringent. There is a flashback in my mind of my father cutting hay with an old fashioned scythe, raking and gathering it into piles with a hayfork. There is also a recollection of a season when I helped my dad with this work. Many of the farmers, my dad included, reaped their winter's supply of hay [illegally] from the numerous sloughs near our homestead. These sloughs abounded in rich luscious, tall grasses. Most of the neighborhood farmers hoped to be the first to get this luxurious harvest. Nonetheless on that particular occasion my dad and I were there first, busily gathering up the bountiful harvest. At noon, my dad made tea in a tin can that he had suspended over a bonfire to heat, and we ate our lunch. When the hay was dry we pitched it into a hayrack, hitched Dan and Kate to the rack, and drove home. It was such a glorious day. Perched high up on the hayrack, seated on the freshly mowed hay and inhaling its sweet fragrant aroma, I was on top of my world.

Without electricity and gas energy, modern conveniences such as dishwashers, dryers, automatic washing machines were unavailable. All household chores were done by hand. Hand operated washing machines helped to a certain extent in the process of laundering, but the clothes still had to be scrubbed on the washboard [especially the socks] and the whites still had to be boiled to get them really clean. This strenuous task was an all day affair. The wood floors had to be scrubbed once a week with a stiff brush and lye soap. Of course, Hélène scrubbed with the brush [she always insisted on doing the hardest jobs] and I rinsed and wiped the soap off. It was almost impossible for me to keep up because Hélène just whizzed through her portion of the work. The ironing was done with a flat iron heated on the stove. It was indeed difficult to get the irons hot enough in order to do a decent job. Besides, as the garments were mostly made out of cotton, everything had to be ironed. That task seemed interminable. It dragged on to all hours of the night.

The meals were prepared on a wood burning stoves as electric and gas ranges were unavailable. In winter that didn't present any problem. In summer however the heat became unbearable; especially on the days on which we baked bread. And mountains of bread was consumed every week. So it took all day and sometimes most of the evening to bake that many loaves. It goes without saying that all that time the oven had to be heated by a red-hot fire in the wood burning stove. The heat in the house became intolerable, suffocating!

Coal oil lamps were used to provide light during the long winter evenings. It was by the dim light of these lamps that Hélène and I spent hours studying till late in the night. It did not seem to matter at the time. It certainly did not deter either one of us.

All these struggles and inconveniences were accepted as being inevitable. They were indeed mere trifles in comparison to the obstacles confronting every pioneer upon his arrival in the west. Not only were these unfortunate pioneers bamboozled concerning the golden opportunities lucrative in the west, but no sooner had they settled on their homestead that the government came up with another devastating brain-wave in the guise of trying to give the farmers a start. Each settler was persuaded to buy a herd of cows that was purchased somewhere in a warmer climate and pay for it by applying a mortgage on his homestead. The cows were unable to adapt to the severe temperatures of the northern prairies and every last one of them died. It was a severe financial blow from which most settlers never recovered, including my parents. Plagued by one misfortune after another, most settlers were unable to repay the mortgage on their farms. Needless to say, only their incredible resourcefulness and invincible courage enabled them to survive at all, let alone pay for a herd of dead cows, or the blunder of someone's idiotic scheme.

It is little wonder that my poor dad would at times become exasperated with frustration. He was struggling against impossible odds facing one failure on the heels of the other. Herculean fortitude would have crumbled under such duress. It is little wonder that he paced back and forth from the barn to the house grumbling to himself in frustration. Our dog Ti-Moose, feeling my dad's misery, paced with him in the opposite direction meeting him halfway every time. During all those days of my childhood I knew my dad was not happy. I could sense his frustration, yet I did not understand the reason for his discontent. Understanding and compassion are the gifts of maturity.

Yet my dad did succeed in his own field, the field of his own domain, the forest! For in that realm he was indeed a virtuoso, a master craftsman. Working in the lumber industry both in the States and Quebec, he had acquired all the skills of the trade and had become an expert. Year after year he managed to salvage the family from financial destitution with the proceeds of the railway ties he contracted every winter. On occasions his even sold cord–wood. Although the work was strenuous, it was the work in which my dad was successful, the work in which he was rewarded for his labour.

Meanwhile my mother struggled relentlessly to make ends meet in a situation that was beyond the bounds of all possibility. Raising fourteen children in a one–roomed log cabin without electricity or running water. Indeed without availability to a reliable water supply in this modern age would be unthinkable. Yet, even though in poor health she managed to struggle through those arduous times by cultivating acres and acres of garden vegetables, sewing the family's clothes, and countless gimmicks she invented in order to provide additional income for the well being of her household besides that of those who always found refuge on her doorstep. Yet, while my dad had been separated from the things he valued most when he came west, my mother had brought her music, her books and all the things she cherished the most, things that provided her with a refuge from the brutal reality of her existence.

"Besides the welfare of those who never failed to find refuge at her doorstep," doesn't begin to tell the events that were daily happenings and part of the accepted routine at our humble home. For my mother's unshakable philosophy was not to be tampered with. "No matter how little you have you must share it with anyone in need." And that is what she was dead set on doing come hell or brimstones, regardless of who or what he was. Any vagrant and his dog was sure to find sanctuary in our home. And so it was that so many drifters, young men in search of employment, found their way to our doorstep.

But drifters were not the only ones who found sanctuary at our house. We had practically adopted a family who lived about five miles away. These people lived at our house most of the time. I remember them sitting at the table with the rest of us at mealtime. I also remember my mother sending food to their home for the smaller children to eat. Previously I referred to them as the Pollyannas because there wasn't one of them who had the resourcefulness or the ability to earn a living. They were the living personification of the grasshopper in Lafontain's "The Grasshopper and the Ant" for they played music and danced all day. Had they lived in this modern age they would have made a fortune as entertainers. Unfortunately they lived in the wrong place at the wrong time.

After they moved to Mildred, we visited them twice. On one occasion we went to pick raspberries and the next time we had been invited to the oldest girl Alida's wedding. Needless to say, on both occasions we traveled in a horse drawn wagon.

Later the family came down with scarlet fever and barely survived. To make matters worse, the shelter they had constructed for themselves had been built without necessary precautions and was therefore unreliable. As the men in the family had no building skills they had put it together as best they could. My dad regretted that he had not been there to help and guide them in that task. Be that as it may when the family was severely afflicted with that horrible disease the roof of the cabin collapsed. A beam fell on one of the girl's head and killed her. The victim, Marie-Rose, had been my friend. She was the one who had always played and picked fruit with me. It was a monstrous tragedy! All my family, especially my dad, lamented the fact that we had not been there in their time of need.

Although all these factors appear to give an entire negative aspect about that era, that wasn't entirely the case. There were many positive attributes pertaining to the age, attributes that seem to have been lost with the rapid development of technology. For instance, neighbors in a community were as members of a large family, joining together to celebrate in times of joy, and helping each other in times of need. The festivities, picnics, concerts, dances, and holiday celebrations were full of rejoicing. Doors were always left open, welcoming a neighbor in to share a meal with the family.

Children in the pioneer era had to contribute to the welfare of the family. They were expected to do their share of the chores involved in the general upkeep of a household, and at times, even had to contribute to the economical aspect of the family. Besides, they were mostly responsible for their own learning. Teachers and parents were too busy to devote much time in the preparation and explanation of each lesson. There were no televisions or calculators etc. to spoon-feed the material to them. Consequently the children had to be resourceful. They had to develop responsible behavior, the ability to think for themselves, and to handle independently, efficaciously, any emergent situation. Consequently, as they were continually engaged in constructive activities, they had no opportunity to be bored or to seek excitement to occupy their would-be extended leisure hours. Sometimes finding excitement involved negative behavior. Childhood obesity apparently was not a problem, or was rare as it did not seem to be a major concern. Apparently being constantly employed in doing worthwhile activities, children had little time to sit for hours watching television and eating junk food.

Another commendable aspect of that age was the fact that families had closer ties within their midst. Family members were devoted to each other. They worked and played as a team. During the day everyone was occupied at one task or other, but at mealtime the family all gathered around the table. It was a time when everyone had a place and felt a sense of belonging in the group. The evenings were also a time for family get-togethers. That was the time when daytime incidences were recounted, time to commiserate or rejoice, a time for laughter!

Nonetheless the contrast between the now and then is so extraordinarily blatant that many times I feel as if those from my generation have been transported and dumped on this planet from another universe. Although the modern generation feels that the differences are mostly in the improved living standards and material appropriation, these factors are the least of the transformations that have transpired. It is truly a brave new world, as Orson Wells has so aptly pin pointed it. Brave! You'd better believe it! But better? That is indeed debatable! It depends on the mentality and opinion of the appraiser.

In my opinion it is the human intellect, his powers of reasoning, and his perception of the truth that has made the most significant and glaring transformation. Indeed, the human psyche has been subjected to an entire makeover and his essence is unrecognizable from his former nature. In the good old days the individual struggled to live a righteous existence according to the laws of our Creator and forefathers while following the dictates his conscience. Whereas the modern individual is convinced that he is superior and above all this nonsense. He believes these stringent rules are old fashioned and to abide by them is not "cool" or if one does he is a "geek". In a mad obsession to gratify all his desires, every whim or every caprice, the modern individual must reject whatever impedes his comfort and seek any means at his disposal, regardless of the consequences. Making sacrifices for the well being of others is inconceivable, in fact the word itself is a dirty word never to be spoken or heard. This new self-concept is a veritable cult, the creed of "me-ism". It goes without saying that the commandments of God and the pursuit of righteousness are not acceptable to this way of thinking. These laws were too restrictive and set limits beyond which one cannot go! Therefore, the new trend or morality challenges the laws of our Lord and portents to either repudiate them or ameliorate and modernize them with laws of its own making, a moral code that will be acceptable and in keeping with this brave new world.

I have indeed gone overboard in my analysis of society in general. For my criticism apply to a small percentage of the general population, that is to the elite and those who have allowed power and riches to go to their heads, and have forgotten that all men are created equal. They are those who deny their responsibility to their brethrens, negate the sacredness of life and the dignity of man as a spiritual being. The majority of people in a society are righteous and honorable. Those in my immediate surroundings have always been virtuous and upright citizens. Indeed judging from all those who have so generously supported me in my trials, most are magnanimous. To enumerate all those would be interminable and would fill volumes.

Yet it is true the most spectacular distinction between the now and then has occurred in the human perception of truth and his concept of what constitutes the difference between right and wrong. In other words the greatest transformation has occurred in the human intellect. There are however other sensational and outstanding distinctions that have transpired during the last century.

I have already alluded to the children's luxurious homes. The contrast between these homes and the log cabin in which I was raised is phenomenal. These spacious and impressive homes have all the attributes of belonging to the higher echelon of society. The exquisite décor, the luxurious carpets, the furniture, and the spacious rooms, all add to the comfort of the residents. It is however the commodity of the appliances that facilitates the routine of daily living, rendering them utterly dissimilar to the daily routine of the past.

The log cabin in which I was raised can in no way be compared to these modern and luxurious homes. That is beyond the shadow of a doubt. Four walls of hued logs formed the frame of the cabin, the crevices between the logs being plastered with mud. The main floor, one large inclusive room; served as kitchen, dining room and living room. The second storey was framed in lumber whitewashed regularly with lime. This spacious room served as a bedroom for the whole family. In the center of the ceiling a trap door opened up to access an attic, a makeshift storage and hiding place for the more adventurous and daring members of the family. In the center of both the main floor and the upstairs area stood a humongous post. On the upstairs section my dad had set up a shelf which provided access to the attic. It goes without saying that privacy was a luxury that did not exist.

Reflecting upon the past and considering the circumstances from which I originated it is amazing that I was able to make the transition and adapt to this new world. Hailing from the primitive living standards of pioneer life to a situation in which technology reigns supreme was very difficult. It is very probable that the children and I were suffering from culture shock. It may well be that this adaptation was our most crucial problem. This situation compounded by the stress of getting settled in a new environment made the situation almost overpowering. My situation as it stood was comparable to that of a jungle dweller who had suddenly found himself plunged from the primitive jungle to the sophisticated glare of a modern technological arena. Truly I found myself in a world that was completely transformed from the world in which I had emerged. And my feelings were a mixture of apprehension and gratitude, thankful for the many opportunities it offered, yet fearing the many hazards it involved.

Many have wondered at the factors influencing my ability to surmount the overwhelming obstacles confronting me on the way. Indeed there were too many to be counted. The most crucial was of course my dogged determination to provide for and my undying love for those that God had entrusted in my care, followed by the magnanimous help my family and friends gave me. For these generous souls held me by one hand while Providence mercifully pulled me through with the other. But that wasn't all! For transcending all was my overwhelming gratitude of having the children with me, a gratitude that obliterated all the obstacles in my sight. Stumbling and blundering along my way, instead of feeling sorry for myself I counted my blessings, for there were many of those. And I was free to count them one by one each and every one.

The intangible factors were the most crucial in my unwavering determination to carry on and were indeed what got me through these troubled times. For although I was most grateful for the conveniences of modern technology which facilitated daily chores, my fixation was such that I would have been undeterred even though the task would have had to be done with a pick and shovel.

However for the many conveniences of technology I was indeed grateful. A world in which the laundry was done by simply pressing the on switch and the water automatically filled the machine instead of the time and fatigue involved in scrubbing clothes on the old-fashioned washboard, dishes that were washed in the same way, and bath water that filled the tub by turning on the tap. In my childhood in comparison, water was not as easily accessible. Indeed water was the main problem. My poor dad had dug a well besides the house, one by the lake, one at the bottom of the hill upon which the house stood and one by one they went dry.

I remember hauling two pails of drinking water up that hill time after time. (I enjoyed it. It was an opportunity to build castles in the air.) For all other purposes water had to be hauled from the lake. I remember harnessing Kate, a docile mare, to a stoneboat laden with two huge barrels, driving to the lake, filling the barrels with lake water and then returning home. In winter it was a different process altogether. The men cut huge blocks of ice on the lake and piled it in an enormous mountain of ice in front of the house. The blocks were brought in and put into a large barrel where they were broken into smaller pieces with an ice pick. This water was used for all purposes during the winter months except for doing laundry. If my memory is not playing tricks on me, we melted snow the day previous to washday. Having experienced the trials involved in obtaining a sufficient water supply for our needs, I am indeed grateful to get it by just turning on a tap.

I counted my blessings when I considered that modern homes (mine included) were heated with natural gas and that it was easy to control the temperature with a switch. In rural areas in Saskatchewan schools and homes on the other hand were heated by burning wood in a tin heater or a huge iron furnace. The logs had to be sawed into appropriate lengths, split and then brought and piled inside the buildings. Most of the time all this work had to be done by hand. While living at home and during the winters when the men were working in the north, Hélène and I were responsible for this heavy labor besides all the other outdoor chores.

For the electricity that provided the magic of light I was (and am) eternally grateful. On the farm and even while teaching in Saskatchewan we had no electricity; therefore coal oil lamps provided us with light during the long winter evenings. It is amazing that anyone could read and study in such dim lighting.

When I think about all these new gadgets that technology has provided for our comfort and I am astounded. Television, telephones, radios, and even automobiles were inaccessible to most who lived in the country not many years ago. In fact we bought our first television when we arrived in Edmonton. It is the computer however that blows me away. How a machine can be so efficient and actually able to "think" is beyond me! Truly as I contemplate all these wonders in this brave new world, I know that I must be from Mars or perhaps from another weird universe or that indeed the universe in which I grew up has had a complete transformation. It is quite evident that during my life span I have experienced that complete transformation from A to Z.

Meandering slowly along the tortuous journey destiny has led me, I am inundated with memories and flashbacks of events and images that persistently keep coming oh so vividly before me. Most are mundane everyday events that transpired as I traipsed along the interminable and dramatic path of my journey. In my childhood they were events that symbolized the general atmosphere and environment of those who shared the rigors of these tough economic times during the depression. Later these images were of critical moments that transpired in the life of my family in its desperate struggle to survive. In those moments, I am transported back to that momentous episode and the sensation is so real that I am virtually reliving that crucial moment with all the emotional ramifications involved be they joyful or bathed in sorrow. Those reoccurring images that keep flashing before my eyes are strikingly clear and realistic. Indeed I am there in mind and spirit, going through the same motions, experiencing the same emotional tribulations as I dwell in the past!

Many times I see my dad sitting on a straight back chair with a most efficacious and delicate file in his hand sharpening a huge crosscut saw. I hear the scrish scrish of the file as he glides it skillfully on each side of the saw's myriad teeth. It is a procedure that requires great skill and my dad will not allow anyone to touch his precious saw. For he claims that it is impossible to work with a dull saw and that no one else has the expertise to perform such an intricate task.

Needless to say my dad was a master in the lumber industry. His tools were of the highest quality and required considerable care. He was also very particular about his co-workers. "With superior tools" he claimed, "very little effort is required to get results." Indeed he insisted that no pressure was needed using the sharp saw's handles to fell a tree, the momentum of pulling it across the trunk was sufficient to accomplish the deed. He insisted that the saw was the agent that cut through the trunk of the tree. An inexperienced worker who insisted on using pressure at one end was felt as dead weight by his partner at the other end. My poor dad often suffered from sheer exhaustion when he had been compelled to work with such as these.

Sometimes I see myself scrubbing the floor with Hélène. It is a rough floor made out of unpolished lumber. But it has been scrubbed so often that its surface is as smooth as if it had been waxed and polished every week. Besides, after it had been scrubbed to a "T" it practically gleamed. Scrubbing that floor however was no cup of tea. It is virtually a major enterprise! Hélène, as usual, was the one doing the most strenuous part of the operation. Using a floor brush and either lye soap or diluted ashes she scrubbed the daylights out of every section while I rinsed away the soap and wiped it clean. My sister was so strong and worked at full speed while I hopelessly tried to keep up with her. Try as I might my efforts were in vain. I didn't have a prayer! She always had to wait until I finally finished rinsing and drying my section before we could move on to the next section.

At times, Hélène and I are weeding the garden which has been overtaken by weeds. I am not exaggerating; the weeds are at least fifteen inches high and have utterly obliterated all traces of the vegetable plants. I wonder about this situation. Perhaps other tasks were more pressing or perhaps the area of the garden was so huge that this portion had to be neglected. At any rate Hélène and I are at it full speed ahead or rather Hélène is at it full speed ahead. I see the weeds being mowed down ahead of her as if a grass fire was sweeping swiftly through them. And there I am frantically trying to keep up with her. I stare in amazement wondering how in the world she does it.

Many times we are studying in the middle of the night. Her concentration is unwavering in spite of the fact that it is almost three in the morning. I of course, am trying to follow her example. I try to pace and read at the same time so that I will not fall asleep. Forget it! The first thing I know my book is on the floor and I am sleeping on my feet. Again I marvel at her extraordinary endurance, her fortitude, and her courage. As I ponder over all this I have come to realize and accept one obvious truth. "Surely she is made of better metal than me."

I often have a vision of mother spinning away. On one occasion I see my mother at the spinning wheel and Hélène busily carding the wool at her side. As usual the conversation centers around our studies.

"I am reading this poem," Hélène says, "that is rather difficult to understand. It is called Michael."

"Read the poem to me," my mother said, "and we'll discuss it. We may be able to make some sense out of it."

As usual, although it was not in my course, I could not resist listening in when the topic had even a trace of literary content. Literature is music to my ears! At school instead of attending to my assignments, I was enchanted while listening to the stories included at the different levels in the reading program. So as my sister and my mother studied the poem "Michael" I was fascinated by its beauty and by the depth of the author's ability to express such deep emotional sentiment. Indeed I was so impressed by its content that I memorized most of it and am still able to recite some of the most significant excerpts it contained and I quote. " Lay now the corner stone, Luke, and hereafter when thou art gone away, think of me my son and of this moment. Hereto for turn thy thoughts and God will strengthen thee. Amid all fears and temptation I pray that thou mayst bear in mind the life thy fathers lived, who being innocent did for their cause bister them in good deeds." I was most distressed when upon relating this incident to my sister she did not seem to recall any part of it.

There was another incident that occurred when we were very young and of which my sister hasn't the vaguest recollection. Even though the family was in dire economic straits, my mother always did her utmost to celebrate Christmas ceremoniously. She always trained the choir and the musical components to give a magnificent performance during the midnight mass. As this mass was one of the highlights of the year followed by joyful festivities, the religious aspect of the holiday was deeply instilled in our spirits. Mother also made sure that there was a gift for every one of the children.

One year Mother had bought both my sister and me a doll. As Hélène was older than me her doll was more expensive than mine. Her doll had eyes that could open and shut and mine was just an ordinary doll. Something must have happened to my sister's doll. I still have a vision of the doll's eyes sunk into its head and how broken hearted my sister was as she hid the doll away. I remember being devastated and wishing that there was something I could do. In fact I was so distressed that if she had accepted it, I would gladly have given her my doll.

At the time, transportation being a major problem, it was more convenient for rural families to purchase flour in one hundred pound cloth bags. In our family the bags were bleached, embroidered and made into pillowcases. Of course the flour had to be shaken out before the bags could be washed. The laundry was, among other things, one of the weekly chores allotted to Hélène and me. On one occasion, some remnants of flour must have been strewn besides the washing machine where the floor was wet. At any rate I came rushing at seventy miles an hour to rinse something at the washstand. Needless to say, I never made it. At once both my feet slid out from under me and hit the wall under the washstand. I still envision myself, sitting in that ungodly mess with both my feet firmly anchored against the wall, and everyone looking down at me, trying desperately not to burst out laughing. It was hilarious! I just sat there, stunned! Or more precisely, floored! To everyone's relief I finally managed to get up on my feet from that slippery gooey floor. Then everyone roared with laughter (including myself).

The reoccurring flashbacks and images of my childhood are most frequently scenes in which Hélène and I are involved. It is not surprising that those images are most often of Hélène and me as the two of us always did things together. We worked together, studied together, build castles in the air together, in fact we did everything together. Indeed my sister's momentous influence on my life may have set the stage for my future success in achieving a career. I tried to imitate her exceptional courage and her unwavering determination as she struggled to pursue and realize her goal.

At other times I see my brother Laurence sitting on a rocking chair in the middle of the room enjoying his favorite dish, bread and milk! Not only is this his favorite snack, but he claims that it is a sure cure for any threat of illnesses. "When I feel that I'm coming down with something," he maintains, "I lunch it out." And that was with numerous snacks of his favorite dish.

Jeannette Romaniuk

A flashback of Laurence scrapping the edges of a large five-gallon can of ice cream fills my heart with delight. All of us were enjoying this rare treat but it was Laurence who is apparently in his seventh heaven. He is relishing every spoonful of that scrumptious ice cream with such ecstasy, such gusto that I am experiencing simultaneously with him the taste of that delicious ice cream just by observing his delight as he savors every tiny bit. I cannot even taste mine, or perhaps did not even bother, being so engulfed by my brother's sumptuous repast.

Strolling around the lake today it occurred to me that there is something about who I am that has been inadvertently omitted. It was best described by my sister as I dashed out of the hotel in Mexico determined to set foot at long last on solid ground "like a bat out of hell" she said. Well, that is the way I have traveled along the path of my momentous journey, "like a bat out of hell." I was driven by a Herculean, monstrous taskmaster, a compulsion; indeed it was a veritable obsession driving me constantly beyond the limits of human feasibility. It was like a thirst that could never be quenched or a craving that could never be satiated. There hath no slave driver's ruthlessness like that of the frenzy that dwells in the human innermost self. The manner in which I drove myself was beyond the realm of logic, a faculty often sacrificed due to human frailty. Be that as it may I must have driven everyone around me crazy, especially Hélène who didn't have a clue what possessed me. (That makes two of us!) We'd be shopping, which was one of Hélène's favorite pastimes but not my preferred occupation at the best of times. It seems to me that window-shopping is a waste of time besides being very boring. Needless to say I was soon chafing at the bit, itching to go home. Hélène wondered why I was in such a panic.

"Why are you in such a hurry," she'd say, "is someone waiting for you at home, or do you have to get back to make Carol's lunch?"

There was of course no logical reason. There was however a million illogical reasons! All the interminable tasks twirling around in my mind waiting to be done while I loitered nonchalant in the shopping center. Naturally to explain this was out of the question a complete "no, no." And so I was silent pretending that there was no excuse. Yet nagging at my very inner-self was a feeling of guilt, of being a work-dodger and of neglecting my duty. "How can I be such a maniac," I'd ask myself. Yet I could not escape the monstrous obsession that was frantically and mercilessly pressuring me along.

There was no remission! The compulsive impact of that brutal obsession was relentless. I would be doing one task and in my mind there were myriads of others lined up and begging to be done at the same time. So I would dash through every task "like a bat out of hell" and ask myself, "Why am I so slow? I should have the floors washed and polished, the laundry and ironing finished, besides the week's baking done." Mercifully the problems of the whole world were not added to the list. Man is his own worst enemy or in other words when man has conquered himself he has conquered the whole world they say. How true! As I look back and try to make some sense out of this stupidity, I am endeavoring to mend my ways. It is indeed a tremendous challenge trying to tear down what it has taken a lifetime to build!

Perhaps it was that mad and relentless obsession that compelled me to make another rash decision. During the early years after we arrived, the city had organized what was called "Miles for Millions" to raise money for charities. Needless to say the family budget did not allow me to support any charitable organization. So in order to ease my conscience I decided to participate and do the walk. As I have inherited my father's strength and ability to walk great distances without fatigue the walk was not a sacrifice. It was rather a lot of fun. Time was the problem. However I managed to walk at least four times and enjoyed every step of the twenty-five mile tract. My first walk was with Sister Good Counsel, the second with a friend, the third with Betty, a girl from the post office and then with Carol, my daughter. Every time my partner could barely make it to the finish line but I wasn't suffering from exhaustion in the least.

Today as I gazed upon the lake's glittering and undulating waters, even the threat of the mighty breeze has failed to deter my restless spirit and I find myself lured for the umpteen time strolling along the path that encircles it. I am indeed fascinated by the enchantment, the wonder, the magic, and the beauty that these waters hold over me. Trudging along slowly my spirit floats among the sparkling crystals over the turbulent and agitated waters, crystals reflecting and exalting the radiance, the magnificence of the prestigious sun. And then my thoughts catapult into the here and now, and the nostalgia for what is no more overwhelms my soul. A feeling of abandonment creeps into my soul as I marvel at the wonders of God's creation. For many have departed, loved ones, family members, dear friends and one whose loss fills my heart with pain, Charlie. Yet here I stand, longing for them to be here. Still how can I have the audacity to feel this way when those who are the essence of my being {except Charlie} surround me and embrace me with their love?

Less I should be tempted to ramble on and on I have decided to set forth a bird's eye view or a brief representation of the situation in which those who are so dear to me find themselves at the moment. It will not be an accurate portrayal as life is so transitory and situations in people lives change from day to day. As Mr. Hall so aptly stated, "All this will pass. Today's cares will be forgotten tomorrow." There is one truth however that that noble gentleman did not consider. He should also have considered the fact that life is sometimes overflowing with joy and that the rapture that we experienced today will be cherished in our hearts forever!

Of all my brothers and sisters, there are only four of us left, Hélène, Juliette, Raymond and me. The others are gone. Gone to the Great Celestial Beyond! Yet their spirits still walk with me as I tread along the thorny path of my long and dramatic journey onward. Yvonne always hovers over my shoulder when I am making soup, giving me specific instructions about what, and how much ingredients to put in that soup. I feel her presence as realistically as when she stood behind me in the kitchen making sure that the soup would turn out just so. I also know she is there in my prayers, as many times as we prayed together one of us would have a distraction and go off on a tangent, then unable to restrain the hilarity of it all, we would be convulsed with laughter. I know John is there when I am making salad dressing, for he made the most luscious dressing you ever tasted, and he guides me step by step through whole process. Needless to say the dressing turns out to be an outstanding success. Laurence is there when upon savoring a scrumptious dish, I can still taste the delight he experienced scraping and smacking his lips drooling over the flavour of the ice cream at the church picnic. Perhaps I have never outgrown my world of fantasy, my chimera, for the spirits of those loved ones are with me as I trudge awkwardly along the way. They have never left; their spirits dwell forever in the bosom of my heart.

Yet what is incomprehensible and so strange is the fact that although the spirits of those dearly departed are with me constantly I miss the ability to converse with them, to reminisce with them, to weep with them and to laugh with them. I long to pick up the phone and say, "Do you remember when…" Or ask for the recipe of one of my mother's favorite dishes. For often when I was uncertain about some details concerning events that had transpired in the past I would say, "I'll ask John." I still do. But alas he cannot help me any more and no one else can, for no one remembers! How I ache for those card games Yvonne and I played together, when she beat me every time. At last she'd give up and

Jeannette Romaniuk

say, "You're no fun to play with. You lose all the time." Reminiscing about those incidences, innumerable incidences, brings back memories of those with whom I have shared an unforgettable part of my life. They are those who will be with me forever.

Then, lost in thought, I contemplate the distance my children and I have journeyed together. I am absolutely astounded as I speculate at the contrast of what was then and what is now. Considering the situation we were in upon our arrival in Edmonton, almost penniless, unable to find accommodation, it is utterly beyond any stretch of the imagination that we survived let alone emerged all in one piece. Considering the circumstances, it is evident that providence and my dogged determination to care for those children come hell or wild fire pulled us through! All in one piece may well be an exaggeration, for the path we traveled was strewn with thorns and wound over steep and treacherous precipices. But undaunted, when assaulted by perilous and tempestuous hurricanes, each took the bull by the horns and courageously, frantically, struggled through. It would be debatable to say which of these storms was the most treacherous to weather, for while we were caught within each tempest's deadly grip, it seemed inconceivable that anyone could come through unscathed. And many oh so many times, the situation seemed desperate, and it was only my Herculean determination and my passionate love for the children that gave me the courage to carry on.

When we arrived in the city the lack of facilities and living accommodations seemed to be an insurmountable dilemma. Yet with untold apprehension and unease (besides the heartbreak) the children were placed in some Catholic institutions until we could take possession of the house I had purchased. In a similar situation I doubt if I would take these measures, especially knowing the effect it had on the boys, but how I would solve the problem is beyond me. After we moved into our new home, being together

- 338 -

should have been a little bit of heaven until I discovered that we had landed right smack in a district where most were low-income families. It goes without saying that many of the parents, being in unfortunate circumstances, were faced with situations beyond their control and were unable to supervise their children adequately. Consequently, left to their own device, many were delinquent. That of course posed a formidable problem, a problem that was beyond my control. There was no alternative; I had no other choice but to work. Needless to say the children were left alone on many occasions. In the country, without negative influence, it had not been a problem. In an urban surrounding however, the situation is completely different. Not only do the children have more time on their hands but they are apt to follow their peer group. And heaven help those who are surrounded by malfeasants. We were. And it appears my boys were led astray by those whose behavior was irresponsible. The were allowed to get away with anything and everything without being held culpable. During those years the family went through hell, fire and brimstone no less. Mercifully as the boys matured, they turned their lives around and became righteous and honorable citizens.

After struggling and suffering through these tribulations it appeared that these troubles were trivial compared to the anguish, the pain we endured when Charlie was taken from us. For in death there is no means of reparation, no means of rectification or of setting things to right as we had done so many times in the past. This was the end! There was no way back. The finality of death can lead to desperation!

Throughout these tribulations I incessantly asked myself, "What could I have done differently in order to prevent this from happening. What if... if... if... if...?" I if'ed my self to kingdom come but always ended against the darkness of a blank wall.

Jeannette Romaniuk

I know we have been twice blessed and that the heavens smiles down upon us when I contemplate the children's life style, their standard of living and the castles that are their homes. I am also perfectly amazed when I consider the contrast between life as it was then and life as it is now. Being born and raised in a one-roomed log shack along with the rest of my brothers and sisters, I am overwhelmed by the grandeur, the splendor of my children's luxurious homes and their luxurious style of living.

When I consider the path I have traveled on my perilous and chaotic journey, I marvel at the distance we have covered and how we have emerged from a situation that seemed desperate to a situation that is more or less within the realm of stability. The term from rags to riches aptly describes the success each member has achieved while struggling against seemingly impossible odds.

Walter's dream has been realized. At some time or other he bought himself a little piece of land on which he build a lovely home for his family. Later he bought a few heads of cattle. Now what was at first just a little piece of land got larger and larger and the number of cattle got bigger and bigger, until that little piece of land became a sizeable farm and the few heads of cattle became a considerable herd.

For most farmers farming is a means of earning their livelihood, but not so for Walter. For Walter it is a passion, a livelong dream that has come true. No matter how exhausting the labor, the enthusiasm and zealousness by which he tackles every task is phenomenal. It is as if his whole soul was in every operation and the opportunity to perform this strenuous labor was a privilege. Indeed he seems to be enjoying every minute of this farming process and to him it is not work but play. In fact at times I get this loony idea that he seems to be playing house. One of his neighbors seemed amused by Walter's attitude.

"To the rest of us," he told me "farming is a means of making a living. And cows are just cantankerous beasts. But not to Walter! Sometimes I see him standing in the middle of the field, leaning against his fork, and gazing at those beasts with such pride and fascination you'd think they were statues of pure gold. It blows me away."

Fate must have smiled down upon Walter for transcending all his success and his good fortune is the fact that he has been blessed with a happy marriage. For lacking a stable relationship all else comes to naught. Lorraine, his spouse, understands Walter's infatuation with the farm. Although she may have some other aspirations, she has made a commitment to make their project a success. It means hours of punishing labor, yet no sacrifice is too great. While Walter is hell bent on paying the debts incurred in the establishment of the farm and works all over kingdom come, the entire management of the farm becomes Lorraine's responsibility.

Walter and Lorraine's Wedding

Following his retirement from Syncrude, Walter worked for a year in Newfoundland. That experience proved to be a worthwhile adventure for the whole family (as he had taken his family with him). Touring the island proved to be a fascinating and pleasurable experience. It also gave the family an opportunity to explore the Maritime Provinces. All in all it turned out to be a most valuable adventure as the family gained a great deal of knowledge, insight, and appreciation concerning the monumental role these provinces played in the history of our country.

Walter's next venture was a year in Venezuela. That was scary! Then he signed a contract to draw plans for the projected expansion of Syncrude. At first the project was located in Calgary but it was later moved to Fort McMurray. Walter says that he will retire at Christmas. We're all holding our breaths and keeping our fingers crossed.

There are three children in Walter's family. Angela and Michael are from his first marriage and Kalee from his second. All three are brilliant, a gift they have inherited from their parents.

As for David it is a little difficult to give an accurate account of his situation at this time. David has always lived on the edge and although he is bending over backwards trying to find some semblance of stability, his situation is still quite precarious at this time. Being adventurous and fearless in youth he has embarked on many daring and bold projects. While his brother's wages are necessary for the upkeep of the farm, David's wages are utilized to keep his many enterprises afloat. Filled with apprehensions and uncertainty concerning the wisdom of his recent marriage and tormented by myriads of business problems he struggles to maintain an even keel. Yet, David is undaunted! "Don't worry, Mom" he says, "the Big Man upstairs will look after me." He always has, for no other living soul could have survived through the predicaments that David has endured.

There are three boys in David's family, Trevor, Travis and Kelly. They are men now, but when they were very young they lived with me so much of the time that it seems they are part of the family. The boys have formed a close bond with Cherrie. They practically grew up together under the same roof. Indeed the affiliation is so strong that the four of them consider themselves brothers and sister, or a second integral family. It is heart-warming to see the four of them being there for each other in times of joy and in times of need.

Kelly, Travis and Trevor Romaniuk

A few years after her divorce, Juliette remarried. Her husband Dan is a steadfast down-to-earth individual, and the two of them have established a firm and stable relationship. Dan has accepted the children graciously. In fact he seems to appreciate having become part of an extensive family composed not only of his wife's offspring but also of all the brothers, sisters, aunts, uncles, etcetera.

They have no financial problems and have a high standard of living. Dan is retired and Juliette is close to retirement. They intend to travel a great deal of the time, spending the winters in a warmer climate. For a person who has struggled all her life to make ends meet, who has lived in constant apprehension and misery, to be in a situation where security and stability reigns is like being released from the jaws of hell into the felicity of paradise.

Juliette had four children by her first marriage, Kevin, Joanne, Daniel, and Debbie. They are all grown up now of course, but to a mother's heart (and a grandmother) they will always exist as those precious little cherubs that she cherished. Much as I'd like to dwell on the drama of their lives, it would be most irresponsible to do so in this volume, as each one's life is a saga that would fill a volume of its own. Trying to condense the life of a unique and precious individual in a few banal sentences is indeed cruel and unacceptable and is best left alone. This is of course the very thing that I am doing with the lives of my own children, but wait, should time and fortitude permit, I have full intentions of redeeming myself as the narrative progresses.

Kevin, Joanne, Juliette, Debbie and Danny

Carol is still bravely trying to deal with the loss of her beloved husband. Indeed we all are! For anyone who had known Danny it would have been impossible not to have been touched by his unique and prodigious personality. We all miss him dreadfully! But if the rest of his family and friends miss him so, what a crushing blow his death must have been for Carol! She must have been devastated. Yet she courageously struggles on trying to manage the incredible burden she has been left to bear on her own. She teaches to provide for her household, her daughter Michelle, and her granddaughter, Erin, who is her Nicole's child.

Not only is Carol saddled with the challenging duties of a primary teacher, but she must perform the role of a mother, housekeeper, business manager, besides playing an active role in the social relationships of both Danny's and her own family. How she is able to attend to all these obligations is inconceivable. It is little wonder that she works till all hours of the night.

After the death of her husband we were all very worried about Lucille. She felt disorientated, lost, as if the bottom had fallen out from her world, leaving her with no place to go. Rick had been her whole life and all her aspirations revolved around him. Theirs had been a marriage engendered in heaven, so perfect it seemed to be! They did everything together and their aspirations were always toward the same goals. Lucille's dedication to her work, her studies, her jogging and myriads of other occupations failed to alleviate the anguish that had shattered her heart to shreds.

Mercifully the Good Lord, commiserating with her suffering and desperation, sent an angel, a cherub, to comfort her and to assuage some of her pain. This child, Alicia's son and Lucille's grandson, is an emissary sent from above to console and bring joy to his grandmother's heart. His radiant angelic smile can bring joy even to the most despondent heart. For the saving grace this beautiful child, Kayden, has brought we will be eternally grateful. He has brought solace when all else had failed.

It is most unfortunate that this tragedy transpired in Lucille's life. Previous to this devastating blow she seemed to have been born with the legendary golden touch. Everything she touched seemed to turn to gold. She is a very capable and ingenious business executive and is very successful in her career. After 19 years with the C.N.R. she moved on to an executive position in litigation for the Government of Alberta. Feeling the need for a change she applied for positions at different institutions. She recently accepted a position working in the Office of the President at the University of Alberta. She was forever taking business courses in the evening, always graduating as an honor student.

Lucille has a son, Johnny besides her daughter Alicia. He should not have been mentioned at the last for he is not least; he is great. He is Johnny!

Charlie is not with us any more. Our lives will never be the same without him. Yet everyday I ask myself how this could have happened, and every day I wonder if I could have done something to save him. I am constantly tormented by recriminations and doubts concerning his demise. Sometimes I feel somehow responsible for his death and that I didn't do enough. And I miss him, oh Lord I miss him so! For he was with me longer than the others and he took part in everything I did, either criticizing or praising my efforts. Yet it seems that his spirit is always with me, wherever I go or whatever I do, even in my dreams.

Then there is Keith. Hélène says that Keith is my golden boy and she is not mistaken. Keith and his spouse, Debbie, have two daughters, Terra, and Carla. Both girls are married and live in Sherwood Park. Terra and her husband have a set of twins, Cassie and Reid. Needless to say that makes Keith a grandfather. I thought he'd have a fit when he turned forty let alone becoming a grandfather. I remember the trauma he suffered when he turned 30. He was devastated on that day. He kept pacing the floor and moaning, "I'm an old man. I'm an old man!" When I mentioned this to him he simply said,"I'm used to being old now so it doesn't matter any more." As for being a grandfather, he is as proud as a peacock. He struts around with a baby in each arm as if he owned the whole world.

0/02/2005

Keith and Debbie with children Terra and Carla

Keith and Debbie's grandchildren: the twins, Reid and Cassie.

Keith is the family anchor. He is there for us: he is always there, rain or shine. In times of trouble, he is standing by your side no matter how painful it may be for him. He will not leave until the crisis has past and he is certain of your ability to manage on your own. In times of joy he celebrates with the best of them. He has the reputation of being the family comedian, no less! I find it impossible to find a single flaw in Keith's character, in fact it appears that he doesn't have any. That may be because I'm a replica of mother bear who was convinced that her cub was the most beautiful baby in the world and that others couldn't even be compared to him. This of course triggered a feud with the other mothers in the animal land who also believed their babies to be the most beautiful. So before I incriminate myself my sister Juliette will judge the issue. Needless to say Keith is a veritable treasure, a gift from the skies. But then they are all treasures, treasures that have been bestowed upon me in spite of my unworthiness. They have been the essence of my existence. I will be merciful and won't go down the list enumerating the merits of each, merits anchored and cherished only in a mother's heart.

Last but not least is Cherrie. Cherrie's personality is vivacious, dynamic, buoyant and cannot be eclipsed. Although her marriage was unsuccessful she was able to pick up the pieces, start over again and make a good home for her two children, Christopher and Victoria. She bought a house in the elite suburb of St. Albert, did some improvements to it, and at one time had it fully paid for. She considers herself (at times) part of David's family. When his three boys became welders, she decided that she had to follow suit and she became a welder too. She makes fabulous wages but she realizes that welding is very strenuous labor. At present she is investigating other fields or trades which she could pursue should welding become too difficult for her. Like her mother, Cherrie is very intelligent, dedicated and she will undoubtedly succeed at whatever she sets out to do.

Cherrie, Victoria, and Chris

It had never dawned on me to consider how very fortunate I was that I had been blessed beyond every figment of the imagination. There were too many things to do, things that were crucial to the well being of the family. Teaching, correcting books, doing the laundry, baking bread, ironing till all hours of the night, and on and on and on. Dashing ahead hell bent to meet the dead lines there was no time to think. Or perhaps I was too exhausted to have the ability to think. Be it as it may when the truth finally occurred to me it was a revelation, and a whole new perspective was revealed wide open before my eyes. I was stunned! It was incomprehensible why the truth had never occurred to me before. But then there are those who are oblivious to the truth until it hits them in the face or they are struck by a bomb.

It was Christmas Day. Several of the kids had come to my house to celebrate the holiday and for dinner. They were all there. David came marching in with a microwave and plunked it on the cupboard. I had insisted that a microwave was not essential, but David was not to be deterred. He had brought a guest and his three boys with him. Carol, Danny and the two girls were there. Keith, Debbie and the girls were there. Charlie and Cherrie must have been there also. Walter, Juliette, Lucille, and their families for some reason had been unable to come. At any rate the whole house was full. I had set tables in one bedroom upstairs and a large table downstairs in the family room. Debbie was trying to teach me how to use the famous microwave and not having too much success. Everyone had brought presents and David had brought beer of course. The turkey with all the trimmings, the potatoes, and the vegetables had been prepared before the guests arrived but Carol and Debbie were rushing around getting the last minute preparations ready. Everyone enjoyed the dinner. After it was over, some played games. While others were delighted just to be together enjoying each other's company: talking, joking, and reminiscing over the comical things they did in their childhood. Everyone was having so much fun and having such a good time.

Jeannette Romaniuk

The whole house was reverberating with laughter and happiness. And suddenly as I beheld all this jubilation my heart overflowed with rapture. In that one moment, the truth flashed before my eyes and my life took on a new meaning, a new significance.

The moment of truth. For in that instant the whole panorama of what was important in my life flashed before me, and what had previously been a "devoir", a commitment, became a blessing. My anger turned to joy. All the struggles, the fatigue, the countless nights of labor, the tears, all vanished before my eyes and I was overwhelmed with rapture. No longer were these children a responsibility but they had become a source of great delight. No longer was I there for them but their existence had become the essence of my very being, and they were there for me. What had been resentment because I had been left alone to provide for the children turned to pity for my husband. He had been cheated out of the joy of seeing his children grow.

As the years went by, there were many of these family celebrations and the happiness that each of these celebrations brought to each member of the family is beyond any stretch of the imagination. On my seventieth birthday after church I was taken to the Chateau Louis for brunch (supposedly). But lo and behold when I entered the dining area, the whole family was there. Husbands and wives, grandchildren, they were all there! Besides, close friends had been invited and everyone had brought a gift. I was overwhelmed! The grandchildren had pitched in and bought me a very expensive watch which is stored jealously in a drawer because it seems too good to wear. There were plants, pictures, and everything under the sun. But the biggest surprise awaited me at the house: a grandfather clock no less! That of course was icing on the cake. I had always told the children that before my demise I had three wishes: visit the Louvre, get a grandfather clock, and a white fur coat. And there it was, standing right there in the corner where it belonged, staring me in the face. I will cherish that clock forever!

Gift from Family on 70th Birthday

Lucille, Jeannette, Nicole and Michelle – 70th Birthday Party

Jeannette Romaniuk

The next grand extravaganza was a family Christmas celebration. I had hoped to celebrated Christmas with all the children on what I felt would be the last before I would be physically unable to do so. Everyone thought it was a good idea. The event was planned to a "T". It was quite evident that my house could not host the whole clan. So we rented the party room at the church. Each family was to bring something, a salad, a dessert, a vegetable or whatever to contribute to the feast. Keith was to cook one turkey and I was to cook the other. As far as I was concerned cooking a turkey was easy. Well, on the day of the celebration everything was in readiness. Everyone was seated around the tables that had been covered with Christmas tablecloths. Looking back it seems that Walter had been unable to come as he was working overseas at the time. We had even invited some friends to join in the feast. We were twice blessed as a cousin from Quebec, who was taking a course at the University, joined the celebration. A festive ambience filled the air as all the guests, delighted to be together on this special occasion, chatting, laughing, joking and enjoying each other's company.

Something rather incomprehensible yet rather amusing happened during the last minute preparations of the dinner. I am still scratching my head wondering how it could have happened. As usual I wasn't allowed to do any of the work. Keith, Debbie, Juliette, and Carol had gone ahead to the church to set up the tables, carve the turkey, and get the food ready to be served. When I came in the kitchenette Keith was picking something out of the stuffing. Whatever it was that he was picking seemed to be a never-ending task as if he had been picking pebbles out of the sand.

"What on earth are you doing, Keith," I asked.

"I'm just picking the bones out of this stuffing," he replied, "to make sure that the little ones don't get a bone caught in their throats and choke."

"How did those bones get into the stuffing?" I asked.

Poor Keith, he was lost for words. He had hoped that he would not have been caught in the act. "Well," he answered, "the stuffing that you brought was full of little bones and I was trying to get them out."

Then it was my turn to be struck dumb. To this day I haven't been able to figure out how these bones happened to be in the stuffing. Needless to say they were bones from the neck and I distinctly remembered taking the neck out before stuffing that turkey. Unless of course the bird had two necks, which is debatable! Keith never finished the endless task. And the stuffing? It landed in the garbage of course, where it belonged. But I was never able to live that one down.

We celebrated two other events in the party room at the church, a wedding and a baptism. Alicia, Lucille's daughter, was married in Hawaii. Although the immediate family was invited it was impossible for most to attend because the cost was beyond their means. To commemorate the event, a celebration was held at the church for the immediate members of both families. Again it was great to get together and have the opportunity to meet Alicia's new family.

Alicia and Brian's Wedding Celebration – St. Chares Church

After Joanne's daughter Emily was baptized at St. Charles Church the family celebrated the event in the party room at the church. It was a joyous occasion. Joanne and Brent had invited some of their close friends. They who added a great deal of excitement and sparkle to the celebration.

Joanne and Emily – Baptism

Samantha and Erin following the scripture at the baptism

When the twins were born we celebrated the event in the reception room in Lucille's luxurious condo complex. These twins, Terra and Stu's babies created quite a stir in the family as twins are bound to do. Keith is very proud of those twins. It is little wonder that Emily feels short-changed and protests in no uncertain terms. "It's not fair," she says," Keith has two babies and we don't have any, not even one."

As the years went by there were innumerable celebrations that brought great joy and unity to the family as a whole. Some of those events were minor incidents yet were memorable and deeply touching in essence, while others were flamboyant elaborate affairs. Weddings, graduations were usually spectacular and ostentatious affairs while birthdays and recognitions of certain events tended to create less fanfare.

Family weddings were all sensational events. With the exception of personal preferences including those who chose to have quiet ceremonies, these events were celebrateted with all the accompanying paraphernalia. Church ceremony, reception, followed by entertainment where all the relatives and friends participated.

The only wedding deviating from the normal in which something spectacular happened was Travis and Nicki's. The ceremony was held in Fort Saskatchewan as both the bride and groom lived in that town. Five family members had promised to give me a ride to the church for the ceremony. But there was a misunderstanding. Each one thought that someone else had picked me up but at the scheduled hour I was still at home in my wedding attire and madly pacing the floor. All is well that ends well so they say and true to form when Juliette became aware of the situation she was fit to be tied.

"I should have known," she stormed," I have to do everything myself or else it never gets done."

Meanwhile the whole wedding party was waiting impatiently for my arrival.

"I simply will not get married without grandma's presence" declared Nicki indomitably. And she proceeded to ask the Father if he would be gracious enough to wait until I was present.

Subsequently Danny was sent to fetch me. Needless to say I felt like two cents and wanted to sneak in unobserved. In fact my greatest wish at the moment was to become invisible. No such luck! No sooner had I emerged from the car that the whole lot of them shouted, "Hey Grandma" at the top of their voices whereupon I was duly escorted to my seat by the ushers. The whole town must have been alerted and wondered what was all this fuss was about. At last the ceremony could go on. It was indeed a blessing that the priest didn't have a commitment at the time and was free to await our pleasure. That episode made Travis and Nicki's wedding memorable.

Nicki and Travis

There are innumerable graduation ceremonies that bring back fond memories and pride in the graduates' accomplishments. Three of these tend to be spectacular because of certain distinctive events. At the time Debbie was studying to be a teacher's assistant at Grant MacEwan College. At her graduation ceremony in April of 1996, all the school dignitaries spoke with their usual comments and congratulations. Then a native school administrator rose up to speak. He began by singing a song in his native tongue and although he explained its meaning it is no longer with me. But as soon as that man began to speak a hush descended upon the audience. All attention seemed riveted to every word he spoke. His speech was not a mere litany memorized for this occasion, his words emanated straight from the bottom of his soul holding the audience spellbound. Many had tears in their eyes. It appeared that he was directing his message to each individual present, and each was deeply stirred by his impassioned message. That gentleman's words will remain forever engraved in my soul.

Being a teacher's assistant was the first step in Debbie's career. She proceeded to achieve excellence in a most specialized field of education. She is an interpreter for the deaf. She translates what the teacher says into sign language for her student.

Angie's son, Ronald, also created a sensation at his graduation. He managed to do this with his unique and sensational hairdo. Being a little blind and sitting way out in the auditorium I couldn't spot him among all the students. Joanne had the solution to the problem. "Look for the student with a crest of white hair standing high above his head," she said "that's Ronnie." It was indeed the solution for I was soon able to discern the crest of white hair and got a dim image of the one who was wearing it.

The next graduation that made an impression on me was of coarse Michael's. He had shown such courage and determination in going back to school and graduating with honors that as he appeared on the stage distinguished as an honor student my heart was bursting with pride.

Michael's Graduation – NAIT Electronic Engineering

I must not fail to give recognition to the others. Michelle not only graduated with honors from the grade twelve bilingual program but she also succeeded in graduating with a degree in science from university. That is not surprising for whatever Michelle does she does with a vengeance. Besides, because of her striking personality she always stands out in a crowd.

When Johnny and Alicia graduated they received the famous Romaniuk scholarship, which is a nickel and dimes scholarship. What can you do when nickel and dimes is all there is in that mingy fund. In principal upon graduation a grade twelve student with average marks is awarded one hundred dollars and an honor student is awarded five hundred dollars. Perhaps the assumption that this is based on merit is not altogether fair because some students must work twice as hard just to succeed as those who achieve excellence.

There are, besides these all-important family celebrations, events that are noteworthy. Some of those events are hilarious while others are so bizarre it doesn't seem possible that they could happen to anyone else in the whole wide world except the Romaniuks. One of these was subsequent to my efforts as an author.

Charlie had always been a writer. He wrote poetry, prose and expressed all his experiences in words. His ability to use picturesque and dramatic language was amazing. Indeed some of his poetry has been published. Alas not so with me. However I had this mad obsession that my mother's heroism should be written in the annals of history, at least in the history of her loved ones; those for whom she had sacrificed her whole existence. So I set to work willy-nilly. My emotions spilling all over the lines of the script, script lacking miserably in skill. I reluctantly allowed Charlie to read my first draft. Poor Charlie, he just shook his head. It was quite evident that as a writer I did not measure up to his standards. After a few suggestions from Charlie I plunged right back into the task, hell-bent on achieving my goal. Well by hook and by crook the book did get finished. But that wasn't the end of it. I couldn't type so Trudy graciously volunteered to type it for me, and Lucille put it in a format to be bound and printed into a book.

After all this pandemonium, the hundred copies of the book were examined by the conspirators, namely Trudy, Lucille and me. We were sitting at the table very pleased with the results. Lucille kept congratulating Trudy and Trudy kept congratulating Lucille. They were telling each other what a good job each of them had done. This went on and on! I was beginning to feel left out as if I had had nothing to do with the whole thing. At last naïve (bonnase) as usual I said in a meek little voice, "What about me?" The look in the girls' eyes was something to behold. They just seemed to say "Oh, oh we seem to have forgotten somebody." And of coarse we burst out laughing. When Rick, Lucille's husband heard this story he couldn't stop laughing.

On another occasion, after we moved into this condo, the girls took it upon themselves to arrange things in a convenient manner. Still recuperating from a mild stroke I was unable to help. Feeling somewhat guilty because everyone was working so hard and I was not helping it seemed appropriate to at least express my gratitude. So I kept saying, "You're doing great, girls. You're doing fantastic." Seeing me sitting there doing nothing and saying, "You're doing great girls." was too much for Rick to take. He just roared with laughter. In fact Rick couldn't get over all the outlandish predicaments the rest of us always got into. It was to him incredible that anyone could repeatedly be caught red-handed in such shenanigans. He had never heard of anyone driving into a gas pump, hurling dishes out of the kitchen window, using a broomstick to throw someone out the house, etcetera; that is not until he had met our family! Every one of these bizarre situations was hilarious to him and he'd laugh until the tears rolled down his cheeks. It was indeed heart-warming to see Rick laugh so heartily.

On another occasion Trudy and Dave had asked me to take the boys to the circus. They must have trusted me a great deal more than I trusted myself for my driving skills were considered hair raising at best. In fact I was the one who drove right into the gas pump. We set out with the car loaded with kids, the three boys, Joanne, and Cherrie. Everything went well until we were on the way home As luck would have it a road crew was doing some construction on the road. There was no sign of the road. It had been entirely obliterated. To say that I was terrified is to put it mildly. The road crew must have sensed my terror for they stopped all the incoming traffic, cleared the way for me to cross the incoming lane and waited. At the back of the car Joanne was keeping things in toe. "If you make a sound" she threatened, "I'll kill you." With everyone looking out for me I managed to get us all home safely. Needless to say I vowed that I'd never attempt such a reckless venture again.

Jeannette Romaniuk

There were many hilarious incidences during all these years. So many that it is impossible to recall or to recount them all. These incidences brought joy to our hearts and made the tribulations easier to bear.

Part VIII

Reminiscing

As the days go by I still meander around the lake daily and faithfully. As I stroll leisurely along the wonders of nature unfold before my eyes. The majesty of the many varieties of trees as they ostentatiously flaunt the magic of their green attire. As I stroll along this lovely spring morning newly hatched goslings are scurrying hither and thither beside the path jealously guarded by the threatening honk of the proud parents. Further ahead a brood of ducklings bursting with new life are skirmishing rapidly through the grass. Just a little speck in the shimmering grass, they are making a mad dash ahead to discover the whole wide world. The frustrated mother is unable to keep track of her brood as some are hightailing it miles ahead while some stragglers are still crossing the path far behind. Not unlike many humans who live in the fast lane, these adventurous high-spirited ducklings had places to go, things to do and people to see. The mystical and mysterious marvels of nature's spectacular beauty leaves me hypnotized and I gaze in wonderment at the panorama stretched before my eyes. Surely the artist who created this magic must have been supreme, omnipotent. And my soul sings in praise to the Lord, "How Great Thou Art! How Great Thou Art!"

In the twilight of my years, at almost eighty-seven as I finish this seemingly endless narrative, and have come to the end of my prolonged journey in this magnanimous world, I am overwhelmed with nostalgic memories of all that has come to pass. When I behold all those who are so dear to me, my beloved children, and all those who have made my existence worthwhile, my heart overflows with rapture and gratitude. I am filled with wonder and incredulity looking back at the distance we have traveled, always asking myself how such a miracle could have been achieved. The answer, my friends, is written in the wind! Words of wisdom created by the famous Bob Dillon.

The members of the family have been fortunate indeed, successful in their careers, living in mansions, high standards of living, and having the opportunities to travel or enjoy other aspects of leisure. Most live in Edmonton or St. Albert except Walter who has a farm in Thorsby. Needless to say residing in such close proximity makes it convenient when the family plans to get together.

I am the matriarch of a rather large family, eight children, eighteen grandchildren, and twenty-four great-grandchildren with two more on the way. All of them are precious of course! I never fail to fall in love with each one of them. At first I thought the grandchildren were the most adorable babies in the world. That is until the great-grandchildren came along. Now the whole matter is up in the air!

At the risk of being tedious I will endeavor to introduce these most prestigious great-grandchildren by tabulating their names and identity in some sort of order.

Walter's Grandchildren: Angie's son and daughter, Ronald who graduated from grade twelve last year, and Danielle.

Ronald's Grade 12 Graduation

David's grandchildren: Trevor's son and daughters, Cole, Jade, and Amber; Travis and Nicki's son and daughters, Mason, Grace, and Shae Lynn; and Kelly and Melanie's son Chase.

Juliette's grand-children: Kevin and Jean's sons Mitchell and Michael; Joanne and Brent's daughter Emily; Danny and Leslie's daughters Jennifer, Danielle and Samantha; and Debbie and Ross's son and daughter, Ashley and Matthew.

Carol's grandchildren: Nicole's daughter and son, Erin and Darcy.

Lucille's grandchildren: Alicia and Brian's son Kayden and soon to be granddaughter Eva Grace.

Kayden Janz (Alicia and Brian)

It goes without saying that all of these are the most beautiful in the world and I love them dearly. But as they get older it's scary. Am I to become a great-great grandmother? Heaven forbid!

I am content in my own little world, plodding along slowly, just one foot ahead of the other. True my childhood dreams were never realized, but perhaps these dreams were unrealistic. And if my childhood dreams were unreasonable, mere fantasies, as an adult they appear completely Utopian, far-fetched; utterly out and out!

My first dream as a child was to become a detective. I was reading a serial story in a French daily paper, *La press*, about an indomitable lady detective, Mme. Storey. Because of her wisdom and her insight into a situation this amazing heroin managed to solve one crime after another. Needless to say I fell madly in love with this fearless lady and come rain or shine I was going to follow in her footsteps. In spite of the fact that I possessed neither her wisdom nor her insight not to mention her stature (she was six feet tall) I was undeterred. I was going to be a detective! It goes without saying that as soon as the paper arrived I grabbed it before anyone had had a chance to look at it. As the years went by I realized that being a detective was out of my reach, as I did not have the talents such a career demanded.

My next fantasy was of becoming a pilot. Whew! What a pilot I would have been! I can't even drive a car. Indeed I am a menace behind the wheel! So much for that dream. Fortunately the whole thing was soon forgotten.

"Well," I thought," if I can't be a detective or a pilot, there is only one thing left for me to do. I have to be a writer!

When all these dreams came crashing down one after another and after my mother in an effort to help me find my place in the world had given me an opportunity to become a registered nurse (a career that was ill-suited to my personality) it is a wonder that I didn't give up. And I did! For some years I was lost, wondering if ever I would find a place where I belonged. That is until the door was open for me to become a teacher. I knew then that that was where I belonged and I never looked back.

As I speculate and meditate in the last stretch of my journey, I regret that of all eleven of us; Hélène, Juliette, and Raymond are the only ones of my siblings left. The others have all departed. George, Laurence, Marie-Anne, Germaine, Yvonne, Cecile and John have gone to claim their celestial reward in Paradise. There are of course those who died in infancy, Paul –Emile, Leon, and Gerard. All the dearly loved ones who are no more have left a void in the hearts of those of us left behind.

Yet at this monumental epoch, my life is filled with events that bring me great joy, events that leave my heart awed with wonder and nostalgia. Events that are a bonus to the many that I experienced in my travels abroad and are so numerous that it would be a miracle if my memory could recall and incorporate them all without any major omissions. For instance, the delight I experienced when Carol and I located and were reunited with my cousins on Victoria Island is beyond any stretch of the imagination!

Indeed destiny has chosen to lead me towards extremely divergent spiritual realms. From the ecstasy of Paradise I was often plunged into the torment of the Inferno. Moments of ultimate jubilation were interspersed by moments of extreme anguish. Days of radiant and blazing summer sunshine followed by the stormy gloom of winter's frigid fury. And in between these two extremes were events incredibly outlandish and hilarious rendering life exhilarating and tolerable.

Yet when I contemplate all that has come to pass I am over whelmed with gratitude I as consider the treasures I have gathered along life's tortuous way. Most precious of them all are those that God in his magnanimous beneficence has fit to trust in my care.

The joy these have brought to my humble existence transcends all. The pure delight the family experiences as we gather together for a celebration is beyond compare, be it a Christmas, religious or wedding celebration. It is at these family gatherings that I realize the many blessings the Lord has showered upon me. Were I to count those many blessing the list would be endless, from here to kingdom come! The children would be first of course, and then my brothers and sisters followed by my many students and dear friends, etcetera.

All eight of my children together at Danny & Leslie's Wedding
Keith, Juliette, Dave Lucille, Walter, Cherrie, Charles, and Carol

To the many magnanimous souls who have held my hand and shared my path along the way, I am eternally grateful. They have filled my life with joy. They have showered me with treasures precious beyond my wildest dreams. They have scattered jewels before me as I journeyed along the way.

It is incredible that I have failed to emphasize the monumental contribution and influence my students have played in the overall success of my career and the realization of my dreams. For as soon as my classroom door closed I was in a different world. Gone were all the burdens, the cares, and the tribulations that weighed heavily and constantly upon my shoulders. Gone was the fact that I was raising a family alone in an illusive dream. Gone was the fatigue, the worry about tomorrows' provisions and even the beast [la bête noire] vanished into thin air. That door barricaded the exterior world and left a sanctuary of peace in the classroom. And in that sanctuary only one thing mattered, the light of anticipation in those beautiful children's eyes. And my most fervent desire was to teach these precious children not only the basic skills such as reading, writing and arithmetic but to teach each and everyone of them that they were special, unique and gifted each in his\her own way. Needless to say, all my efforts to help my students and the gifts that I may have been able to bestow upon them cannot be compared to the gifts they have given me. For because of their love and the love of all those in my milieu, I had the courage to conquer the troublesome aspects of my personality. I no longer hide in the shadows but am able to confront whatever comes my way. In fact I am walking tall. This conclusion came after many days of deliberations of course. At last I concluded, "If so many love me, I mustn't be that bad. In fact I must be all right!"

How could I have been guilty of such a significant omission? These children most certainly have not been forgotten for I hold the memory of each and every one of them engraved in my heart. Surely they have not forgotten me! For wherever my path leads me: walking around the lake, buying groceries, in church, or even at the doctors office someone pops out of no where and gives me a great big bear hug. At times I am at a loss as the contrast between a grade one student and a six-foot giant is huge. I am grateful that many of my students have become professional doctors, lawyers, nurses, etc.

There is an episode that happened at St. Kevin School that illustrates my attitude and perspective concerning the teaching profession. I regarded the role of a teacher as a privilege and a sacred trust. Anyone entrusted with such a privileged position should be grateful indeed. A grade five teacher was sitting at the table in the staff room and was apparently exhausted.

"Anyone who says they love teaching has to be insane." she sighed. Needless to say there was no comment on my part as I happened to be one of those. Besides she was one of the most competent teachers on staff.

Later I read a story written by a teacher saying that he would pay to have the privilege of teaching. It was indeed a relief to find that I wasn't the only one who suffered from insanity.

What is indeed more astounding is the fact that I have completely forgotten about la bête noire, that ferocious beast that was hell bent on my destruction, forever threatening to ruin every future opportunity that stood before me. It is almost unbelievable that the monstrous beast has disappeared. It has vanished without a trace! Surely the enormity of my allies: my brothers, sisters, children, students, colleagues, and friends convinced the miscreant of the impossibility of its evil intent. Realizing that it was hopelessly outnumbered it gathered its vicious venom and in the shadows of the night silently slithered away.

BIBLIOGRAPHY

1. Dickens, Charles, David Copperfield, 1998 Modern Library ed. Shakespeare, William, *Julius Caesar*, Act IV Scene 3.

2. Encyclopedia Britannica, 1964 Edition.

3. Hine, Stuart. *The Magnificat,* Manna Music Inc.,1953-1955.

4. Steinbeck, John, *The Grapes of Wrath,* The Viking Press, 1939.

5. Steinbeck, John, *Travels with Charley*, Curtis Publishing Co. Inc., 1961 & 1962

Appendix A

Family Tree

Jeannette Evangeline Romaniuk (nee Gaumond)

and

John Romaniuk

Walter Joseph Romaniuk

Diane Carson		Lorraine Tessier
Angie	Michael	Kalee
Jean-Paul Ladouceur		
Ronald	Danielle	

David Joseph Romaniuk

Trudy Draper						Nadia
Trevor		Travis			Kelly	
Tracy		Nicole			Malanie	
Cole	Jade	Amber	Mason	Grace	Shae	Chase

Juliette Mary Klymko (nee Romaniuk)

Vince Walsh								Dan
Kevin		Joanne	Danny			Debra		
Jean		Brent	Leslie			Ross Fagan		
Michael	Mitchell	Emily	Danielle	Jennifer	Samantha	Ashley	Matthew	

Caroline Mary O'Shea

Danny Yanew		
Nicole Elaine		Michelle Lynn
Carl		
Erin Michelle	Darcy	

Lucille Mary Murdoch (nee Romaniuk)

Richard Edward Murdoch		
John David Murdoch	Alicia Marie Janz (nee Murdoch)	
	Brian Janz	
	Kayden Richard	Ava Grace

Charles Joseph Romaniuk

Linda Baron

Keith Arnold Romaniuk

Debbie Johnson		
Terra		Carla
Stewart		Dean
Cassie	Reid	Ashley

Cherrie Lynn Romaniuk

Al Jackson	
Chris	Victoria

Jeannette Evangeline Romaniuk (nee Gaumond) was born in the French community of Shell River, Saskatchewan on November 26, 1919. Much of her secondary education was done through correspondence. She went on to get in Bachelor of Education at the University of Alberta. Teaching became Jeannette's passion. After retirement in 1984 she continued to tutor many children at various levels. In more recent years her passion to write about her life experiences became an obsession. Her first published works was a peom entitled "In Memory of Mother Theresa and Princess Diana" in the mid 1980's.

ISBN 1425176801

9 781425 176808

Edwards Brothers Malloy
Oxnard, CA USA
April 18, 2013